The Performance
of the
British Economy

The Performance
of the
British Economy

EDITED BY

Rudiger Dornbusch and Richard Layard

CLARENDON PRESS · OXFORD
1987

Oxford University Press, Walton Street, Oxford OX2 6DP

Oxford New York Toronto
Delhi Bombay Calcutta Madras Karachi
Petaling Jaya Singapore Hong Kong Tokyo
Nairobi Dar es Salaam Cape Town
Melbourne Auckland

and associated companies in
Beirut Berlin Ibadan Nicosia

Oxford is a trade mark of Oxford University Press

Published in the United States
by Oxford University Press, New York

British Library Cataloguing in Publication Data
The Performance of the British economy.
1. Great Britain—Economic conditions—1945–
I. Dornbusch, Rudiger   II. Layard, Richard
330.941'0858   HC256.6
ISBN 0-19-877272-6
ISBN 0-19-877271-8 Pbk

Library of Congress Cataloging in Publication Data
Data available

Phototypeset by Cotswold Typesetting Ltd, Gloucester
Printed in Great Britain
at the University Printing House, Oxford
by David Stanford
Printer to the University

Contents

Introduction

The British economy has worried people for decades. The reasons are not far to seek, as the table shows. In the 1960s the main worry was the slow productivity growth in Britain, compared with other countries. By the 1970s a new worry had emerged: more rapid inflation than elsewhere. During the 1980s, there was a further worry: unemployment. Britain today has substantially higher unemployment than any other major country.

To throw light on the problems of the 1960s, the Brookings Institution commissioned a major study of Britain's economic prospects in 1966 (Caves *et al.*, 1968). A repeat performance was undertaken in 1978 (Caves *et al.*, 1980). Both of these volumes were written entirely by North American authors. We thought the time had come for a further appraisal of the story since around 1970. But we also thought that British authors could be trusted to do most of the work. For since the 1960s the relative performance of British economics has certainly improved, even if the same cannot be said of the British economy.

Our first three chapters are concerned with the demand side of the economy, and the next four with the supply side. As is well known, the aggregate demand for output is crucially dependent on interest rates, government expenditure, tax rates, and the forces affecting the trade balance. Thus the first three chapters deal with monetary policy, fiscal policy, and the forces affecting external balance, focusing on North Sea oil.

In the chapter on monetary policy, *Stanley Fischer* starts with the broad story of Britain's macroeconomic performance since 1970. He then turns to the role of monetary policy. Until 1972, Britain was on a fixed exchange rate as part of the Bretton Woods system. This provided an anchor for the price level. But after the collapse of the Bretton Woods system, Britain, like other countries, looked around for some nominal anchor for the economic system, and interest focused increasingly on the monetary aggregates. This interest was spurred greatly by the largely fortuitous coincidence of rapid growth in M3 in 1972/3 followed by an inflationary explosion in 1974/5. From 1976 onwards public targets were announced for M3, and this practice continued until very recently.

Until 1979, monetary control was only one instrument of economic management, and fiscal policy was used, in part at least, to maintain the level of real aggregate demand. But from 1979 onwards the notion of managing real aggregate demand was largely abandoned, and the reduction of inflation was treated as the overriding object of policy.

This philosophy was enshrined in the Medium Term Financial Strategy, in

Productivity, inflation, and unemployment

	1966–9	1970–9	1980–5	1985
Growth of GDP per worker (% p.a.)				
UK	2.9	2.2	2.2	2.2
OECD	3.9	2.4	1.6	1.6
Inflation (% p.a.)				
UK	4.2	12.9	9.0	6.1
OECD	3.9	8.1	7.1	4.7
Unemployment (%)				
UK	3.1	4.4	11.1	13.2
OECD	2.7	4.3	7.5	8.1

Notes:
Inflation in year t measures the GDP deflator in year t relative to $t-1$. Productivity growth is similarly defined.
Unemployment is the OECD standardized rate; the all-OECD rate is for 16 major countries; the 1st column shows data for 1967–9.

Sources: OECD *Historical Statistics*, 1960–80. OECD *Economic Outlook*, December 1982, December 1983, and May 1986.

which, from 1980 onwards, the government committed itself to specific nominal targets for monetary growth and public borrowing over a run of years. To try to hit those targets, interest rates were raised substantially. This (together with tighter fiscal policy and a high exchange rate) eventually dampened down inflation. But the economic cost was high.

At the same time, the velocity of circulation of M3 became increasingly unstable (and downward-trended). Thus less and less weight could be put on M3 as a target variable. Interest shifted (rightly, in Fischer's view) to the monetary base M0, to nominal income, and more recently to the exchange rate. In 1986 a major issue had become whether Britain should revert to a semi-fixed exchange rate, by joining the exchange rate mechansim of the European Monetary System. On balance, Fischer favours this, while keeping an eye on M0.

While high real interest rates have been one reason for low aggregate demand in the 1980s, another reason has been tight fiscal policy. As *David Begg* shows in a telling figure, fiscal policy in the later 1970s was 'broadly neutral' but moved into a substantial cyclically-adjusted surplus in the 1980s. This was due mainly to a big increase in the share of taxes in national income.

The ostensible reason for tighter fiscal policy was to make it easier to achieve the M3 target. Begg dismisses this explanation on the grounds that the relation between public borrowing and monetary growth is tenuous. He then examines other possible justifications. One might be to prevent an explosion of the public debt. But, as Begg shows, the net public debt is now much lower than in the 1950s and 1960s (relative to national income), and has recently been very stable. The same is true of the *net* liabilities of the public sector (that is, its debt minus its assets).

Since the monetary base is only about 5 per cent of the national income, the government has little incentive to print money as a way of financing a government deficit. It is however possible that pre-commitment to nominal targets for public borrowing may raise the public belief in the government's commitment to fight inflation; for if inflation went up, nominal debt interest would rise and real fiscal policy would thus automatically tighten (to contain nominal borrowing). However, it is unclear how far inflation was in fact reduced because people believed in the commitment rather than because unemployment went up so much.

Turning to the balance of trade, the dominant factors have been North Sea oil, and the oil price. As *Charles Bean* shows, Britain started the 1970s producing no oil and by 1985 was the fourth largest producer in the free world. Over the same period the price of oil rose sharply in 1973/4 and again in 1979/80. What was the effect of all this?

Bean uses a three-sector econometric model to perform two simulations. The first looks only at the effects of the changes in oil production and known reserves (given the actual history of the oil price). This suggests that North Sea oil raised the real exchange rate by around 10 per cent in the early 1980s (rather under half the actual increase that occurred). But, contrary to common belief, manufacturing output was not reduced by this, owing to the fact that the appreciation made it easier to contain wage pressure without excessive falls in activity. In the second simulation, Bean adds to the effects of oil production the effects of the two changes in the oil price (with non-accommodating money). This combination does indeed explain falls in manufacturing output and employment of the order of 2 per cent. But in the 1980s the induced growth of services employment is such that total employment is roughly unaffected. These estimates are broadly consistent with those of other studies and suggest that high unemployment and de-industrialization should be blamed not on North Sea oil, but rather on factors such as wage pressure (discussed below).

Before coming to the labour market, we look at the effect of the other big exogenous change that has affected Britain in the last fifteen years—entry to the Common Market. *Francesco Giavazzi* begins by examining the microeconomic effects of this. The Common Agricultural Policy appears to have cost Britain about 1 per cent of GDP when compared with free trade in agriculture and no subsidies to farmers. As regards manufactures, entry into the EEC customs union has radically reoriented Britain's trade. It has raised manufactured exports to Europe to 50 per cent of all Britain's manufactured exports, but raised imports from Europe even more—to 60–70 per cent of all manufactured imports. Finally, Giavazzi considers the issue (also considered by Fischer) of EMS entry. He shows that membership of a system of fixed but adjustable parities involves high interest rate volatility before readjustments, but suggests this may be preferable to high exchange rate volatility.

Richard Layard and Stephen Nickell examine the labour market, as one key component of the supply side of the economy. They see the labour market as being in equilibrium (at the non-accelerating inflation rate of employment, or NAIRU) when the intended real wage determined by wage-setters equals the intended real wage implied by price-setters. Unemployment has to be high enough to bring intended real wages to this equality. The NAIRU thus rises when there is an increase in wage pressure. Since 1970 wage pressure has increased owing to increased union militancy, increased taxes, and easier social security. In addition, the major negative demand shocks of the early 1980s have caused a huge rise in long-term unemployment. Such unemployment exerts little or no downward pressure on wages, and the short-run NAIRU is in consequence higher than the long-run NAIRU. This explains why wage inflation did not fall between 1982 and 1986 despite high unemployment. Long-term unemployment also explains why there can be so many vacancies despite the large numbers unemployed. Another reason for the co-existence of vacancies and unemployment is a mismatch between the pattern of vacancies and unemployment. But this mismatch, though serious, may not have worsened over time. It could be reduced if relative wages were more flexible.

Labour productivity growth since 1981 has been quite good (roughly back to the levels of the 1960s). This is due to three main factors: first, total factor productivity growth has recovered; second, workers' effort per hour has increased; and, third, there has been extensive scrapping of the least productive plant. But some, at least, of these influences cannot persist indefinitely.

The efficiency of the economy depends on the workings not only of the labour market, but also of the product market. *J. A. Kay and D. J. Thompson* review the history and workings of public policy on this issue. After the war, economists were acutely conscious of the extent of 'market failure', especially among the natural monopolies. This led to some nationalization, and to the establishment elsewhere of a regulatory framework to promote competition. In recent years the pendulum has swung sharply. Many economists are now acutely conscious of the degree of 'regulatory failure', and the Conservative government has embarked on a major programme of de-nationalization. The authors review carefully the evidence on the success of nationalized and private industries. They conclude that the key desideratum is competition, and that ownership is much less important. To promote competition among private firms they favour more specific rules about acceptable commercial practice, rather than judging each case on its merits in terms of its conformity to the public interest. They also favour clearer rights of private litigation. Where industries are publicly owned, they favour separating those activities involving natural monopoly (e.g., ownership of supply lines) from those that are in a more competitive business (e.g. supplying appliances).

Finally, *A. B. Atkinson, J. Hills, and J. Le Grand* examine the role of the welfare state, concentrating on policies for health, housing, and social security. They first describe the evolution of policy and find more continuity of policy between governments of different colours than is often supposed. The more obvious differences have concerned council house rents, building programmes, and unemployment benefits. The degree of continuity can be seen fairly clearly from the time-series of real expenditure on the different programmes. Where there have been changes in policy, these have emerged more as the result of small incremental movements, than as the result of dramatic policy initiatives.

The authors also look at the effectiveness of the policies. For instance, they point to the continuing decline in inequalities in life expectancy over the past twenty years (when measured over individuals, rather than between social classes whose sizes have changed). By contrast, while the proportion of the population living in poverty or on its margin fell during the 1970s, it rose sharply between 1979 and 1983, the main cause being the increase in unemployment and the increasing incidence of low pay. In housing, while the 'traditional' problems of lack of amenities (such as an indoor toilet) and of a crude shortage of dwellings relative to households have been largely resolved, new problems have emerged, such as the increasing disrepair of the housing stock and a recent rapid rise in homelessness.

So the picture of Britain's economic performance is mixed. The country as a whole is richer than ever before. But it is also more unequal than at any other time since the Second World War. And the greatest evil is mass unemployment.

We hope that this volume will help in the development of better policies. The papers were presented to a conference held in Chelwood Gate, Sussex, in May 1985 and organized by the London School of Economics Centre for Labour Economics. The conference was generously financed by the Economic and Social Research Council, and we are extremely grateful to the Council, and to Marion O'Brien, who was a superb conference organizer.

Rudiger Dornbusch
Richard Layard

References

Caves, R. E. *et al.* (1968), *Britain's Economic Prospects*. Washington: Brookings Institution.

Caves, R. E. *et al.* (1980), *Britain's Economic Performance*. Washington: Brookings Institution.

CHAPTER 1

Monetary Policy

Stanley Fischer

Massachusetts Institute of Technology

The rationale for British monetary policy in the past 15 years has fluctuated along with the macroeconomy. From the reticent pragmatism of the 1960s, British monetary policy-makers have progressed to voluble frankness in the search for a guideline or indicator that would solve the trade-off dilemmas that face them.

Figure 1.1 summarizes the outcome of policy and the shocks hitting the economy since 1970.[1] After the inflationary outburst at the beginning of the Thatcher government, the inflation rate has been brought down rapidly and steadily, at the cost of a continually increasing unemployment rate. Unemployment increased with frightening speed: from 4.7 per cent in the fourth quarter of 1979, it reach 12.8 per cent only five years later, and it continues to climb even in 1986. With inflation finally back to the levels of the 1960s, the key issue now is whether the massive unemployment will be reversed, and if so whether that can be done without re-igniting inflation.

The picture for the United Kingdom is similar to that of the rest of the OECD–Europe. Until 1980 the UK had a higher inflation rate and lower unemployment rate than OECD–Europe, as Table 1.1 shows. Since then it

Table 1.1

Inflation and unemployment, UK and OECD–Europe

	OECD–Europe		UK	
	Inflation	Unempl.	Inflation	Unempl.
1967–73	5.7	3.4	7.0	2.4
1974–80	11.8	5.7	16.0	4.7
1980	14.3	7.0	18.0	6.1
1981	12.2	8.4	11.9	9.5
1982	10.5	9.2	8.6	11.1
1983	8.2	10.2	4.6	12.1
1984	7.4	10.7	5.0	12.6
1985	6.6	11.0	6.1	13.1

Source: OECD: *Historical Statistics* and *Economic Outlook*, various issues; UK: data from 1980 are from *Economic Trends*.

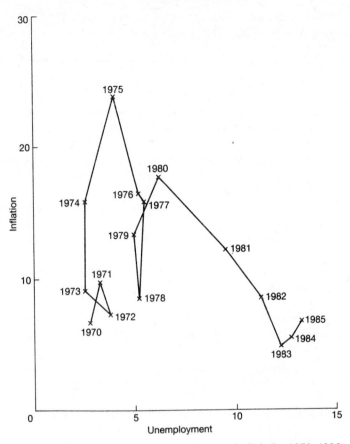

Fig. 1.1 Inflation (CPI) and unemployment in Britain, 1970–1985.

has crossed over, becoming a relatively low-inflation–high-unemployment country.

Although the Bank of England carries out both monetary policy and debt management, it is less independent than the US Federal Reserve Bank or the German Bundesbank. The Chancellor of the Exchequer is ultimately and actively responsible for monetary policy. Monetary policy decisions and strategies, although supported and explained by the Bank and its Governor, are not necessarily the Bank's decisions. The Chancellor's pronouncements on monetary policy are decisive. None the less, I shall in this chapter refer interchangeably to the monetary policy of the government and that of the Bank.

The rhetoric of British monetary policy moved sharply towards monetarism during the 1970s. In 1971, competition and credit control still emphasized the use of interest rates to control credit growth. Two years later the Bank of

England adopted internal monetary targets for M3, and in 1976 sterling M3 (£M3) targets became public. Despite frequent failures to meet the targets, £M3 remains one of the announced monetary targets, with the money base (M0), M1, and a broader measure of liquid assets (PSL2) having also appeared at different times.

The growth rate of £M3 seen in Figure 1.2 reached 27 per cent in 1972 and 1973 and was again high in 1980 when the Corset was removed. Bank rate was abandoned during the period, replaced by the minimum lending rate (MLR), which in turn was abandoned in 1981, after hitting an historical high of 17 per cent in 1979. The Treasury bill rate (TBR) was in the double digits from 1974 to 1976, and reached near 17 per cent in 1980. The public sector borrowing requirement (PSBR) is also shown in Figure 1.2. After exceeding 6 per cent of GNP in 1975, it fell rapidly, then increased to 5 per cent of GNP in 1979, before being brought down again in the early 1980s despite rising unemployment. Cyclically adjusted, the PSBR shows a growing surplus in the 1980s. (Biswas, Johns, and Savage 1985).

Along with the volatility of money growth, interest rates, the Budget, and oil discoveries, came volatility of the real exchange rate (Figure 1.3). Most striking is the rapid real appreciation of sterling from 1978 to 1980, in part as a result of the discovery of oil.[2] The current account moved into surplus in 1980 but has generally declined since then. Note the positive relationship in Figure 1.3 between the real exchange rate and the current account.

Figures 1.1–1.3 provide the background for the discussion of monetary policy that follows. I start in Section 1 with a brief description of the money supply process. Section 2 presents a chronological review of the search for monetary guidelines; in Section 3 I discuss the transmission mechanism for monetary policy, and the trade-offs that have to be faced by the policy-makers. Alternative targets for monetary policy are discussed in Section 4. As the promise of monetary targets has waned and the inflation rate has fallen, the attraction of joining the European Monetary System (EMS) has increased, until in 1986 membership becomes increasingly probable. In the last section I examine the issue of joining the EMS.

1. Money Supply Determination

The standard textbook exposition of money supply determination assumes that the central bank controls the monetary base, and that the public and the banks maintain stable portfolio proportions between currency and bank deposits and bank reserves and other assets, respectively. The money supply is given by

$$M = \{(1 + cu)/(re + cu)\}H \qquad (1.1)$$

where M is the money stock, cu the currency–deposit ratio, re the reserve ratio, and H the stock of high-powered money.

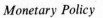

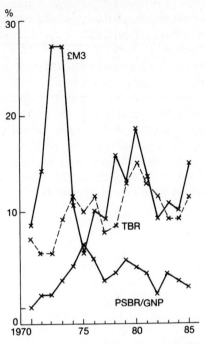

Fig. 1.2 UK money growth, Treasury bill rate, and PSBR/GNP, 1970–1985.

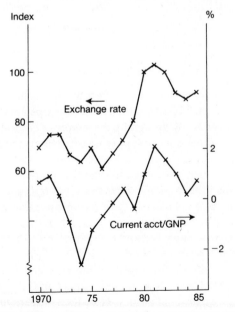

Fig. 1.3 The UK exchange rate and the current account, 1970–1985.

Reserve requirements in Britain are minimal: banks and licensed deposit-takers keep non-interest-bearing balances of 0.5 per cent of their eligible liabilities at the Bank of England, primarily to provide the Bank with revenue. In addition, London clearing banks and some other banking institutions voluntarily hold further working (non-interest-bearing) bankers' deposits with the Bank to facilitate daily transactions.[3]

The money multiplier formula is an identity (which would hold even of banks' reserve ratio were zero), and thus is one way of thinking about money supply determination in Britain. But it is not the preferred mode. Rather, descriptions of money supply determination in Britain combine a standard money demand function, as in Figure 1.4, with the Bank's ability to determine interest rates. Given a stable money demand function, the Bank determines the quantity of money by its choice of interest rate.

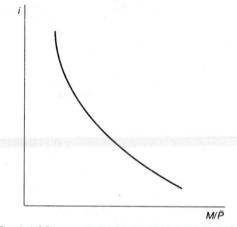

Fig. 1.4 Money supply determination in the UK.

This simple description raises two questions. First, how does the Bank determine the interest rate? It determines it through open market operations, through its control over H. By tightening the supply of liquidity, the Bank can raise nominal interest rates, and by supplying extra funds to the market it can reduce them.

The Bank's work is much more difficult than that of the US Federal Reserve Bank (the Fed) because the Bank manages the Treasury's accounts, which are held mainly with the Bank. Treasury cash receipts dominate the day-to-day movements of high-powered money in Britain, whereas in the United States the Treasury attempts, through Tax and Loan Accounts, to limit its impact on the monetary base.

Second, Figure 1.4 shows the demand function for *real*, not *nominal*, balances. The standard textbook model (equation (1.1)) determines the nominal, not the real, quantity of money. How then is the nominal quantity of money determined? In the first instance, the price level can be taken as predetermined at a moment of time, so that changes in nominal balances are also changes in real balances.

More fundamentally, with slow-moving prices, a feedback process with the nominal money stock as target makes it possible to determine the nominal money stock by controlling the nominal interest rate.[4] Given, say, an M3 target, so long as the Bank controls the interest rate, and if the demand for M3 is interest-elastic, the Bank can determine M3. Of course, the demand function for M3 may shift in such a way that the interest rate needed to attain the target money stock is inconsistent with the goals of policy, and then one or both targets have to be modified.[5]

Given that (1.1) is an identity, why is it not used to describe the determination of the money stock in Britain? The reasons are probably that the Bank does not formally pay attention to control of H, the monetary base, and that re, banks' reserve ratio, may vary substantially. If the Bank did fix H, and with both the reserve ratio and currency–deposit ratio declining functions of the interest rate, we could include an upward-sloping money supply function in Figure 1.4 to show how the money stock is determined, given the money base and price level.

2. The Search for Policy Guidelines

In the first comprehensive post-Second World War examination of monetary policy, the Radcliffe Committee strongly opposed the view that monetary policy should be controlled by any single guideline or target.[6] It is famous for the statement, '[W]e cannot find any reason for supposing, or any experience in monetary history indicating, that there is any limit to the velocity of circulation . . .' (p. 133), for its emphasis on the importance of the quantity of liquidity, for the notion that the interest rate structure was the key indicator and transmission route for monetary policy, and for its insistence that monetary policy worked only by affecting aggregate demand. Radcliffe argued that whatever significance attached to the supply of money was a result of its importance as part of the wider liquidity structure of the economy. The Committee was also quite explicit that the monetary authorities had to face trade-offs among the objectives of economic policy.

As the Bretton Woods system weakened through the 1960s, British monetary policy began a search for a new analytic basis and policy guidelines that would lead to the right choice among possibly conflicting objectives, although it very rarely confronted those conflicts explicitly.[7] The increasing inefficiency and ineffectiveness of direct controls over lending, coupled with rising inflation, led in September 1971 to Competition and Credit Control.

The competition came in the ending of the cartel agreement on the fixing of interest rates in the British banking system. Credit control was in principle to operate through interest rates, with monetary policy inducing reductions in the quantity of credit by producing higher interest rates. All banks were to hold reserves in the form of cash at the Bank of England and other highly liquid assets, against sterling deposits obtained from outside the banking system. The Bank of England retained the right to call for special deposits on which interest would be paid at the Treasury bill rate.

Both the name of the policy and official explanations of the change[8] stressed credit as the mechanism through which the policy would affect the economy. At the same time, monetarism was gaining strength internationally, not least in Britain, where the 1970 finding of a stable demand function held out the promise of M3 as the right target for policy (Goodhart with Crockett 1970). Against this background, 27 per cent growth rates of M3 in 1972 and 1973 with inflation rates already above 7 per cent led to fears of an inflationary explosion—even though part of the M3 growth was the result of re-intermediation as direct controls were removed.[9] By the end of 1973, the inflation rate was accelerating.

The result was the imposition of the Corset, supplementary (non-interest-bearing) special deposits (SSDs).[10] SSDs were imposed on the base of interest-bearing eligible liabilities (essentially, interest-bearing sterling deposits) on the theory that the rapid growth of M3 was the result of liability management. Beyond a specified permitted growth rate of eligible liabilities, banks had to make deposits with the Bank of England, with progressively higher ratios as deposit growth increased. The Corset was put into operation three times between December 1973 and June 1980, being operative about half that time. Practically no supplementary special deposits were ever made at the Bank of England, except during the third imposition, which ended in July 1980. This was the result of not only the success of the Corset in reducing the growth of credit, but also the ability of the financial system to divert into other channels credit that had previously moved through banks.[11] None the less, it is argued that the Corset provided a valuable constraint on potentially expansionary bank lending.

At the same time, the Bank adopted M3 targets for internal use. The simplest, but incorrect, explanation for the shift to a money target would be that a monetary anchor was to replace the exchange rate anchor lost in 1972. Although this rationale was invoked in 1978,[12] it does not seem to have been significant in 1973. Rather, by that time monetarism had made considerable inroads among both academics and market participants. If the foreign exchange and financial markets were beginning to interpret policy changes in monetarist fashion, the Bank would have to take account of that trend by itself watching the behaviour of monetary aggregates. With inflation accelerating, the Bank would have an extra reason to look to money targets as a means of keeping inflation under control, at least in the medium term. The failure to announce the targets suggests a lack of confidence that they could be achieved—or perhaps opposition from the Treasury.

The stability of the M3 demand function through 1970 was certainly one factor in the choice of an M3 rather than M1, or base, target. In 1973 it was still possible to believe that the shifts in demand since 1971 were merely a one-time disturbance associated with Competition and Credit Control.[13] Another factor was the two-for-one attraction of being able to relate the growth of M3 to the public sector borrowing requirement—the choice of M3 allowed the Bank to target a monetary aggregate while remaining close to the credit view of the monetary mechanism.[14]

Monetary targets were publicly announced in 1976, the year of the IMF loan.[15] The inflation feared in 1972 and 1973 had indeed occurred, leading to increased confidence in the existence of a link between M3 and inflation—even if some of the 1974–5 inflation was related to the oil shock rather than the prior money growth. The official rationale for the targets stressed the fight against inflation and the need to provide an anchor for expectations.

The advent of the Thatcher government and the subsequent abolition of exchange controls led to the removal of the Corset, on the argument that direct controls on credit creation by the domestic banking system could easily be circumvented by offshore intermediation. The notion of the Corset as a direct control is common, though not persuasive, for it was essentially a variable reserve ratio rather than a direct limit on lending. The problem was not so much direct controls but rather the fear that intermediation would be driven outside the banking system in any prolonged use of the Corset.

The Medium Term Financial Strategy (MTFS), the Thatcher government's more fundamental policy change, placed even more weight on the M3 (by now £M3) target. Fiscal and monetary policy were to be co-ordinated, with PSBR being determined in the light of the need to reduce the growth rate of £M3 gradually without causing excessive increases in interest rates—and with the ultimate aim of gradually reducing the inflation rate (see Lawson 1981). Table 1.2 shows the 1980 plan for both the PSBR and £M3 growth, along with the outcomes.

Table 1.2
MTFS, 1980, and the outcome

	PSBR		£M3	
	Target	Actual	Target	Actual
1980/1	3.8	5.4	7–11	17.7
1981/2	3.0	3.3	6–10	14.1
1982/3	2.3	3.2	5–9	10.9
1983/4	1.5	3.2	4–8	8.6

Note: PSBR is given as a % of GNP. Targets are those announced in 1980 for the following four years.

Source: Davies (1985).

The failure to meet £M3 targets in the first two years of the MTFS was in part a result of re-intermediation following the removal of the Corset, and also of the end of foreign exchange controls. Because £M3 appeared to be an unreliable indicator, M1 was added as a monetary target in 1982, as was PSL2, a broad measure of liquid assets including building society shares and certificates of deposit (CDs). M1 was replaced by M0, the monetary base, in 1984. This was because M1 included a rapidly growing share of interest-bearing deposits, and M0 has had a higher correlation with GNP.

In 1985 £M3 once again went above its target range. With M0 exactly at the centre of its range, the government in October temporarily abandoned £M3 and made M0 the monetary target. In the 1986 Budget the behaviour of £M3 was validated by specifying a high target range, and a more moderate growth rate was given for M0. As I discuss below, though, the temporary adoption of the monetary base as the target of monetary policy does not mean that the Bank is moving to control the money stock through the base-money multiplier textbook mechanism.

There should be no doubt about the overall success of MTFS in achieving its main goal, the reduction of inflation. Restrictive fiscal and monetary policy indeed worked. The following discussions of the role of monetary policy take place against a background of success in achieving the ultimate targets of policy.

3. The Monetary Mechanism

Monetary policy affects the economy through three interrelated channels:

1. interest rate effects on prices and aggregate demand;
2. exchange rate effects on prices and aggregate demand;
3. expectations effects on wages, prices, and interest rates.

The effects of monetary policy on asset prices—interest rates and the exchange rate—are immediate, whereas the effects on demand and wages are slow. As a result, monetary policy changes the real exchange rate and the real interest rate.

UK econometric models show a larger exchange rate channel than interest rate effects. Easton (1985) traces the routes through which interest rates affect aggregate demand in five econometric models.[16] In all cases residential investment is affected;[17] so too, typically, are inventories and durables. In simulations in which the nominal interest rate is reduced by 2 per cent, Easton finds a wide range of estimated multipliers for both inflation and output. The multipliers depend on whether the exchange rate is held fixed or allowed to depreciate, on whether the change is expected to be transitory or permanent (in the Liverpool model), but also, significantly, on the model. The Bank of England and NIESR models show virtually no effects on real output and employment, the Treasury and LBS show significant increases, while Liverpool produces a contraction.[18] In the non-Liverpool models, an interest rate decline increases inflation in those simulations in which the exchange rate depreciates.

In simulations in which the nominal exchange rate is held fixed, the real effects of the interest rate decline are substantially reduced, particularly in the LBS model. In each case the inflation rate is higher when the exchange rate is allowed to depreciate; in the Treasury model an interest rate decline reduces inflation when the nominal exchange rate is held fixed.

The comparisons imply substantial exchange rate effects on both inflation and output. Such effects are found too in simulations of the NIESR and Treasury models attempting to account for the 1979–82 disinflation by Artis *et al.* (1984). In the Treasury model, a 15 per cent appreciation within the first three years reduces the price level and average earnings each by 5 per cent, with only a 0.5 per cent effect on GDP. The beneficial inflation effects take a year longer to become very large in the NIESR model, but cause significant output losses.[19] A related simulation of the Treasury model by Melliss starts with a 5 per cent exogenous depreciation, described as the result of a decline in confidence. Real GDP rises for three years, peaking at an increase of 0.7 per cent above base; the inflation rate peaks in year 2 at 1.2 per cent above the base-line rate, with the cumulative effect at 3 per cent above the initial price path within five years (Melliss 1984). The current account follows a J-curve, the surplus increasing by about 0.4 per cent of GNP within three years.

Small-scale price–wage determination models contain several routes for the exchange rate to affect prices. For instance, Layard and Nickell (in Chapter 5 below) show import-price effects in their labour demand equation, wage equation, and price equation. The reduced-form magnitude of exchange rate effects is not clear from their reported results,[20] but may well be large.[21]

The Radcliffe Committee argued that monetary policy affects the economy through aggregate demand. Expectations provide another potentially powerful and more rapid mechanism. The exchange rate mechanism operates rapidly because the exchange rate is an asset price, the response of which to monetary action depends on expectations of future exchange rates and policies. The extent to which short interest rate movements affect long rates, and thus some components of investment, depends on expectations working through the term structure. Asset market expectations can be crucial too in the choice of a monetary target and, particularly in an open economy, in forcing policy changes to stop an exchange rate rout.

But monetary policy may also affect labour market expectations and wage-setting. The hope that firm policy guidelines would shift the Phillips curve must have been part of the rationale for the MTFS. Such a link cannot be ruled out *a priori*, but it does not appear to have played a significant part part in the British or US disinflations.

The Shifting Phillips Curve and Monetary Policy

The key issue defining future British macroeconomic policy choices is the need to explain the continuing shifts of the Phillips curve. Two hypotheses are broadly consistent with the data. First, the natural rate of unemployment may have been increasing over time, and now could be above 10 per cent. This is the Layard–Nickell thesis (Chapter 5 below). With a time trend, the simplest Phillips curve with annual data produces a strong unemployment *level* effect. For the period, 1963–85, using annual data, with the rate of change of wages (*DW*) as the dependent variable, the relationship is

$$DW = 0.920 - 0.030INFE - 3.069RU_{-1} + 0.553RU_{-2} + 1.429TIME$$
$$(0.48)\quad(0.12)\qquad\quad(3.65)\qquad\quad(0.50)\qquad\quad(3.85)$$

$$\bar{R}^2 = 0.67,\ \text{Durbin–Watson} = 1.99 \tag{1.2}$$

where *INFE* is a constructed expected inflation rate, the weighted average of the previous three year's rates (weights are 0.5, 0.3, and 0.2); *t*-statistics are in parentheses.

Second, with the time trend omitted, the Phillips curve becomes a relationship between the rate of wage inflation and the *change* in unemployment.[22] The equation is:

$$DW = 5.740 + 0.808INFE - 3.019RU_{-1} + 2.952RU_{-2} \tag{1.3}$$
$$(3.00)\quad(4.30)\qquad\quad(2.73)\qquad\quad(2.48)$$

$$\bar{R}^2 = 0.43,\ \text{Durbin–Watson} = 1.58.$$

Autocorrelation correction did not much change the coefficients, moving the two coefficients on lagged unemployment to -2.684 and 2.624 respectively, each with *t*-statistics well above 2. Nor does constraining the coefficient of expected inflation to 1 substantially affect the remaining coefficients. In neither this equation nor the previous one did exchange rate effects appear significantly.

The rising natural rate view focuses policy attention on structural labour market policies. Despite the success of (1.2), the absence of a significant expected inflation rate rate from that equation renders it suspect. The second view is related to the hysteresis argument that rising unemployment increases the natural rate.[23] The present formulation does offer the prospect of moving the inflation rate down without causing unemployment if expectations are not determined purely by actual inflation behaviour. If expectations of inflation cannot be affected other than by reducing inflation, the possibility that the rate of change of unemployment enters the Phillips curve is bad news indeed, for any change in inflation brought about by increased unemployment can be preserved only at the cost of higher unemployment.[24] Only favourable shocks that reduce the rate of wage increase, or more subtle effects omitted from the equation such as those from exchange rates, offer hope of bringing down the inflation rate without creating a permanent rise in unemployment.

Although the policy dilemmas raised by equation (1.3)-type Phillips curves are severe, they do not have major implications for monetary policy in particular. Whatever the optimal path chosen for the economy, monetary policy will have a role to play. A particular role would come if the policy mix could have differential effects on output and inflation, given nominal GNP. This would occur if the exchange rate or import prices appeared directly in the wage–price sector, as they do. In that case, a disinflation accompanied by an appreciation—the tight money–loose fiscal US combination—will have more rapid effects on prices than the opposite mixture.[25]

It makes little difference to the analysis of the effects of a one-time monetary policy intervention whether the action is taken as a change in the money stock or a change in an interest rate, provided that change is brought about in the same way. Of course, it does make a difference whether the interest rate is changed through moral suasion, through direct controls, through an open market operation, or through fiscal policy. And of course, a policy that increases the growth rate of money is different from a policy that increases the ratio of money to debt in the economy, even though in the short run both policies may start with an open market purchase.

4. The British Approach to Monetary Policy

While British monetary policy rhetoric has turned to monetarism and money targeting, British policy thinking is far from monetarism in the US sense. The essential difference is that interest rates are entirely central to British monetary analysis and are incidental to monetarism. In April 1986, the Chancellor confirmed that 'Short-term interest rates are the essential instrument of monetary policy.'[26]

The importance of interest rates arises at two levels. First, as noted in Section 1, British monetary analysis sees the nominal money supply as being determined proximately through the choice of a nominal interest rate. In his 16 April 1986 speech, the Chancellor explained that 'no Government that is interested in controlling the quantity of money can be indifferent to its price'. And second, there is evident concern about the adverse consequences of interest rate variability. The desire to smooth interest rates, or the existence of interest rate targets, is the key to understanding several important policy episodes.[27]

The first is the MTFS, which ties fiscal to monetary policy. Neither US monetarists nor Keynesians would tie monetary and fiscal policies together closely, at least not in the short run. In the long run, the government Budget constraint does connect monetary and fiscal policy more closely, if fiscal policy is defined with reference to the primary Budget.[28] But the MTFS initially specified its deficit and money growth paths for consistency with a desirable interest rate path.

A second example is base control, which was extensively discussed in 1979 and 1980, in the process that led up to the Green Paper on *Monetary Control* (Cmnd 7858).[29] The Green Paper first discusses the operation of a base-money control mechanism without mandatory reserve requirements, arguing that such a system would not be possible in the UK unless the Bank withdrew the lender of last resort facility. By this, it means presumably withdrawing the right of the discount houses to have access to the Bank. In fact, there is no need whatsoever to give up the lender of last resort function, but only the automatic provider of reserve money function. The Bank would still be free under a base control system to provide added reserves as it saw fit, including in those the circumstances in which the lender of last resort function should be exercised. The report then goes on to say that, even if balances with the Bank of England were to become 'the only effective form of primary liquidity', base control would not limit the money supply because banks' reserve ratios would vary.

Turning to a system with a required reserve ratio, the report raises several issues, including the choice between lagged, current, and lead accounting. In tentatively rejecting base control, the Green Paper emphasizes the danger of dis-intermediation if a serious penalty scheme is set up for violaters of the reserve requirement. Goodhart (1985) also notes the likely instability of money market rates under such a scheme.

There appear to have been three objections to the base-money approach to monetary control: a fear of interest rate volatility, a fear that Goodhart's law would strike by taking intermediation away from institutions controlled by the Bank, and a belief that credit rather than money was the right variable to control.

The fear of interest rate volatility and the implicit assumption of nominal interest rate targets at both the short and long ends link both the above examples. The Green Paper says: 'Using the basic weapons of fiscal policy, gilt-edged funding and short-term interest rates, the monetary authorities can achieve the first requisite of control of the money supply—control, say, over a year or more' (Bank of England 1984a, p. 138). This statement makes sense only if the long rate is taken as given; otherwise monetary control can be achieved through open market operations that determine the quantity of base-money.[30] At the same time, the Treasury (through the Bank) can sell whatever amounts of gilt-edged it wants. Open market operations, if necessary at the short end, and gilt-edged sales between them would affect interest rates.[31]

Fear of interest rate volatility and the constraint of gilt-edged sales can be seen too in the government's reluctance to sell gilt-edged securities in a falling market.[32] It is remarkable that the authorities do not trust the London market, with its supposed breadth and strength, to absorb without excess interest rate variability the rolling over, and additions to a national debt that is very long-term and amounts to only 50 per cent of GNP. This attitude to the sale of gilt-edged is a vestige of the period when the national debt was three times GNP. There is no good reason now why debt sales should not be moved off tap and into auctions, in which case the implicit interest constraint would either come into the open or be abandoned.[33]

Interest rates are not only targets, but also instruments. Official descriptions of Competition and Credit Control (CCC) refer to the interest rate as a means of controlling the volume of credit. The notion that it is the availability rather than the cost of credit that matters for spending plans is at the base of this approach, even though CCC was intended to move away from direct control over credit allocation. The alternative is to think of the quantity of credit as determining the interest rate, and the cost of borrowing in turn as determining investment and durable spending.

Similarly, as described in Section 1, the interest rate was seen as the mechanism for determining £M3. An increase in the interest rate would reduce the demand for credit, thereby reducing bank loans, and, via the balance sheet identity, reducing £M3. The shift to monetary targeting became a constraint on fiscal policy because the authorities knew what interest rates they wanted, knew what money growth rates were needed to keep the markets happy, and therefore had to find another instrument—fiscal policy—to produce the right money growth.

A final example of the role attached to interest rates comes from Charles Goodhart (1985), who suggests that variables that serve as a monetary target should have an interest-elastic demand function. The basis for this argument is set out in Section 1. A US monetarist would be quite happy even with a totally interest-insensitive money target; for in that case disturbances to interest rates that originate elsewhere in the economy would not directly affect the quantity of money demanded, and, more positively for a monetarist, a given change in the money stock would not be dissipated through interest rate adjustments.[34]

Although the Chancellor, in his April 1986 Lombard Association speech, made inflation the main nominal target, monetary targets continue to be specified. In the US case, the money targets adopted in 1979 provided cover for disinflationary monetary policy that pushed nominal interest rates to record levels. With disinflation in hand, and the £M3 velocity relationship having broken down, the British government, like the Fed, appears to be relegating monetary targets to their appropriate position as indicators of the policy that will be followed if no disturbances—including velocity shifts—appear.

There are three separate issues here. The first is whether there should continue to be monetary targets. The answer is yes, monetary targets do provide information about policy plans, and do force policy-makers to explain their actions rather than flying by the seat of their pants. The second is whether it is advisable to pay attention to interest rates in setting money targets, and in deviating from them. The answer again is yes: velocity shifts make singleminded devotion to money targets inadvisable, and the authorities should have regard to interest rates.

The third question is whether £M3 is a good monetary target as opposed to indicator. The answer is no. There are too many steps between what the Bank does and £M3 for it to serve as a good guide for monetary policy. Further, the analysis underlying £M3 tends to build in interest rate targets that may never be thought about under the present procedures, which should be changed to break the close link between monetary and fiscal policy so that the policy mix can have a chance to be used. Further, there is some evidence that restrictive monetary policy, which raises nominal interest rates, may increase rather than reduce £M3.

The narrower monetary magnitudes are controllable, and are more likely to be inversely related to market interest rates. They would be preferable indicators of and targets for monetary policy in the short run of several months, when GNP data are still difficult to interpret. With M0 now playing an increasingly important target role, the Bank should move to base targeting and consider changing the monetary system so that it can control the base. This does not necessarily stop interest rate targets from affecting policy, but it does ensure that the monetary consequences of alternative interest rate targets are weighed explicitly.

The continuing fear of the Bank that any variable that is controlled loses its meaning is correct, more so the broader the target, but that is just a fact of life. That is why it is important for the Bank to target a variable like the base, which it can control. Attachment to credit as a quantitative target is particularly inappropriate, because new credit routes can open up with extraordinary speed. Interest rates and the cost of credit are the variables that should be targeted if the aim is to affect aggregate demand through credit variables. And interest rates can be controlled through narrow money targets. The desired level of the target is bound to be changed, both in the short run in response to disturbances, and in the longer run as institutions develop.

Attention to interest rates is far from sticking closely to interest rate targets. Like money targets, interest rate targets should be used, constantly reappraised, and changed as often as circumstances require.

Nominal GNP targeting has received considerable attention in Britain (see Bean 1983). On this, the appropriate conclusions have been drawn. Nominal GNP targets will be implied by any coherent policy, and can be announced year by year. Beyond this there is no reason why the government should not announce a long-term target path for nominal GNP, which is a more plausible target path than one for the money stock or the Budget deficit. It will be understood that year-by-year policy is chosen consistent with this target path, so that money targets can vary as velocity shifts and fiscal policy can be adjusted, and that the target path may be changed. The policy mix provides some hope of affecting inflation and real output differentially, so that policy choices may suffer from being constrained by an overall nominal GNP target.

It is hard to believe, though, that divergences from a specified nominal GNP path arising from changes in the policy mix could be especially large.

Whatever value attaches to long-run nominal targeting is bound to be greater if the target is plausible. Numerical nominal GNP targets are more likely to continue than any specific money growth targets. That is the case for long-term nominal GNP targeting. Such targeting makes no sense as part of a short-run monetary policy strategy, which has to be specified in terms of variables more closely under the control of the authorities.

With the exchange rate as the main transmission mechanism for monetary policy, direct exchange rate targeting would tie monetary policy more closely to the ultimate objectives of policy. The Bank has typically acknowledged an exchange rate objective. For instance, in explaining why base control was not accepted in 1979–80, J. S. Fforde (Bank of England 1984a, p. 72) states: 'For by then the need to have regard to a range of indicators, including the exchange rate, when judging the appropriateness of policy in respect of ultimate objectives, was becoming very evident.'

The Governor clarified the exchange rate commitment in October 1984:

There are even those who still insist that we have some kind of exchange rate target. How they can still think this after the exchange rate movements in both directions which have occurred in recent years and months—not only against the dollar but also against the generality of currencies—defeats me.

Let me repeat without qualification that we do not have an exchange rate target. But this is quite a different matter from saying that we are not concerned about the movement in the exchange rate. We are—because there are times when the movement in the exchange rate is telling us something about domestic monetary conditions, telling us for example that the indications from the target aggregates do indeed need qualification. [Bank of England 1984b, p. 476]

The case for paying more attention than that to the exchange rate is strong, given the pervasive influence of exchange rate changes on the economy. The fear of the authorities is that exchange rate targets are useless because they are certain to be overwhelmed by capital flows if the market disagrees with the government—and that the market is not always right.

Even if Britain stays out of the EMS, it should still give more weight than it has to exchange rate targets. Although it has been difficult to establish effects of exchange rate variability on trade (see Bank of England 1984c), the large variations permitted in 1984 cannot have been useful in an economy in which exchange rate changes affect domestic prices and output. Capital flows will make it impossible to fix the exchange rate when there is no formal commitment, but allowing greater interest rate variability will provide more control over the exchange rate—and, given the relative effects of interest rates and exchange rates on the ecomomy, increased interest rate variability can be traded off for less exchange rate variability.

The discussion of this section is remarkably and unabashedly generous in its range of monetary indicators; for both quantities and asset prices, including the exchange rate, provide information on the disturbances affecting the economy. British monetary policy has been moving in the direction of explicitly taking into account a wide range of monetary variables. In his 16 April 1986 speech, the Chancellor, in addition to describing short-term interest rates as the essential instrument of monetary policy, noted that increasing attention was being paid to the exchange rate and narrow money measures as indicators of future inflationary pressure.

Despite the pragmatic shift from a rigorous £M3 target to a wide variety of monetary indicators, and discussion of nominal GNP targeting, there has been no change in the ultimate target of British macroeconomic policy since 1979: the inflation rate. The government has taken the view that monetary policy controls the price level, and that the real side is determined largely by microeconomic considerations.[35] Monetary policy has thus been directed to bringing the inflation rate down, and it has succeeded.

The success came at the cost of extraordinarily high unemployment. Whether it could have been attained at lower cost depends in part on whether the monetary–fiscal mix affects output and inflation differentially, as the US experience and econometric models discussed above suggest. It depends also on whether a slower path of nominal demand reduction, with due attention to the difference between the full employment and actual Budget deficits, could have brought inflation down with a less rapid and smaller increase in unemployment.

5. Joining the EMS

There are two serious arguments *against* joining the EMS. The first is that, by joining, Britain would give up its policy autonomy. The second is that only Germany has succeeded in the EMS without capital controls and trade intervention. If joining the EMS required Britain to re-impose controls, and to interfere with trade, these objections would be strong.[36]

The argument *for* joining the EMS is that the autonomy that Britain would give up is the autonomy to inflate, which it would prefer to be without, and which is the source of the doubts about future policy that make any moves to expansion difficult at present. Further, whatever obstacles to trade arise in the EMS are a consequence of the EEC, not the EMS. That leaves the important issue of capital controls.

Even with Britain not in the EMS, the sterling exchange rate against the Deutschmark has been far more stable than the rate against the dollar. It is entirely possible that Britain can operate in the EMS without the use of capital controls if it stays on the present low-inflation course. And it is far more likely to stay on that course if it does belong to the EMS.

The issue of British membership should give as much concern to the rest of the EMS as it does to Britain. The EMS is currently an arrangement for France and Italy to purchase a commitment to low inflation by accepting

German monetary policy. With Britain in, there would be two major international currencies in the system, reducing the dominance of the Deutschmark. In the absence of capital controls, specifically British disturbances would be transmitted to Europe through the exchange rate commitment. The German anchor would become relatively less weighty. Presumably the Europeans, including the Germans, are willing to accept that.

In brief, the case for Britain to join is that exchange rate variability is costly, and that the implied commitment to low inflation will cement the gains of the last few years on inflation. The credibility of the exchange rate commitment is far more valuable than the credibility of the MTFS in affecting inflationary expectations.

The decision to join the EMS is long-term, and should not be made in light of the particular problems of the day. None the less, the present conjuncture provides a good test case of the value of policy autonomy. The major policy need at present is for a sustained attack on unemployment. Supply-side policies to reduce the incentives for continued unemployment and induce wage flexibility are an essential part of the package. So is fiscal expansion, which can build on the disinflationary oil shock.

Could such a package be undertaken along with a commitment to the EMS? Obviously, the supply-side measures would not damage the EMS commitment. Exchange rate appreciation would—but Europe too may be expanding with the oil shock. Exchange rate appreciation should not in any event be allowed to get too far out of line, and EMS membership will ensure that. The fear in any serious reflationary package is that it will be seen as a signal of a change in resolve on inflation. That is less likely to happen in the EMS than out of it. There is indeed a serious case in favour of Britain joining.

6. Summary

British monetary policy can be characterized in terms of its announcement, targeting, and operating procedures. Since the 1960s, the notion that monetary policy is best conducted in silence and ambiguity has given way to increasingly explicit announcements of operating and ultimate targets of policy. Explicit monetary targets were introduced in the early 1970s and were made public from 1976 on.

Until 1979, the ultimate targets of policy were both inflation and unemployment, though monetary policy in Britain as in other countries assumed special, if during the 1970s unsuccessful, responsibility for maintaining low inflation and the value of money. Since 1979 the low-inflation goal has been primary, with the government expressing the view that real variables are essentially independent of macroeconomic policy. Discussion of monetary policy since 1979 takes place against a background of its success in achieving its goal of sharply reducing inflation.

Although the adoption of internal monetary targets in the early 1970s followed the end of Bretton Woods, monetary targets were probably not at the time a substitute for an exchange rate target. They were adopted because monetarism was at that time gaining popularity, among both market participants and researchers, because the demand for M3 appeared empirically stable, and especially because the inflationary outburst of 1974–5 was preceded by rapid growth in M3.

Monetary targets became explicit in 1976. The instability of the M3 demand function led to the adoption of other monetary targets, both broader and narrower. Most recently, the monetary base M0 has received increasing emphasis, though there has been no move to base control as a means of controlling money growth. There have been no formal exchange rate targets, and wide fluctuations in the exchange rate. Monetary policy does sometimes respond to exchange rate movements.

The Medium Term Financial Strategy tied monetary and fiscal policy together, thereby precluding countercyclical fiscal policy or the use of the fiscal–monetary policy mix. MTFS could have emphasized nominal GNP targets as the appropriate goals of policy, but instead specified deficit and money growth targets as a guide to expectations and policy. The many advantages of nominal GNP targeting may eventually lead to its replacing the targeting of policy variables.

There have been no publicly announced interest rate targets, though the Bank has at times had internal interest rate objectives. Interest rates none the less play a central role in monetary policy. Monetary policy is eased or tightened by lowering or raising rates. Viewing the demand for high-powered money as unstable because reserve ratios are extremely low, the Bank sees itself achieving its money targets by affecting interest rates. It thereby moves individuals along their demand functions to the point where they demand the targeted quantities.

Interest rates are thus entirely central to the authorities' view of the monetary mechanism. Not only are they important in their own right as determinants of economic activity, but they also determine nominal stocks of assets in the short run. So long as there is an active nominal target, the use of operating interest rate targets need not be the source of any instability.

The main issue confronting monetary policy in Britain at present is whether an explicit and strong exchange rate target should become the centrepiece of policy, by joining the EMS. The balance of the argument favours this course.

This paper was prepared for the Conference on the British Economy, Chelwood Gate, Sussex, May 1986. I am grateful to my formal discussants Sir Terry Burns and Charles Goodhart for constructive and detailed comments that have improved the paper, and to Christopher Allsopp, Rudiger Dornbusch, John Flemming, Laurence Harris, Richard Layard, and Marcus Miller for their help. Financial assistance from the National Science Foundation is acknowledged with thanks.

APPENDIX: ANNUAL DATA, 1970–85

	RUET	IP	GRIP	GDPR	REGR	GDPN	NGR	INFGDP	CAE-TRAT
1970	2.600	90.2	0.6	190.26	2.2	51.50	9.7	7.3	0.783
1971	3.100	89.7	−0.6	195.33	2.7	57.84	12.1	9.4	0.988
1972	3.500	91.3	1.8	199.64	2.2	64.05	10.7	8.3	0.157
1973	2.400	99.5	9.0	215.46	7.9	74.00	16.5	7.1	−0.749
1974	2.400	97.5	−2.0	213.04	−1.1	84.10	13.6	14.9	−2.252
1975	3.700	92.2	−5.4	211.50	−0.7	106.26	25.2	27.3	−0.990
1976	5.000	95.2	3.3	219.59	3.8	126.44	19.6	14.6	−0.512
1977	5.300	100.2	5.3	221.82	1.0	145.57	13.9	14.0	−0.064
1978	5.200	103.1	2.9	230.31	3.8	167.84	15.7	11.0	0.432
1979	4.800	107.1	3.9	235.44	2.2	196.38	17.1	14.5	−0.293
1980	6.100	100.0	−6.6	230.01	−2.3	230.01	16.3	19.9	1.135
1981	9.500	96.6	−3.4	226.80	−1.4	253.47	10.7	11.8	2.139
1982	11.100	98.4	1.9	230.00	1.4	276.04	8.9	7.4	1.473
1983	12.100	101.9	3.6	237.95	3.5	300.11	9.2	5.1	0.931
1984	12.600	103.1	1.2	242.15	1.8	318.09	6.2	4.2	0.248
1985	13.100	108.2	4.9	250.36	3.8	351.15	8.8	5.4	0.800

	GH	GM1	GM2	GM3	INF	TBR	DW	PSBRR	RER
1970	11.6	9.3	9.4	8.6	6.1	7.01	12.4	−0.050	72.3
1971	−5.1	15.1	13.2	14.0	9.4	5.57	11.0	1.197	75.5
1972	21.2	14.2	27.9	27.2	7.3	5.54	13.0	1.610	75.7
1973	31.5	5.1	27.5	27.1	9.2	9.34	13.5	3.011	67.8
1974	4.1	10.8	12.9	11.0	15.8	11.37	17.6	4.360	64.6
1975	10.1	18.6	7.1	5.8	24.3	10.18	26.6	6.356	70.0
1976	19.9	11.3	11.6	9.8	16.6	11.12	15.6	5.013	64.0
1977	5.3	20.8	9.5	9.4	15.8	7.68	10.2	2.752	67.5
1978	9.8	16.3	14.6	15.6	8.3	8.51	14.6	3.761	72.4
1979	9.8	9.1	12.5	13.2	13.5	12.98	15.3	5.052	81.3
1980	−2.9	4.0	18.5	18.7	17.9	15.11	18.8	4.325	100.0
1981	3.8	17.7	27.8	13.5	11.9	13.03	13.4	3.468	102.7
1982	4.3	11.3	11.4	9.3	8.6	11.47	11.4	1.565	99.3
1983	2.8	11.1	13.0	11.0	4.6	9.59	8.6	3.413	92.4
1984	4.0	15.4	12.3	10.1	5.0	9.30	5.7	2.700	90.0
1985	4.4	17.1	13.9	15.0	6.1	11.55	11.2	1.893	92.3

Notes:
RUET = %unemployment rate, *Economic Trends*; *IP* = industrial production, IFS; *GRIP* = growth rate of *IP*; *GDPR* = real GDP, IFS; *REGR* = growth rate of *GDPR*; *GDPN* = nominal GDP; *NGR* = growth rate of *GDPN*; *INFGDP* = inflation rate of GDP deflator, IFS; *CAETRAT* = current account as a percentage of GNP (current account from *Economic Trends*, GNP from IFS); *GH* = growth rate of high-powered money (IFS, line 14); *GM1* = growth rate of M1 (IFS, line 34); *GM2* = growth rate of M2 (IFS, line 351); *GM3* = growth rate of M3 (*Economic Trends*); *INF* = inflation rate of CPI (IFS); *TBR* = Treasury bill rate (IFS; *DW* = growth rate of wages (IFS, line 65); ave. monthly earnings; *PSBRR* = PSBR as % of GNP (PSBR from *Economic Trends*, GNP from IFS); *RER* = real exchange rate (IFS; relative value added deflators).

Notes

1. The Appendix table presents annual data for the major macroeconomic variables.
2. Buiter and Miller (1981) give oil a relatively small, and tight money a larger, share of the credit for the appreciation.
3. The article 'The Role of the Bank of England in the Money Market', in Bank of England (1984), describes much of the money supply process.
4. See McCallum (1986) for a demonstration that the price level is not indeterminate when the nominal interest rate is controlled, so long as the government has some nominal target that directs the policy.
5. In discussion at the conference, I noted that monetarists would regard an interest-inelastic money demand function with equanimity, whereas the Bank's explanation of the money supply process laid stress on the need for the demand to be interest responsive. The difference results from the use of expression (1.1) as a model of money supply determination by at least US monetarists, whereas British monetary economists appear to think in terms of a model like that of Figure 1.4.
6. Radcliffe Committee (1959, pp. 22–3). Radcliffe's definition of the goals of external policy included the ability to make a contribution to world economic development.
7. Bank of England (1984a) and Goodhart (1984) cover the historical record. See also Spencer (1985).
8. For example, in speeches and papers reprinted in Bank of England (1984b).
9. P. D. Spencer (1985, Ch. IV) calculates that the removal of controls accounted for about a 10% increase in M3 during the 1970–3 period.
10. See 'The Supplementary Special Deposits Scheme' (Bank of England 1984a, pp. 117–28).
11. The main channel was the so-called bill leak. Banks accepted private paper, providing a guarantee that in effect turned the paper into bank credit that did not, however, appear on the bank's balance sheet.
12. In the Governor's Mais lecture (Bank of England 1984a, p. 54).
13. Hacche (1984) shows that M1 demand and personal M3 demand showed smaller forecast errors for the 1971–3 period than M3.
14. The flow of funds relationship is: change in M3 = PSBR − (public sector debt sales to private non-bank sector) + (increase in bank lending) + (net external flows) − (increase in non-deposit bank liabilities). Domestic credit expansion (DCE) is the sum of first three items. DCE targets were imposed in the UK by the IMF in 1967 and 1976.
15. Walters (1986, p. 107) states that, although the adoption of monetary targets was much influenced by the state of sterling, the targets were not imposed by the IMF.
16. The models are those of the Bank of England, London Business School (LBS), HM Treasury, NIESR, and University of Liverpool.
17. The short, rather than the long, interest rate is the relevant variable in four of the models.
18. This last result occurs because the only exogenous variable that Easton could find with which to shift the nominal UK interest rate was the US interest rate; accordingly, the policy shift led to an appreciation of sterling as opposed to a depreciation in the other models.
19. The comparison here is between Tables 2 and 4 in Artis *et al.* (1984).
20. I have not been able to calculate a rule of thumb corresponding to the claim in the USA that a 10% appreciation reduces the price level by 1.5%. Dornbusch and

Fischer (1986) find a total effect exceeding 2%, as a result of direct exchange rate effects in both the price and wage equations. Prices of imports, along with wages, have significant effects on price inflation. In addition, given the rate of unemployment, exchange rate appreciation reduces the rate of wage inflation. Dornbusch and Fischer attribute this last effect to sectoral pressures on demand in industries (for example, motor cars) especially vulnerable to import competition.

21. Layard and Nickell attribute 1 percentage point of the increase in unemployment between 1965–74 and 1975–9 to higher import prices, including oil (Ch. 5 below).
22. When the coefficient on the expected inflation rate is constrained to unity, the time trend drops out of equation (1.2).
23. See for example Blanchard and Summers (1986) and Sachs (1986).
24. Sachs (1986) does not include expected inflation in his analysis of optimal policy with hysteresis. I am ignoring the fact that the coefficients on RU_{-1} and RU_{-2} are not exactly equal in absolute value.
25. The other possibility, already noted, is that money growth has a direct effect on the expectations that affect wage-setting.
26. Speech to the Lombard Association, 16 April 1986.
27. Internal interest rate targets were acknowledged in connection with the ending of the Corset.
28. Patrick Minford offers as a long-run relation that the PSBR-to-GNP ratio should be half the target inflation rate (Minford 1985, p. 2).
29. The relevant part of the Green Paper is reprinted in Bank of England (1984b). For further discussion see Goodhart (1985); see also Spencer (1985, Ch. 11).
30. Changes in methods of monetary control introduced in 1980 and 1981 did envisage greater use of open market operations to affect interest rates.
31. In discussing MTFS, I argued that a concern over interest rates produced the link between fiscal and monetary policy. It should be noted that, by holding the budget deficit constant in the face of declining income, MTFS implicitly tightens fiscal policy in recessions relative to a policy that fixes spending and tax rates. Although the fiscal policy tightening would produce lower interest rates, it would accentuate rather than offset the recession.
32. A comparison of the volatility of interest rates in the USA and the UK shows that first differences of all rates were more stable in the USA over the 1974–9 period, and more stable in the UK in the period 1979(4) to 1985(4). (Data are Treasury bill and long-term government bond yields, quarterly, from IFS.)
33. In his comments at the conference, Charles Goodhart noted that the markets had not yet developed to the point where gilts could be sold into a falling market, or where auctions were likely to work well. Such institutions would have been developed if the authorities had thought they were important (see 'Comments' below).
34. There remains the difficult question of how monetary policy effects would be transmitted to the economy if the interest rate did not play that role. Direct and immediate effects of a change in M on P or Y are difficult to imagine.
35. See Nigel Lawson's Mais Lecture (Lawson 1984).
36. Goodhart (1986); see also Davies and Morrison (1986).

References

Artis, J. J. *et al.* (1984), 'The Effects of Economic Policy 1979–82', *National Institute Economic Review*, no. 108, 54–67.

Bank of England (1984a), *The Development and Operation of Monetary Policy, 1960–1983*. Oxford: Clarendon Press.

—— (1984b), 'Some Aspects of UK Monetary Policy', *Bank of England Quarterly Bulletin*, 24, 346–9.

—— (1984c), 'The Variability of Exchange Rates: Measurement and Effects', *Bank of England Quarterly Bulletin*, 24, 474–81.

Bean, Charles (1983), 'Targeting National Income', *Economic Journal*, 93, 806–19.

Biswas, Rajiv, Johns, Christopher, and Savings, David (1985), 'The Measurement of Fiscal Stance', *National Institute Economic Review*, no. 113, 50–64.

Blanchard, Olivier and Summers, Lawrence (1986), 'Hysteresis and the European Unemployment Problem', *NBER Macroeconomics Annual*, 15–78.

Buiter, Willem H. and Miller, Marcus (1981), 'The Thatcher Experiment: The First Two Years', *Brookings Papers on Economic Activity*, 315–67.

Davies, Gavyn (1985), 'The Macroeconomic Record of the Conservatives', Goldman Sachs, London.

Davies, Gavyn and Morrison, David (1986), 'UK Monetary Policy, Target Zones, and the EMS', Goldman Sachs, London.

Dornbusch, Rudiger and Fischer, Stanley (1986), 'The Open Economy: Implications for Monetary and Fiscal Policy', in Robert J. Gordon (ed.), *The American Business Cycle*, University of Chicago Press.

Easton, W. W. (1985), 'The Importance of Interest Rates in Five Macroeconomic Models', Bank of England Discussion Paper, October.

Goodhart, Charles A. E. (1984), *Monetary Theory and Practice*. London: Macmillan.

—— (1985), 'Monetary Control—the British Experience', in C. van Ewijk and J. J. Klant (eds.), *Monetary Conditions for Economic Recovery*. Amsterdam: Martinus Nijhoff.

—— (1986), 'Has the Time Come for the UK to Join the EMS?', *The Banker*, 136, 26–8.

—— with Crockett, Andrew (1970), 'The Importance of Money', *Bank of England Quarterly Bulletin*, 10, 159–98.

Hacche, Graham (1984), 'The Demand for Money in the United Kingdom: Experience since 1971', in Bank of England (1984a).

Lawson, Nigel (1981), 'Thatcherism in Practice: A Progress Report'. Paper given to Zurich Society of Economics, 14 January.

—— (1984), 'The British Experiment', *Mais Lecture*, 18 June 1984.

McCallum, Bennett T. (1986), 'Some Issues concerning Interest Rate Pegging, Price Level Determinacy, and the Real Bills Doctrine', *Journal of Monetary Economics*, 17(1), 135–60.

Melliss, C. L. (1984), 'Some Experiments with Optimal Control on the Treasury Model', Treasury Working Paper no. 67, April.

Minford, Patrick (1985), in University of Liverpool Quarterly Economic Bulletin.

Radcliffe Committee (1959), *Report of the Committee on the Working of the Monetary System*, Cmnd 827. London: HMSO.

Sachs, Jeffrey (1986), 'High Unemployment in Europe: Diagnosis and Policy Implications', National Bureau of Economic Research Working Paper no. 1830, February.

Spencer, P. D. (1985), 'Competition, Innovation, and Disequilibrium: Problems of Monetary Management in the United Kingdom 1971–1981'. Unpublished manuscript.

Walters, Alan (1986), *Britain's Economic Renaissance*. Oxford: University Press.

CHAPTER 2

Fiscal Policy

David Begg

Birkbeck College, London

1. Introduction

Fiscal policy refers to government decisions about its revenue and expenditure. Since 1970 Britain has been governed successively by the Conservatives (1970–4), Labour (1974–9), and the Conservatives (since 1979). Table 2.1 presents some familiar indicators of fiscal policy corresponding to these terms of office. Over the period as a whole, popular discussion may have overstated the magnitude of increases in spending, debt interest, and tax revenues. If this table has a simple message, it lies in the increase in transfer payments (most notably unemployment benefit), financed to a large extent by higher government borrowing.

It is instructive to recall that until 1970 most discussion of fiscal policy would have adduced statistics similar to those presented in the table; and this was true as much in university lectures as in the popular press or on the floor of the House of Commons. Since 1970, economics has given considerable emphasis to intertemporal decision-making in which expectations play a key role, and has made explicit the accounting framework which relates current flows to the evolution of stocks over time, not least in the public sector balance sheet. Hence I take as my starting point the statement that the only coherent

Table 2.1
Simple indicators of fiscal policy, 1970–1984
(% of GDP at market prices)

	1970	1973	1979	1984
Government spending on:				
goods and services	22.3	23.1	22.4	23.8
transfer payments	12.0	12.5	14.9	17.7
debt interest	4.1	3.6	4.4	4.9
Taxes and other revenues	41.2	36.6	38.4	42.6
PSBR	0.0	5.6	6.4	3.5

Sources: Annual Abstract of Statistics; Economic Trends.

I should like to thank David Currie, Rudiger Dornbusch, Gareth Evans, John Flemming, Robert Gordon, Richard Layard, and Marcus Miller for helpful discussions. Gareth Evans and Charles Johnson provided invaluable research assistance. All remaining errors are my own.

definition of *current* fiscal policy is today's plans for spending, taxes, and borrowing—not just today, but over the indefinite future.[1]

It is not simply the description or measurement of fiscal policy that has been amended since 1970: its very focus has altered. Until 1970 demand management had been seen as much the most important objective for fiscal policy in the postwar period. Yet in the mid-1980s, with high and persistent unemployment, fiscal policy was very tight. If my review of UK fiscal policy since 1970 has a single theme, it is the story of how demand management ceased to be the overriding objective of fiscal policy in the UK.

To this end, my discussion is organized as follows. Section 2 considers how to measure fiscal stance, the impact of fiscal policy on aggregate demand. Section 3 reviews briefly the history of demand management in the UK. Having set the scene, I then discuss the rationale for following such policies. Section 4 examines whether tight fiscal policy was required either by considerations of sound finance and the need to avert a domestic debt crisis, or by the need for sound money to hold inflation in check. Section 5 discusses whether tight fiscal policy became necessary for supply-side reasons. Conclusions are offered in Section 6.

2. Indicators of Fiscal Stance

I begin with the traditional role of fiscal policy as an instrument of demand management. The systematic use of policy to reduce the fluctuations of output around its natural or potential level is possible only if two conditions hold. First, policy must have an impact effect on demand. Second, changes in aggregate demand must not contain the seeds of their immediate undoing through near-instantaneous induced changes in the price of goods, labour, credit, and foreign exchange.

In principle, both conditions may fail to hold. An example of the first is the Barro–Ricardo neutrality theorem, which argues that, under certain (implausible) conditions, a temporary increase in the budget deficit arising from a temporary substitution of bond for tax finance will have no aggregate demand impact whatsoever (see Barro, 1974). More generally, the permanent income hypothesis warns us that many types of temporary fiscal changes may have a very small impact effect on private expenditure. The second condition will generally fail in models of the New Classical variety in which market-clearing is effectively instantaneous. Here let me simply state that while I believe both caveats contain important insights, I regard them both as much too extreme to be practical descriptions of the real world. Policy can affect aggregate demand, not least because the textbook assumption of perfect capital markets is nowhere close to practical fulfilment; and deviations from potential output are not immediately eliminated because short-run sluggishness of wage and price adjusment is a reality, for which modern macroeconomics is gradually providing plausible microfoundations.

In short, I begin from the viewpoint that demand management is not an empty box or a pointless exercise. Grant this and it becomes essential to develop an indicator of fiscal stance if one is to measure and hence evaluate the operation of demand management in the UK since 1970. Before describing such an indicator, I must issue a series of important health warnings.

First, *no* indicator of fiscal policy can be model-free. For example, the consequence of a particular fiscal stimulus will depend critically on the initial level of Keynesian unemployment (if any), the speed with which prices adjust, and the extent of capital market imperfections. Second, no fiscal indicator can be independent of other *policies* in force. For example, it will depend on the extent of monetary accommodation and on the exchange rate regime. Third, as I emphasized in the introduction, a complete description of fiscal policy requires a statement of current perceptions about future fiscal variables which, *inter alia*, requires a specification of how information evolves and expectations are formed.

Even in the abstract world of pure theory, we have precious few examples of models worked out in this degree of detail, though that in Blanchard (1985) is a laudable attempt. A realistic empirical index of fiscal stance would require a convincing macroeconometric model—a supply-side, expectations-forma-tion, serious intertemporal decision-making by the private sector, an account of dynamic adjustment, and so on—into which one could plug the evolution of beliefs about current and future fiscal actions given similar beliefs about other policies in force. While it is right to remind ourselves of this ultimate goal in the pursuit of more sophisticated policy analysis (see e.g. Buiter, 1985, for a powerful plea), it goes without saying that the economics profession is still well short of such an aspiration.

How, then, can we make practical progress immediately? We can get a flavour of what might be involved by looking at Table 2.2, which reports recent simulations undertaken on the operational macroeconometric model of the NIESR. I cite these merely because the source is convenient and some model variables such as the exchange rate are solved using model-consistent expectations, although, like other operational models, the Lucas critique has not been fully extended to all private sector equations. Table 2.2 provides a benchmark set of fiscal ready reckoners.

Even so, it would still be a formidable undertaking to proceed in this fashion to develop an index of fiscal stance, year by year, since 1970. To begin with, we should have to specify, year by year, the evolution of views of current *and* expected future fiscal variables and of how perceptions of monetary and exchange rate policy regimes were revised. For a practical assessment of UK fiscal policy since 1970, we are driven back on a measure that is considerably less sophisticated and, correspondingly, must be interpreted with greater care and subtlety.

I propose to adopt a simple index of fiscal stance based on some elementary adjustments to the public sector financial deficit (PSFD). Although elemen-

Table 2.2

Unanticipated but sustained fiscal expansion in the National Institute model

Fiscal expansion from:	After 1 year				After 5 years			
	GDP (%)	π (%)	U (%)	PSBR (% of GDP)	GDP (%)	π (%)	U (%)	PSBR (% of GDP)
Public expenditure	0.7	0.6	−0.2	0.7	0.6	0.7	−0.2	1.0
Income tax	0.6	0.4	−0.1	1.3	0.8	2.0	−0.3	1.9
VAT	0.7	−2.1	−0.3	1.8	1.2	1.7	−1.1	1.5
National insurance contributions	0.8	−4.1	−1.0	2.2	3.2	4.0	−3.4	1.5

Notes:

Data refer to differences between two simulations in the final quarter of the year indicated. U and π refer to the unemployment rate and inflation rate. The different fiscal stimuli were calibrated to have an approximately equal first-year effect on GDP.

Source: Adapted from Britton (1986).

tary, these adjustments are none the less important. However, since they start from the contemporaneous deficit, they ignore the impact of expected future fiscal variables, the mix of fiscal and other policies, and the differing demand impact of different spending and tax mixes within a given total deficit.[2]

First, it is important to recognize that an inflation-adjusted index of the real deficit must go beyond the mere computation of the deficit at constant prices. Government spending includes nominal interest paid on the debt, and this transfer payment affects private sector disposable income. Yet, crudely, it is some measure of real interest income that is relevant, as many studies of the consumption function confirm (see, e.g., Davidson *et al.*, 1978, Hendry, 1983, and Patterson, 1986).

At one extreme, one could compute the *ex post* real short rate of interest and include only this element in the debt service component of the fiscal deficit. At the other extreme, one could appeal to perfect capital markets and permanent income, and value debt service at the *ex ante* long real interest rate on the outstanding debt stock. Buiter and Miller (1983) advocate the latter, suggesting that most government debt is held by financial institutions which effectively smooth short-term fluctuations in household income streams. For several reasons, for example the fact that lifetimes are finite and uncertain and that debt interest also applies to national savings held directly by households, I think Buiter and Miller overstate their case. Hence I propose to do the obvious and adopt an intermediate position which values real debt service halfway between the value obtained by using *ex post* real short interest rates and *ex ante* real long rates.

The second adjustment follows from the endogeneity of some components of revenue and spending over the business cycle. For example, policy sets tax rates and levels of welfare benefits but the consequent flows of expenditure and revenue depend on the level of activity. To assess fiscal policy in general, and its contribution to demand management in particular, we need to think about the policy variables selected, not the subsequent expenditure and revenue flows. The most straightforward way to accomplish this is to compute the cyclically adjusted deficit, showing what the deficit would have been had output been at its potential level.

In the language of modern control theory, some policy variables can be viewed as open-loop or independent of the state of the business cycle. Typically, such variables act as automatic stabilizers. At given tax and unemployment benefit rates, booms will automatically reduce the deficit and slumps increase it. Other aspects of policy can be viewed as closed-loop, discretionary, or cycle-contingent. Examples include temporary cuts in tax rates during a slump or temporary tax increases during a boom.

It is important to be clear about how accurately the cyclically adjusted deficit allows us to make inferences about fiscal stance and demand management. Suppose that in a slump tax rates are temporarily reduced. Computing tax revenues as if output had been at potential will indeed reveal that discretionary policy had been relaxed in the slump and that demand management had been practised. Thus, variations in the cyclically adjusted deficit over the cycle allow inferences about the direction of discretionary policy.

Two points must be made about the light this measure sheds on the open-loop or cyclically invariant aspect of policy. First, the cyclically adjusted deficit tells us whether open-loop components were lax or tight *throughout* the cycle. In this sense, it tells us about the medium-run stance of policy. Second, one could have two different fiscal designs with the same cyclically adjusted deficit but one having a higher component of fixed expenditure and correspondingly higher marginal tax rates. This design would have stronger automatic stabilization properties than the regime with lower fixed expenditure but correspondingly lower marginal tax rates. For the evaluation of demand management, two conclusions emerge. First, the cyclically adjusted deficit will highlight the nature of discretionary fiscal policy, but will fail to pick up the differences in the design of automatic stabilizers which are also relevant to demand management. Second, the cyclically adjusted deficit will indicate whether fiscal policy on average was tight over the cycle. From the demand management standpoint, a generally tight medium-term policy will be especially costly when the economy is operating below potential output.

Having discussed the relevance of cyclical adjustment, I now select an index for the UK. Clearly, such an index depends both on a view of the potential output and on the model used to infer what the deficit would have been had output attained this level in any particular year. I simply borrow the estimates computed by Muller and Price (1984). In passing, I note that they use a simple trend for potential output, and it would be nice to see their work extended to a more sophisticated model of the supply side. For example, it would be appealing to reconcile such estimates of potential output with the many studies of equilibrium unemployment in Britain (see, for example, Layard and Nickell, 1985, and Pissarides, 1986).

Figure 2.1 shows my adjusted measure of the real fiscal stance combining the inflation adjustment to the fiscal surplus and the cyclical correction discussed above. For comparison, it also shows the uncorrected surplus, and the discrepancy between the two is striking. Whereas the naive surplus suggests that fiscal policy has been expansionary, especially in the mid-1970s, the adjusted measure emphasizes that fiscal policy was very tight in 1970, broadly neutral throughout the mid-1970s, and extremely tight again by the early 1980s. For reference, the figure also shows the path of UK inflation and unemployment during the period.

3. Fiscal Policy and Demand Management in the UK, 1970–1985

Table 2.3 provides a convenient summary of the relevant background information. The right-hand part of the table reproduces from Figure 2.1 the

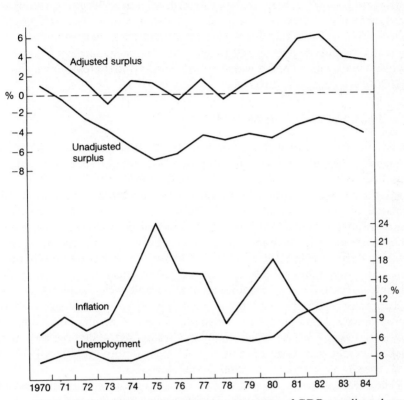

Fig. 2.1 UK public sector financial surplus as a percentage of GDP: unadjusted, and adjusted for inflation and the cycle.

Sources: Muller and Price 1984; Miller 1985; *Economic Trends.*

cyclically adjusted real budget surplus as an indicator of fiscal stance. The left-hand part of the table contrasts forecasts of real GDP growth made in the Budget Statement with actual outturns for real GDP growth. Forecasts can be proved inaccurate either because the impact of the Budget and other forces on aggregate *demand* has been wrongly assessed, or because the government has a mistaken view of aggregate *supply* and potential output. By combining the information in Table 2.3 with our estimates (with the benefit of hindsight) of potential output, we may be able to reach an informed judgement about what demand management policy was attempting to do, and the reasons why things did not turn out as the government had expected.

The Heath Government, 1970–1974

When the Conservatives under Edward Heath won the general election in June 1970, they inherited a remarkably tight fiscal policy from Labour. In part this had been conscious policy. Following the 1967 devaluation, the Labour government had accepted the lessons of the absorption approach to the balance of payments, and the tight Budgets of the late 1960s had aimed (successfully) to hold down demand for non-traded goods and to facilitate a resource transfer to the traded goods sector. Even so, in interpreting policy-making during the late 1960s and 1970s we have to bear two things in mind. First, the notion that equilibrium unemployment might have increased since the mid-1960s had not yet become accepted. Second, the principles of inflation accounting, especially in so far as they applied to the assessment of the government's fiscal stance, had yet to be developed. With inflation creeping up towards 10 per cent, it was probably not recognized quite how tight fiscal policy actually was. Over-optimism about likely output growth in 1970 and 1971 (see Table 2.3) tends to confirm this assessment.

The Heath government was elected on a manifesto emphasizing market forces and the supply-side benefits of withdrawing from demand management in general and the support of lame ducks in particular. Even so, with unemployment rising, the first two years of the Heath government saw a steady relaxation of fiscal policy. Thus, in a macroeconomic sense, the famous policy U-turn of 1972, which cast a long shadow over the early years of the Thatcher government, was less important for the fact that it restored the commitment to demand management than for its supply-side implications: lame ducks (Rolls Royce and Upper Clyde Shipbuilders) were back in business, and an increasingly *dirigiste* incomes policy replaced any pretence at monetary control as the means of fighting inflation. Given the sustained expansion of fiscal policy against a backdrop of an easy monetary policy, it is unsurprising that output growth was rapid; at 8.9 per cent over 1972–3, it considerably outstripped even the optimistic budget forecast of 1972 (see again Table 2.3).

Whatever the conduct of fiscal policy to this point, it is hard to escape the

Table 2.3

Budget forecasts, actual outturns, and fiscal stance, 1970–1984

Fiscal year	Forecast GDP growth (%)	Actual outturn (%)	Forecasting error (%)	Cyclically adjusted real surplus (% of GDP)	Calendar year
1970/1	3.5	2.0	−1.5	5.0	1970
1971/2	3.1	2.1	−1.0	3.3	1971
1972/3	5.9	8.9	3.0	1.3	1972
1973/4	4.5	−2.3	−6.8	−1.0	1973
1974/5	2.5	−0.7	−3.2	1.4	1974
1975/6	1.5	1.8	0.3	1.1	1975
1976/7	4.0	3.0	−1.0	−0.7	1976
1977/8	1.5	3.0	1.5	1.5	1977
1978/9	3.0	2.2	−0.8	−1.0	1978
1979/80	−1.0	−0.7	0.3	0.9	1979
1980/1	−1.5	−3.8	−2.3	2.1	1980
1981/2	1.0	0.7	−0.3	5.3	1981
1982/3	2.0	2.4	0.4	5.6	1982
1983/4	2.5	2.8	0.3	3.7	1983
1984/5	2.8	3.5	0.7	3.2	1984

Source: Financial Statement and Budget Report, various issues; and Figure 2.1.

conclusion that fiscal policy during 1973 was mistaken. The government forecast output growth of 4.5 per cent over the next year and fiscal policy was relaxed still further, so that the Heath government was now running a cyclically adjusted real deficit for the first time.[3] Given the lags that operate in the real economy, it would probably have been more appropriate to begin applying the fiscal brakes. And with hindsight, we can say that by 1973 actual UK unemployment was probably close to its equilibrium level, so a target of 4.5 per cent GDP growth was probably itself optimistic. Given the boom in world trade and commodity prices and two years of easy monetary policy, the fiscal stance adopted in 1973 probably made accelerating inflation inevitable, even without the forthcoming (unforeseen) oil shock. In the circumstances, it is ironic that 1973 also saw the introduction of the only episode of wage indexation in recent UK history. With a trigger-threshold of 7 per cent, accelerating inflation became a racing certainty.

The Wilson and Callaghan Governments, 1974–1979

After the miners' strike and the three-day week, Labour under Harold Wilson won the the general election in February 1974. More importantly, the new government had to cope with the repercussions of the first oil shock.

Domestically, it inherited excess demand, accelerating inflation, and the wage indexation agreements described above.

Those who recall 1974 will remember that much of the analysis of the likely effects of the oil shock centred on its implications for aggregate *demand*; its large and adverse effects on aggregate supply went largely, or at least substantially, unheeded. Thus, the concern of demand management policy was how to prevent the oil shock from not merely neutralizing the Heath boom, but plunging the UK into a major recession. Of course, the simplest element of the strategy was not fiscal but monetary: the accommodation of inflation to prevent a large monetary squeeze. In the event, Table 2.3 suggests that fiscal policy was mildly contractionary during 1974 and 1975, although with inflation in excess of 20 per cent there was a large nominal budget deficit. The combination of a fiscal policy that was unintentionally tight (though perhaps no tighter than appropriate, given the reduction in potential output) and the adverse supply shock itself produced a noticeable and partially unexpected fall in output. Nor, with hindsight, can one really conclude that fiscal policy was inappropriate during these years. Unless the consequences of an adverse supply shock are fully understood and quickly reflected in real wages, a bout of stagflation is almost inevitable. If demand management during 1974–5 is to be criticized, it should probably be in its assessment of the level of potential output and on the extent of monetary accommodation that was allowed.[4]

With unemployment rising sharply, 1976 saw a relaxation of fiscal policy. However, fiscal policy was no longer seen as the major element of demand management. At least since Kaldor (1971), Cambridge economists had emphasized that fiscally induced, consumption-led booms were self-defeating, and that a preferable policy was to induce an export-led expansion engineered by a real exchange rate depreciation, with any inflationary pressures being held in check by incomes policy.

By the end of 1976 a massive speculative run on sterling had driven the government to seek a sizeable loan from the IMF, as a condition of which, in the Declaration of Intent in December 1976, the government gave undertakings on the subsequent paths of £M3 and the PSBR which, though less formal than the subsequent Thatcher MTFS, marked a clear departure from previous policy design. The associated programme of public expenditure cuts, begun in 1976, was reflected in the 1977 Budget, and Table 2.3 shows a sharp fiscal contraction in that year.

The remaining Callaghan years saw an uneasy truce with the unions, collapsing in the 'winter of discontent' in 1978–9. From the trough of 1976 there was a rapid and persistent appreciation of the real exchange rate, the last attempt to hold down sterling being abandoned in October 1977 after a fruitless period of trying to stem capital inflows by a negative short real rate of interest. The pressure of increasing unemployment was judged to satisfy such fiscal expansion as was compatible with the assurances given to the IMF.

Since we now believe that the equilibrium unemployment increased significantly between 1974 and 1979, any greater fiscal stimulus during the late 1970s would probably have been unwarranted.

Thus, I conclude that the period of Labour government between 1974 and 1979 was not a period in which it can easily be said that there were major failures in fiscal policy from the viewpoint of demand management. Important issues of credibility, supply-side economics, and monetary policy design remained to be learned, but during this period as a whole fiscal policy was broadly neutral. When changes in real fiscal stance were adopted, they still had the conventional effects. Thus the period did not show, as is sometimes asserted, that fiscal policy had ceased to be a powerful weapon; rather, it suggests that considerations of sound finance and supply-side incentives had emerged as issues whose importance was at least as great. I shall return to this theme later.

The Thatcher Government (1979 Onwards)

The Conservative Thatcher government took as its starting points the relentlessly rising unemployment of the 1970s, which it (correctly) attributed primarily to the deteriorating supply position of the economy, and the re-emergence of inflation after the 'winter of discontent' in 1978–9. Hence it is unsurprising that the macroeconomic policy stance rejected previous policies, emphasized the importance of the supply side, and rejected co-operative incomes policy as a means of controlling inflation. Not only was the Thatcher government determined to avoid a repetition of the Heath U-turn of 1972, but it also understood intuitively the importance of expectations, credibility, and pre-commitment which, following Kydland and Prescott (1977), academic economists were discovering as the problem of time inconsistency.

Thus, the Thatcher government differed from its predecessors in bringing to macroeconomic policy design a belief in a much more explicitly formulated set of policy rules which would constrain its own future actions and hence could be credibly expected so to do. These rules reflected the government's belief about how the economy worked. First, the government at that time was explicitly monetarist: controlling £M3 would quickly control inflation. Second, and related, the government, unlike its post-Keynesian predecessors, believed that the economy remained close to potential output and the natural rate of unemployment.

Of course, the government did not espouse the most extreme form of instant monetarism embodied in the New Classical Macroeconomics; otherwise, it would have slashed monetary growth 'at a stroke'. Yet the difference remained one of degree: provided monetary growth was brought down steadily but *gradually*, to avoid placing too great a real squeeze on markets which worked well but not perfectly, inflation could be brought down *without* the emergence of Keynesian unemployment. The announcement of a clear and credible plan to do so could only assist this process, by generating lower inflation expectations which in part would be self-fulfilling.

Given this initial conception, what was to be the role of fiscal policy? First, it should be consistent with, and reinforce the credibility of, the tightening projections for £M3 growth as the centrepiece of the fight against inflation. Second, it should directly stimulate the supply-side by reducing government claims on resources, reducing the disincentive effects of high marginal rates in the tax and transfer system, and ensuring that government borrowing did not contribute to higher interest rates more than would otherwise have been the case. In short, given the assumptions that the economy was always close to potential output, and that the supply-side potential of the economy had deteriorated, demand management was much the least important objective of fiscal policy. When stronger claims implied that the fiscal stance might actually exacerbate (small) cyclical problems, that was a small price to pay.

The 1979 Budget began to put these ideas into practice. Table 2.3 confirms a tightening of the fiscal stance. Such trends were consolidated in the 1980 Budget, in which the MTFS, with its projections for £M3 and the PSBR/GDP ratio, was formally introduced. Yet in assessing demand management during this early period, it would be wrong to attribute primarily to fiscal policy the sharp contraction in aggregate demand which led to the dramatic Keynesian recession of 1980–1. The effects of fiscal tightening were swamped by the tightness of monetary policy, whose effects were not merely or mainly domestic in transmission: coupled with the speculative pressure on sterling arising from new discoveries of oil, and revaluations of its worth following the second oil shock in 1979–80, the massive real appreciation of sterling was a major factor in the 1980–1 recession.

Because the 1980 Budget had significantly underestimated the extent of the 1980–1 recession (Table 2.3), it was inevitable that the combination of low tax revenue and higher unemployment benefit payments would lead to an overshooting of the PSBR target for 1980–1, and it was essential for the credibility of the chosen strategy that fiscal policy be visibly tightened in the 1981 Budget, which was achieved in practice largely by suspending the inflation indexation of nominal bands for income tax allowances. Table 2.3 confirms the sharp increase in the cyclically adjusted real surplus in 1981. From the standpoint of demand management, this was a major error of fiscal policy, coming as it did at a time when output was significantly below potential.

In some ways, 1981–2 marks a watershed, not merely in fiscal policy but in the whole macroeconomic strategy of the Thatcher government. Table 2.3 shows that, although still tight, fiscal policy was significantly relaxed during 1983–4. Simultaneously, there was a gradual shift in monetary policy in two respects. First, the errors of 1979–80 were recognized and monetary policy increasingly 'took account of' the exchange rate. Second, and related, it was gradually recognized that neither £M3 nor any other monetary aggregate gave a simple and reliable indicator of monetary stance or the implications for inflation. Hence, in the mid-1980s £M3 was sometimes allowed to grow well beyond its target range; nor was any renewed burst of inflation immediately forthcoming.

To the extent that strict monetary targets have in part been replaced by an implicit nominal exchange rate target, which may also act as a nominal anchor (see, e.g., Artis and Currie, 1981), it would be wrong to say that monetary plicy to control inflation has been abandoned. But, to the extent that a severely tight and rigid monetary stance has been relaxed, it is true that fiscal policy has come to play a more direct role in the anti-inflationary strategy, the mechanism of which I shall describe shortly. For this reason, the extent to which there is any freedom to use fiscal policy for demand management remained strictly limited, and this is reflected in the indicators of real fiscal stance for 1983 and 1984 shown in Table 2.3.

As in the previous period of Labour government, there is nothing in this *ex post* assessment which suggests that demand management had ceased to have conventional effects in the 1980s. Rather, the Thatcher government decided that, if necessary, the pursuit of demand management had to be subordinated to the fight against inflation and to reviving the supply potential of the economy.

Conclusions

During the two decades before 1970, demand management assumed a policy priority unparalleled before or since. Since 1970, fiscal policy has generally been tight and sometimes especially tight, precisely when output was furthest below potential. Even the brief review above is sufficient to illustrate how objectives for fiscal policy have gradually assumed greater importance since 1970. Two aspects of poor economic performance undoubtedly contributed to this switch of emphasis. Persistent and significant inflation led to demands for sound public sector finances and a sound currency. Persistent and increasing unemployment led to demands for supply-side policies which would address the disappointing path of potential output itself. In the next two sections I examine these issues in turn.

4. Sound Finance and a Sound Currency: Debt, Deficits, Money, and Inflation

While sophisticated adjustments to the deficit may give ever more accurate indicators of its impact on aggregate demand, essentially it is the unadjusted deficit which governs the evolution over time of the stock of public sector debt. Large deficits lead people to fear that the government will resort to finance through money creation, either immediately or in the future, as the cumulation of debt interest exacerbates the deficit. Even worse, the government might have to default on its debt obligations. In this section I examine whether such fears provide a rationale for tight fiscal policy.

The Simple Arithmetic of the Public Accounts[5]

The outstanding stock of public sector liabilities comprises high-powered money, bills, and bonds. In such a discussion, bonds should be assessed at market value, not at par: much of the subsequent analysis of unsound finance hinges on the possibility of using unanticipated inflation to inflict capital losses on private bondholders, for which it is necessary to assess government debt at market value.

Economics tells us that nominal magnitudes are pretty meaningless. Most discussion of the public debt focuses on the debt/GDP ratio, which we might expect to be constant in a steady state. Deflation of the debt by GDP captures the idea that, over time, nominal and real spending and taxes, and specifically the economy's capacity to service the debt at given tax rates, will grow. Hence it is a crude attempt to make allowance for all the future variables which should be in the analysis of public finances but are omitted. In passing, I note that using the debt/GDP ratio as an *indicator* in no way prejudges its optimal level or rate of change in the medium run.

Let *s* denote the ratio of nominal debt at market value to nominal GDP. Clearly, we can decompose annual changes in *s* into the arithmetic contributions of the PSBR, which increases the numerator of *s*; nominal income growth, which increases the denominator of *s*; and capital gains on bonds, which revalue outstanding debt.

However, this is not the most illuminating decomposition for policy analysis. First, it obscures the fact that high inflation typically will be accompanied by high nominal interest rates and a high PSBR. Second, it fails to distinguish between expected and unexpected changes in bond prices. Adopting the strong but powerful assumption that the *expected* annual yield on bills and bonds is equated, whence for bonds the coupon payment per pound invested plus the expected capital gain must equal the yield on bills, I show in the Appendix to this chapter that annual changes in *s* may be decomposed into five elments, each expressed as a fraction of nominal GDP. They are: (1) the primary deficit (spending minus taxes), (2) the adjusted cost of debt service (calculated from the excess of the short real interest rate over the rate of real GDP growth), (3) the revenue raised from high-powered money creation (the product of nominal GDP growth and the stock of high-powered money), (4) revenue from asset sales (privatization), and (5) the burden of *unanticipated* capital gains on outstanding bonds.

Table 2.4 shows how the arithmetic of the public finances works out for the UK since 1970. It ignores revenue from asset sales, which was small before 1985, and refers to UK public sector debt net of certain fairly liquid public sector assets. The top part of the table documents the dramatic reduction in

Table 2.4
Net public debt as a percentage of GDP, 1970–1984
(selected years, and annual decompositions)

	s: net debt/GDP (%)				
1969	68.2				
1973	48.9				
1979	41.5				
1984	41.0				

Contribution of (as % of GDP)

	Δs	Primary deficit	Real money creation	Debt interest	Unanticipated capital gains
1970	−2.0	−3.5	−0.7	−1.2	3.6
1971	−7.9	−0.4	−0.8	−3.1	−3.9
1972	−2.9	0.1	−0.7	−2.0	−0.7
1973	−6.5	2.3	−0.9	−3.0	−3.6
1974	−6.3	3.5	−0.8	−0.2	−7.5
1975	−1.3	5.7	−1.3	−4.0	−0.4
1976	2.5	4.9	−0.9	−1.7	0.4
1977	1.8	2.3	−0.7	−2.2	2.0
1978	−3.7	0.4	−0.7	−1.5	−1.9
1979	−0.4	2.4	−0.7	−0.3	−0.8
1980	−3.2	2.0	−0.7	0.6	−5.2
1981	0.4	2.7	−0.4	1.0	−3.0
1982	0.7	−2.2	−0.4	1.5	1.1
1983	1.2	−0.2	−0.3	0.6	1.3
1984	0.4	0.0	−0.3	1.0	0.2
Annual averages					
1970–3	−4.8	−0.4	−0.8	−2.4	−1.2
1974–9	−1.2	3.2	−0.8	−1.6	−1.4
1980–4	−0.1	0.5	−0.4	0.9	−1.1

Notes:
For further explanation, see Appendix. The decomposition is not exact because of miscellaneous transactions in nominal assets which affect net debt but are not explicitly treated in Appendix.

Sources: Bank of England; Miller (1985).

the debt/GDP ratio since 1970, which merely continued a trend experienced during the postwar years. Whereas 40 years ago the UK had one of the highest debt/GDP ratios in the OECD, its trend has been in the opposite direction from that in many OECD countries, so that by the mid-1980s the UK had a lower debt/GDP ratio than many of these countries. In this simple sense it would be a mistake to believe that the UK had faced a crisis of the public finances which required the adoption of tight fiscal policy.

The lower part of Table 2.4 gives an annual decomposition of the elements that contributed to this trend, and displays annual averages for the approximate periods of office of the three governments since 1970. Several features are worthy of comment. First, the fastest reduction in debt/GDP occurred during the Heath years; paradoxically, it has been slowest in the Thatcher years. Second, the differing contributions of the primary deicit are not the main source of this conclusion. Third, revenue from money creation is typically small, being erected on a pinhead since high-powered money is tiny relative to GDP. Fourth, all three governments benefited from the unanticipated capital losses they inflicated on bondholders when nominal interest rates exceeded previous expectations. Finally, whereas the governments of the 1970s enjoyed real interest rates below the rate of real output growth, so that the debt burden was falling relative to GDP, in the 1980s high real interest rates have proved a significant burden on the public finances.

This last observation is of some importance. The existing debt is a burden on the public finances only when the real interest rate exceeds the rate of real output growth. This is surely a feature of the 1980s, but it is not obviously a feature of earlier decades, when real interest rates were often close to zero and sometimes negative yet output growth was significant and sustained. In such circumstances, the net worth of the public sector is effectively infinite. Theoretically, it would be possible to finance all public spending by borrowing. The supply of willing lenders would be growing faster than the government's need to borrow, and lenders would be confident of reselling the bonds to a yet larger army of lenders in the future. It is precisely this reversal of the magnitude of the real interest rate and the real growth rate which lies at the heart of the international debt crisis, and which forms the basis of modern economic analysis of that problem (see, for example, Cohen and Sachs, 1984; Cohen, 1985). But the same point holds good for the solvency of governments borrowing in domestic markets. When the net worth of the public sector became finite once again, everyone had to start thinking about the medium-term programme by which the government would meet the real burden of its debt obligations. In such circumstances, a credible anti-inflation strategy requires that the government provide assurances today that it does not intend to resort to printing money tomorrow.

Although this analysis conveys important insights, it cannot purport to be a complete positive theory of why fiscal policy changed direction in Britain. As we saw earlier, concern about the PSBR and its possible implications for inflation dates back at least to the mid-1970s, when real interest rates were still significantly negative. Fear of inflation must play a more central role in the story. Before addressing that question directly, I wish to stress that neither the PSBR nor the debt/GDP ratio provides an accurate indication of the soundness of the public finances.

Sound Finance and the Solvency of the Public Sector

While public sector debt conveys some information about the liabilities of the public sector, any assessment of its solvency must rest on a comparison of its liabilities and its assets.[6] The tangible wealth of the public sector, assets minus liabilities, is a more satisfactory criterion than debt alone. Such a criterion would, *inter alia*, eliminate the nonsense whereby asset sales (privatization) appear to improve the public finances simply by reducing the PSBR and recorded debt outstanding. Privatization may benefit the public finances, but any such benefit derives not from the ownership transfer *per se*—selling an asset for the right price leaves wealth unaffected—but rather because associated changes in managerial efficiency or less stringent regulation of operating activities raises the market value of the asset.

Even tangible wealth is an inadequate measure of public sector net worth or solvency. The government also has the obligation to make future expenditure and the power to levy future taxation. Essentially, solvency requires that the initial stock of tangible wealth be at least as great as the present value of future operating deficits, suitably measured. Buiter (1985) gives a clear and comprehensive treatment of this issue.

Gathering estimates of the relevant data is a formidable undertaking. Hills (1984) reports partial estimates for three years; 1966, 1975, and 1984. Assets include a valuation of the public sector's physical and financial capital, and of the present value of *some* future tax streams, most notably from North Sea oil. Liabilities include not merely the familiar financial debt obligations but also estimates of the present value of future pension obligations, both to workers in the public sector and to those participating in the national state pension scheme.

Hills estimates that, in 1982 prices, the net liabilities of the public sector fell from £285 billion in 1966 to £60 billion in 1975, rising slightly to £65 billion in 1982. These estimates show the amount that must be matched by the present value of future public sector surpluses on items excluded from his calculations. Broadly, this means general tax revenue (excluding petroleum revenue tax) *plus* real revenue from high-powered money creation *minus* public consumption and transfers (excluding pensions). Two points should be stressed in assessing the required magnitude of these future surpluses. First, debt interest is excluded, since it is already implicit in the discount factor used to compute the present value required. Second, only some fraction of public sector investment should be reckoned as a debit in calculating future surpluses. If all public investiment yielded the market rate of raturn, the present value of its future earnings would equal its purchase price, and public sector investment would drop out of the calculation entirely. Conversely, reckoning the whole of public investment as a charge on the surplus implicitly assumes that its yield is zero. In practice, some intermediate position is plausible.

Suppose one had a comprehensive annual measure of public sector net worth, NW. Letting R denote the expected long real rate of interest, then the permanent income of the public sector, and the annual consumption stream C it could sustain indefinitely,[7] would be given by $C = R \cdot NW$. Thus a fiscal plan to consume more than this is implicitly a plan to leave subsequent governments with a worse fiscal position (see Miller and Babbs, 1983; Buiter, 1985).

How might one build up a measure of this permanent income deficit $C = R \cdot NW$? Suppose some items T^* will be constant. Then their present value is T^*/R, and the relevant deficit is $(C - T^*) = R \cdot NW^*$, where NW^* includes present value estimates of those income streams whose future profile is already known to differ significantly from their current flow value. Specifically, I have in mind oil revenues.

Thus, in what follows I attempt to calculate the real permanent income deficit (surplus) after adjusting for discrepancies arising from oil revenues, from the difference between public exhaustive spending and public consumption, and from the relevant inflation adjustment of debt interest.

Since I have argued that the sale of assets at anything close to the right market price leaves public net worth essentially unaffected, it is necessary to begin from the public sector financial deficit (PSFD), not the PSBR. As in Table 2.3, this should be inflation-adjusted, and instead of actual interest payments we want to multiply the market value of net debt by the real interest rate, though this time it is the expected long rate that is relevant. Since the PSFD already includes rent on publicly owned dwellings and land, and since these may be thought of as index-linked, some crude allowance is already implicit for the role of non-financial assets in T^*. All these adjustments, though not interpreted in quite this way, are embodied in the calculations in Miller (1985), save that he uses a slightly narrower definition of the net financial debt than I used in Table 2.4. Table 2.5, which deflates all magnitudes by GDP, shows the PSFD and Miller's adjusted PSFD. Two further adjustments are then made. First, using estimates from Devereux and Morris (1983) and Odling-Smee and Riley (1985) of the expected present value of oil revenues (which I assume to be close to zero prior to the first oil shock), I replace actual revenues with their contemporaneous permanent income value. Second, I make some allowance for the distinction between public consumption and exhaustive spending inclusive of fixed capital formation. Some public investment (such as road building) yields no direct returns, though indirectly it may increase output and tax revenues therefrom. This I treat as consumption. While other public investment yields returns, it may (as an act of policy) have

The permanent income public sector real surplus, 1970–1984

	£m, current prices			As % of GDP			
	Oil & gas taxes	Permanent income equivalent	Public investment	PSFS adjustment (3)+(2)−(1)	PSFS at long real rate	Permanent income PSFS (4)+(5)	Actual PSFS
	(1)	(2)	(3)	(4)	(5)	(6)	(7)
1970	5	50	1622	3.2	3.6	6.8	1.3
1971	10	75	1668	3.0	1.5	4.5	−0.5
1972	15	100	1781	2.9	−0.5	2.4	−2.5
1973	15	150	2345	3.3	−1.6	1.7	−3.8
1974	20	630	2930	4.2	−2.6	1.6	−5.7
1975	25	822	3476	4.0	−4.3	−0.3	−7.2
1976	81	1050	3860	3.8	−3.6	0.2	−6.7
1977	238	1230	3532	3.1	−1.1	2.0	−4.2
1978	565	990	3442	1.8	−1.9	−0.1	−4.9
1979	2311	1209	3756	1.4	−1.2	0.2	−4.4
1980	3735	2532	4063	1.2	−1.3	−0.1	−4.9
1981	6491	3105	3298	0	0.2	0.2	−3.6
1982	7814	3090	3175	−0.5	0.7	0.2	−2.8
1983	8782	3120	4200	−0.5	−0.1	−0.6	−3.6
1984	12002	3120	4605	−1.4	−1.0	−2.4	−4.3

Notes:

Column (2) is the estimate of contemporaneously calculated permanent income from oil and gas revenues, based on Devereux and Morris (1983) and Odling-Smee and Riley (1985).

Column (3) is public investment, defined as one-half of the joint value of public corporations' investment and public sector investment in dwellings.

Column (5) is taken from Miller (1985), who values debt service costs at the *ex ante* long real interest rate applied to all interest-bearing debt.

Column (6) shows actual public sector financial surplus as a percentage of GDP.

earned less than the full market rate. Thus, I deduct from the PSFD one-half of public sector expenditure on investment in dwellings and one-half of public corporations' investment. By construction (no pun intended), this adjustment errs on the cautious side. Column (6) in Table 2.5 thus shows, year by year, by how much the fiscal plans were unsustainable.

The last two columns of Table 2.5 compare the adjusted index of the underlying public sector surplus and the actual surplus cited in popular discussion. Whereas a naive interpretation might suggest that the public finances were steadily deteriorating, the true position is strikingly different. The penultimate column reveals that the fiscal position improved dramatically in the early 1970s, and thereafter was steadily maintained until 1984. Only in the mid-1980s, when North Sea oil revenue substantially but temporarily exceeded its permanent income value, was fiscal policy exacerbating the solvency problem for succeeding governments. From this I draw two conclusions. First, these calculations of public sector solvency provide no sound-finance justification for the adoption of tight fiscal policy and the sacrifice of demand management at the date this transition actually occurred in the UK. Second, if any government can be deemed to be mortgaging the future to alleviate the present, it is the Thatcher government in the mid-1980s. Both conclusions are probably at variance with popular wisdom.

If the reasons for adopting a progressively tighter fiscal policy cannot be found in considerations of sound finance and the fear of impending insolvency, can we appeal instead to the need for sound money? If the solvency of the public sector can be shown to depend critically on the government's ability to raise revenue through inflation, a stronger fiscal position will be an essential component of a credible plan to eliminate inflation and forgo the revenue it would otherwise have generated.

Inflation as a Source of Revenue

For simplicity, I abstract from inflation non-neutralities in the tax system and in the level of real government expenditure. I also assume that real interest rates and real output growth are substantially independent of inflation.[8] Inflation directly contributes to the government coffers through the inflation tax on high-powered money. Moreover, unanticipated inflation, by raising nominal interest rates, inflicts unanticipated capital losses on holders of nominal bonds, thus reducing the market value of the government's outstanding liabilities.

It is important to stress that in practice the revenue that can be raised through the inflation tax is small. Notes and coin are now less than 4 per cent of UK GDP, and this ratio is in trend decline as financial innovations proceeds apace. Second, the inflation tax, being the product of inflation and real high-powered money (the demand for which falls as inflation rises), has a theoretical maximum for most plausible specifications of money demand; thereafter revenue falls as inflation rises. Precisely where this occurs depends on the interest elasticity of demand for high-powered money, a subject of some current controversy, since it is difficult to get reliable proxies for the changes in real-money demand induced by financial innovations. Buiter (1985), for example, estimates that revenue is maximized when annual inflation is 67 per cent in the UK. But the central point is that this revenue will always be small (see Table 2.4).

Table 2.4 also shows the effects of unanticipated changes in bond prices, the vast bulk of which revenue accrued from inflation effects on nominal bonds. Since the UK twice experienced years of inflation of roughly 20 per cent, which presumably was unanticipated when some of the nominal debt was first issued, Table 2.4 begins to give us an idea of the once-off amount of revenue that a government could raise through this route.

To refine this question, it is of course vital to know more about the composition of the debt. The shorter the debt maturity, the less will the current price deviate from the par redemption value. Moreover, indexed-debtholders cannot be exploited at all through this mechanism. Hence in Figure 2.2 I show the maturity composition of the UK debt, distinguishing indexed and nominal debt, and decomposing the latter into maturities of less than 5 years, 5–15 years, and over 15 years.

Figure 2.2 shows clearly that the maturity structure of the UK debt has steadily shortened during the period since 1970. Taken together with the increased trend for long debt to be index-linked, this implies a dramatic reduction in the possibility of raising significant revenue through a bout of unexpected inflation. One interpretation of the trend is simply that bondholders have perceived the inflation-vulnerability of long nominal debt and demanded a risk premium for new issues which the government has not found it attractive to accept. But it has also been part of a deliberate, and well designed, credible anti-inflation strategy for debt management, by seeking to pre-commit the government to a position in which it stands less to gain by any subsequent unexpected inflation.

I conclude that, in the past, the UK public finances have been a beneficiary of inflation. Thus, if, motivated by some other consideration, UK governments wished to effect a significant reduction in inflation, other components of fiscal policy had to be tightened somewhat. However, given that the index of fiscal stance in Section 1 was already inflation-adjusted, given that the underlying solvency of the public sector was much healthier than popularly supposed, and given the *relatively* small amounts of revenue which in any case had been raised through inflation, it seems difficult to argue that UK fiscal policy has been motivated by the need to sustain the public finances during a period in which inflation was being brought under control. Finally, it should be noted that both market forces (financial innovation and competition) and debt management policy have combined now to place the UK in a position where future revenue gains from future inflation are likely to be significantly smaller than those observed in the past and documented in Table 2.4.

David Begg

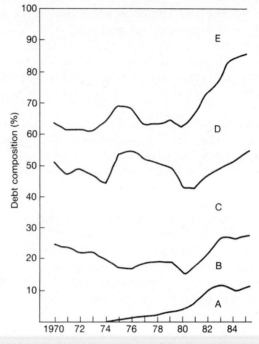

Fig. 2.2 The composition of the UK national debt, 1970–1985 (par values): A, index-linked (gilts and national savings); B, nominal non-marketable debt; C, nominal short marketable debt (under 5 yrs); D, nominal medium marketable debt (5–15 yrs); E, nominal long marketable debt (over 15 yrs).

Notes: National debt is held outside the public sector. This differs from public sector debt primarily because debt of local authorities, for which the central government is not legally responsible, is included in public but not national debt. Non-marketable debt chiefly includes national savings, and should be viewed as short to medium in maturity. For the final year (1985), market values of short, medium, and long marketable debt were all very close to par values (see *Bank of England Quarterly Bulletin*, December 1985).
Sources: Bank of England, Annual Abstract of Statistics.

Deficits, Money Growth, and Inflation

If our understanding of fiscal policy is to be illuminated by the link between deficits and inflation, we must seek this connection not in the impact of inflation on the public finances, but rather in the effect of the public finances on money creation and inflation.

Substantial inflations occur for one of three reasons: an adverse supply shock which the government accommodates to mitigate the immediate recessionary impact; succumbing tho the temptation to print money to raise taxes through inflation; or a fundamental error of policy design. To the extent that the first explanation is of relevance during both the oil shocks, the years of highest UK inflation (1975 and 1980) may owe little to the prior fiscal position. It has been my contention that the second explanation was unlikely ever to have been of major importance, and by the mid-1980s the possibility that it could yield much revenue in future has been even further curtailed. That leaves the third explanation.

For simplicity, I assume initially that all debt takes the form of non-interest-bearing money H. Any primary deficit $(G-T)$ must be financed by printing money. Thus

$$G - T = \Delta H \qquad \text{or} \qquad \frac{G-T}{PY} = \frac{\Delta H}{PY}$$

where PY is is nominal GDP.

By simple arithmetic,

$$\Delta\left(\frac{H}{PY}\right) = \left(\frac{H}{PY}\right)\left(\frac{\Delta H}{H} - \frac{\Delta P}{P} - \frac{\Delta Y}{Y}\right) = \frac{\Delta H}{PY} - \frac{H}{PY}(\pi + n)$$

Hence we can express the simplified budget constraint as

$$\frac{G-T}{PY} - \frac{H}{PY}(\pi + n) = \Delta\left(\frac{H}{PY}\right). \tag{2.1}$$

As a fraction of nominal GDP (PY), the primary deficit $(G-T)$ must be financed either by the inflation tax $H\pi$ or by the real seigniorage nH which accrues to the government when income and money demand increases and the corresponding supply of money can be provided; otherwise it must be financed by increasing the real money stock at a rate which exceeds that justified by money demand given current inflation and real income growth. This latter mechanism is clearly the stuff of which hyperinflations are made. Hence the danger signal is when the primary deficit exceeds the implicit tax revenue derived from the inflation tax and real seigniorage—in other words, when both sides of equation (2.1) are positive. Paradoxically, it is the failure of the inflation tax to rise sufficiently as inflation accelerates which guarantees that accelerating inflation does not automatically generate the tax revenue required to stabilize expenditure and revenue. With the left-hand side of equation (2.1) still positive, the government has no option but to finance this deficit by attempting to make nominal money growth outstrip nominal income growth, thus maintaining a positive value of the right-hand side of equation (2.1). For a vivid illustration of a government chasing its tail in a spiralling rate of money creation, see the discussion of Israel in Bruno (1986).

The argument extends to interest-bearing debt provided there is some limit on the total quantity of debt the private sector is prepared to hold. Once this limit is reached, the government is driven back on money creation if it wishes to persist with its underlying deficit. And, as stressed by Sargent and Wallace (1981), with forward-looking expectations, the inflation may begin as soon as such a future situation is anticipated. Hence we reach the following dilemma. The credibility of an anti-inflation strategy may require pre-commitments (e.g. retiring long nominal debt) to convince the private sector that in future the government will not succumb to the temptation to raise tax revenue through inflation. But, by removing an automatic stabilizer which would generate additional revenue should inflation unexpectedly get out of hand, this pre-commitment must be *reinforced* by a credible statement that the medium-term fiscal strategy does not involve deficits which would then leave no future alternative to money creation.

Given my assessment of public sector solvency since 1970, it should be evident that, in the UK, there was never any real prospect of the fears described above. Doubtless, there was considerable inflation illusion in public as well as private accounting, so that the fact that fears of money creation for budgetary reasons were ill-informed does not mean it was unimportant for policy to confront them.

While the Treasury always made medium-term projections of expenditure, tax receipts, and the evolution of the debt, such calculations must be public knowledge if they are to influence private sector expectations and play a useful role in a credible anti-inflationary strategy. In this regard, two developments stand out in recent British fiscal policy. First, following Labour's Letter of Intent to the IMF in 1976, public commitments were given for the course of £M3 and the PSBR for several years ahead. More importantly, in 1980 the Thatcher government adopted the Medium Term Financial Strategy (MTFS). Because this represented the most important step to date in formalizing and publicizing medium-term policy design, and because it was during the Thatcher years that fiscal policy tightened most significantly, even though output was below potential, the MTFS deserves special consideration.

The MTFS announced an annually updated three-year projection for the PSBR as a percentage of GDP, it being understood that any major revision of the initial projections would constitute a policy U-turn which the government was pledged to avoid. It was a simple form of pre-commitment. The PSBR projections are set out in Table 2.6. In the early years, a 'consistent' path for £M3 was also announced, though in recent years M0 and nominal GDP have assumed at least as much prominence. The MTFS can be viewed in at least three ways: as a statement of the solvency of the fiscal position, as a device for monetary control thereby to control inflation, or as a more direct mechanism for tackling inflation. I discuss each of these interpretations in turn, beginning with solvency.

For reasons I have laboured earlier, the PSBR/GDP ratio need bear no relation to the underlying sustainability of current levels of public sector real consumption at existing tax rates, or to the sustainability of any other plan, including one to reduce the size of the public sector by a specified amount or to reduce marginal tax rates to particular levels. It makes little sense to focus on liabilities but not assets, and to focus on current flows to the exclusion of what

Table 2.6
MTFS Projections of PSBR/GDP ratio, 1980/1–1986/7
(percentages)

	1980/1	1981/2	1982/3	1983/4	1984/5	1985/6	1986/7
Targets							
1980/1 Budget	3.75	3.00	2.75	1.50			
1981/2 Budget		4.25	3.25	2.00			
1982/3 Budget			3.50	2.75	2.00		
1983/4 Budget				2.75	2.50	2.00	
1984/5 Budget					2.25	2.00	2.00
1985/6 Budget						2.00	2.00
Outturn	5.00	3.40	2.75	3.20	3.10	2.00	

Source: Financial Statement and Budget Report, various issues.

is already knowable about future flows. In making no adjustment to *nominal* interest on the public debt, the PSBR/GDP ratio also suffers from inflation illusion.[9] In short, I submit that the announced PSBR targets bear so little relation to the information one would really wish about the sustainability of the currently envisaged fiscal programme that they cannot seriously be viewed as enhancing the credibility of the open-loop component of medium- or long-term fiscal policy. They do, however, have an important implication for the closed-loop or contingent aspect of policy, a point to which I shortly return.

Did the MTFS represent instead an important strengthening of monetary control and a means of influencing inflation through this mechanism? Certainly its architects appeared to believe so at the time. Burns and Budd (1979) emphasized the demand-side linkage. By increasing privately held debt, the PSBR would induce a wealth effect on money demand, leading either to undesirable rises in interest rates of to inflation if nominal money was allowed to increase. Yet this contention is dubious: even Milton Friedman believes that increases in the demand for real-money balances can safely be accommodated without fear of inflation.

Others have emphasized linkages through money supply. In my view it is implausible that there *must* be a close connection between the PSBR and the money supply, even over a period of several years. High-powered money is tiny relative either to other components of the government budget constraint or to broad measures of money which might affect private behaviour. Any relation between deficits and high-powered money, at least over the range in which the UK has historically operated, is largely an outcome of deliberate policy, not economic necessity. Even if such a relation did exist, the further links from high-powered money to broad money (which is almost exclusively private bank deposits) and thence to inflation is tenuous in the short and medium run.

For these reasons, I do not consider that the fiscal component of the MTFS was either necessary or sufficient for the conduct of a tight monetary policy which, especially during its first few years, the Thatcher government believed central to the fight against inflation. The credibility of the government's determination to sustain and win that fight was of course of the utmost importance. Paraphrasing Fforde (1983), when government policy must be capable of being explained in a very few sentences, clear simple rules which signal a radical change in priorities may be more effective than more sophisticated pronouncements. In this sense, the fiscal component of the MTFS may have been less important for its underlying logic than for the fact that it was believed.

Indeed, I wish to take this argument further. Having suggested that this design of fiscal policy was neither informative about the sustainability of the government's open-loop plans for fiscal policy nor essential for the tight monetary policy they in any case would have adopted, I now want to argue that the MTFS contained an effective closed-loop component which impinged directly on inflation, in two ways. The MTFS set targets for the path of the ratio of nominal PSBR to nominal GDP, and these targets were intended to be open-loop. From them, the government would not budge, come what may. Table 2.6 confirms that subsequent revisions have been minimal, albeit with the help of some devices such as asset sales. Earlier, I stressed that the PSBR/GDP ratio fails to inflation-adjust the PSBR for the effect of higher nominal interest rates. A policy that is open-loop in nominal terms is necessarily closed-loop in real terms. Unexpected inflation automatically tightens the real fiscal stance, putting downward pressure on demand, prices, and wages. Since this effect is guaranteed, it is a pretty credible signal that inflation will not subsequently get out of control.

Second, in assessing possible insolvency which might then leave no option but money creation, I stressed the crucial role that *real* interest rates play in determining the net worth of the public sector. Table 2.4 documents the large swing in real interest rates in the 1980s. The MTFS is also a contingent promise to tighten other parts of fiscal policy when real interest rates rise. Hence it offers some assurance that corrective fiscal action will be taken, that public finances will remain sound, and that reluctant money creation will be avoided.

It seems to me that it is these contingent features of the MTFS that have the greatest logical appeal as part of an anti-inflation strategy and may in practice have contributed to its success. And this logic seems, at least implicitly, to have found increasing favour with the Thatcher government during the mid-1980s: the reliability of individual monetary indicators, let alone their connection with the PSBR, has received less emphasis, and projections for nominal GDP correspondingly greater emphasis.

These remarks concern the qualitative design of the MTFS. To explain why the fiscal stance in practice has been so tight, one also needs to evaluate why the particular path for the PSBR/GDP ratio was selected. I claim no special knowledge of the thoughts of the framers of the original MTFS. To the extent that both inflation and real interest rates in the 1980s may have exceeded the expectation of 1979–80, fiscal policy may have been tighter than originally hoped.

5. Fiscal Policy and the Supply Side

In the previous section I discussed the determination to reverse the UK's poor inflation performance of the 1970s and the extent to which the quest for sound finance and sound money had led to the adoption of a tight fiscal stance when demand management considerations would have dictated a fiscal relaxation. But that is only part of the story. By OECD standards, the UK's long-run growth performance had been poor, and the steady rise in equilibrium unemployment also led to a determination to attack deep-rooted supply problems. A detailed analysis of the microeconomic impact of fiscal policy lies beyond the scope of this chapter. Rather, my concern is the extent to which supply-side considerations motivated the macroeconomic fiscal stance and the abandonment of demand management in Britain. Specifically, to what extent must a government choose *between* demand management and supply-side incentives?

Three arguments suggest that some trade-off exists. First, higher marginal tax rates make automatic stabilizers more powerful in the short run but may lead to disincentive effects in the longer run. Second, by analogy with the moral hazard problem in insurance, the more a government guarantees to take whatever discretionary action is necessary *ex post* to fix up full employment, the less individual workers or managers need worry that their own inefficiency will lead to unemployment or bankruptcies. Third, and related, Buiter and Miller (1983) have characterized the process as a game between the government and the private sector. The co-operative solution, implicitly embodied in the 1944 White Paper, is for the government to promise demand management and a full employment commitment while the private sector agrees to strive for productivity growth combined with wage moderation. The co-operative solution is fragile precisely because, with such government commitments, the private sector faces two temptations to renege: it can go slow on productivity (the easy life) without fear of unemployment, and it can push for higher wages knowing that in the short run this will lead to temporary real-wage increases while the commitment to subsequent monetary accommodation will inflate away these real-wage increases before serious adverse employment consequences have time to feed through. In the language of modern dynamic game theory, the co-operative solution may be time-inconsistent. Since the government can foresee that the private sector will face future temptations to renege, it should abandon the wishful thinking embodied in the co-operative solution and design policy on the assumption that the private sector will renege.

Recent research on repeated and dynamic games suggests that this reasoning may be too pessimistic for several reasons. First, it may be possible to devise credible commitments not to renege: in essence, these involve each party volunteering at the outset to lock itself in somehow. Second, once the reputation of the players is made endogenous, the cost of losing reputation by reneging on a prior agreement may dominate the gains to reneging. Finally, as with the so-called 'tit for tat' strategies, it may be possible to commit oneself to take punitive action against another player in the event that they renege. If these penalties are both severe and credible (i.e. would be optimal *ex post* for the punisher to carry out), they may sustain the co-operative solution.

Against this background, how should we interpret the fiscal choices made by UK governments since 1970? First, one must understand the position from which they began. I agree with Buiter and Miller's characterization of the 1950s and early 1960s as a period in which the fragile co-operative solution was sustained. Governments pursued active demand management with considerable success; in return, wage claims were moderate, inflation was low, and productivity growth was not sufficiently poor as to lead the government to conclude that this part of the bargain was in default.

With both inflation and unemployment increasing in the late 1960s, the Heath government took office in 1970 on a manifesto that viewed the private sector—in particular the unions—as having begun to renege on both parts of its bargain. In consequence, it made sense for the government to reconsider its commitment to demand management and the propping up of lame duck firms by specific subsidies. I believe it would be wrong to interpret this policy shift as the implementation of a tit for tat punishment designed to drive the unions back to a desire to co-operate. Rather, it was a fall back on the Nash equilibrium; accepting that the private sector would continue to behave non-cooperatively, policy was designed conditioned on this diagnosis and took a tougher line to attempt to secure a long-run supply-side outcome which was preferable to that being achieved by the interaction of a co-operating government and a reneging private sector. Market forces were to be allowed to operate in the hope of disciplining an otherwise reluctant private sector.

For this to succeed, it was of course imperative for the government to stick to its guns, and to be expected to do so. In fact, as things failed to improve quickly, political pressure forced the famous U-turn of 1972 in which demand management was re-adopted unilaterally without any very credible commitment by the private sector to revert to co-operative behaviour. This U-turn, whether justified or not, was to have a profound effect on subsequent policy design. Specifically, Mrs Thatcher drew the obvious inference that mere promises to be tough were insufficient: a government embarking on such a course must first find a way to tie its own hands so that when, temporarily, the going got tough, the temptation to revert to expediency and reflation could be resisted. Only then could market forces be expected to exercise any real discipline on private behaviour, both in wage push on the one hand and on underlying productivity growth on the other.

The period of Labour government from 1974 to 1979 should be divided into the sub-periods before and after 1976. During the first sub-period, the Wilson years, the policy of the later Heath period was essentially continued. Demand was actively managed, albeit taking account of both the excessive 1973 boom and the deflationary impact of the first oil shock. Policy was primarily accommodating and was known to be so. Nor did extravagant public sector pay awards do anything to dispel the feeling that the government was adopting a distinctly co-operative posture in the belief (hope?) that the private sector would play ball. A realistic assessment of the supply-side implications was not the greatest priority.

Against this background, one should not underestimate the change of direction undertaken by the Callaghan government in 1976.[10] In earlier sections I referred to the tight contraction of fiscal policy and the adoption of targets for £M3. While in part these changes may have been forced on the government by the conditions attached to the IMF loan in 1976, one should note that the change in policy had begun prior to this, and that to some extent the famous Letter of Intent of December 1976 may have been precisely the sort of credible pre-commitment that I discussed above. These developments were important, but I would wish to distinguish their implications for inflation and for demand management. In my judgement, the change in policy was intended primarily to reduce the inflationary bias which a guarantee of monetary accommodation had previously entailed. Public pronouncements notwithstanding, it is not clear that the government had really abandoned demand management of the real economy, as the active attempts to manage the real exchange rate during 1976–7 attest. This evidence, together with the persistent but optimistic attempt to secure a co-operative solution with the unions, culminating in their conspicuous default during the 'winter of discontent' in 1978–9, suggests that prior to 1979 the supply side of the real economy continued to be a low priority.

Viewed in this light, the crucial innovation of the Thatcher government was not the determination to fight inflation. Monetary targets for 1979–80 were barely tighter than those previously envisaged under Labour; and, in both raising VAT and honouring the Clegg awards for public sector pay increases, the 1979 Budget deliberately added to inflation in the short run. Rather, its immediate innovation was to tackle incentives, productivity, and the supply-side in general, significantly downgrading demand management in favour of market forces. The real threat of unemployment and bankruptcies was intended to, and has, gradually changed attitudes of workers and managers. Mindful of the Heath U-turn, it was recognized that it was imperative to make this tough commitment credible. Initially, this was accomplished by persistent emphasis that there would be no U-turn, a tit for tit strategy in which the government volunteered to punish *itself* for any subsequent reneging by so raising the political cost of such a reversal that it would not subsequently be able to undertake it. By 1980, this was reinforced by the formal apparatus of the MTFS which, *inter alia*, Buiter and Miller (1983) describe as a commitment to switch off the automatic fiscal stabilizers. When in 1981 the government responded to an unexpectedly severe recession (and consequent PSBR overshoot) by a severe fiscal contraction, their credibility had largely been established.

Necessarily, supply-side benefits will probably be slow to come through. Muellbauer and Mendis (1983) have argued that the rapid productivity growth of 1982–3 is largely a phenomenon of the Keynesian business cycle, and the subsequent slow-down of productivity growth is consistent with this interpretation. Thus, while it is too early to document significant productivity gains which can unambiguously be attributed to the fiscal stance since 1979, it is also true that the time horizon over which one would expect such a policy to succeed is very long. It would be equally invalid to conclude that this aspect of recent fiscal policy design has been a failure.[11] What can undoubtedly be said is that the Thatcher government has adopted a longer time horizon, or a lower discount rate on policy success, than previous governments. *Per se*, this should be regarded as a beneficial change in policy design.

6. Conclusions

The two decades before 1970 saw a consensus in macroeconomic policy in which the pursuit of full employment and demand management was paramount, and fiscal played a central role. During the 1970s, the combination of high inflation, steadily rising unemployment, and, after 1973, sluggish output growth gradually convinced policy-makers that demand management should be subordinated to other objectives of fiscal policy. This reassessment did not begin with Margaret Thatcher, but its implications were most clearly and determinedly pursued during her government, when the fiscal stance was very tight even though output was well below potential. Demand management had been almost completely abandoned.

Sound finance does not provide a very plausible rationale for this change in emphasis in fiscal policy. The popular debate deals in indicators that bear little relation to a true assessment of the sustainability of fiscal policy. The public finances have been considerably more healthy than is commonly supposed. Nor has tight fiscal policy been essential for pursuit of a monetary policy that would bring inflation under control. Even so, the fiscal component of the MTFS may have reinforced beliefs that the government intended to win the fight against inflation. And it did contain an implicit commitment to tighten fiscal policy should inflation unexpectedly rise.

To an important extent, the adoption of maintenance of tight fiscal policy during a major recession was specifically designed to signal the end of the commitment to demand management in the hope that this would alter private behaviour and gradually improve supply-side performance.

During the 1980s the UK's inflation performance has improved substantially. Yet to date, neither this nor the attack on supply-side problems has led to any significant improvement in the real economy. Since the failure to use fiscal policy to stimulate demand in the early 1980s undoubtedly led to a sacrifice of output, it remains to be seen whether the UK will recoup this output with interest.

APPENDIX: THE PUBLIC SECTOR ACCOUNTS

I adopt the following notation:

H, B, D	= nominal stock of high-powered money, bills, bonds (par value)
q, p, p_k	= price of bonds, GDP deflator, implicit price of public capital
K, r_k, r	= real public capital stock (including physical and resource capital), net return on public capital, bill interest rate
π, n	= inflation rate, growth rate of real GDP
G', T'	= real public consumption, real taxes net of transfers
Y, I	= real GDP, real public investment at market prices
AS	= nominal value of asset sales (privatization of physical assets)
W, L, s	= nominal public wealth, nominal liabilities of public sector, ratio of liabilities to GDP
c	= coupon on nominal bonds
c_i, D_i, q_i	= analogous variables for index bonds
$PSFD, PSBR$	= public sector financial deficit, public sector borrowing requirement

Public sector (tangible) wealth W is defined as

$$W = p_k K - H - B - Dq - D_i q_i \qquad (A2.1)$$

where p_k is the implicit value of a unit of public capital in terms of its discounted future earnings. However, it should be stressed that W is *not* a measure of net worth or solvency. The government also has the power to levy future taxes and make future expenditures. Essentially, solvency requires that negative (positive) wealth be matched by an equivalent present value of future surpluses (deficits) in the relevant sense. (For a clear but comprehensive treatment see Buiter, 1985.) Thus, even an examination of tangible assets and liabilities gives only an incomplete picture of the public finances.

A second identity defines the PSBR:

$$\Delta H + \Delta B + q\Delta D + q_i \Delta D_i = PSBR$$
$$= p(G' + I - T') - r_k K_{-1} + rB_{-1} + cD_{-1}$$
$$+ c_i D_{i,-1} - AS. \qquad (A2.2)$$

Hence, differencing (A2.1), we can relate the PSBR to changes in public sector wealth:

$$\Delta W = PSBR + D_{-1}\Delta q + D_{i,-1}\Delta q_i - K_{-1}\Delta p_k - p_k \Delta K \qquad (A2.3)$$

which makes clear that the market value of wealth changes because of revaluations as well as through a non-zero PSBR. Notice, comparing (A2.2) and (A2.3), that, if the implicit value of public capital p_k equals the market price p at which the government buys or sells investment goods (i.e., if the rate of return on public and private investment is identical), changes in the stock of public capital leave wealth unaltered.

Much discussion of the public finances proceeds on a more restrictive basis, namely, by neglecting assets entirely and focusing on liabilities and the public sector debt. I now define G to be the sum of spending on consumption and investment goods by the government, and T to be tax receipts less transfers less the operating deficits of public corporations. Letting public sector liabilities L be the sum of high-powered money, bills, and bonds,

$$\Delta L = p(G-T) + rB_{-1} + cD_{-1} + c_i D_{i,-1} - AS + D_{-1}\Delta q + D_{i,-1}\Delta q_i \qquad (A2.4)$$
$$= PSBR + D_{-1}\Delta q + D_{i,-1}\Delta q_i.$$

Letting s denote the debt/GDP ratio (L/pY), it follows definitionally that

$$s = \frac{PSBR}{pY} - s_{-1}(\pi+n) + \frac{D_{-1}\Delta q + D_{i,-1}\Delta q_i}{pY}. \qquad (A2.5)$$

However, this is not the most illuminating decomposition for policy analysis. Adopting the strong but powerful assumption that the *expected* one-period return on bills, nominal bonds, and indexed bonds is equated, whence for bonds the expected coupon payment per pound invested plus the expected capital gain must equal the return on holding bills, it is simple to show that (A2.5) may be rewritten as

$$s = \frac{G-T}{Y} + \frac{(r-\pi-n)(L_{-1}-H_{-1})}{pY} - \frac{(\pi+n)H_{-1}}{pY} - \frac{AS}{pY} + \frac{D_{-1}q^u + D_{i,-1}q_i^u}{pY}. \qquad (A2.6)$$

Thus, the debt/GDP ratio rises when there is a primary deficit $(G-T)$, when the interest-bearing debt $(L_{-1}-H_{-1})$ carries an interest rate exceeding both inflation and growth of real GDP, and when there is an unanticipated rise in bond prices (q^u, q_i^u) which represents a private sector gain but a public sector loss. Conversely, the public debt is reduced by asset sales, by the inflation tax on non-interest-bearing money, and by the seigniorage that the government extracts when real-income growth raises real-money demand. Table 2.4 presents the decomposition embodied in equation (A2.6) for annual changes in the UK debt/GDP ratio since 1970. Asset sales are negligible prior to 1985.

Notes

1. More precisely, we require an 'open-loop' path for government variables to be implemented if everything goes according to plan, plus 'closed-loop' or contingent

plans specifying how, if at all, future surprises will be accommodated after they occur.

2. For an attempt to calculate a demand-weighted measure of the fiscal deficit, in which the demand impact of separate tax and spending components are separately computed, see Biswas, Johns, and Savage (1985).

3. Again, the absence of inflation accounting may have led to part of the problem: the March 1973 Budget was portrayed as 'broadly neutral'. In both May and December intentions to cut back public expenditure were announced, though they proved hard to implement (Biswas, Johns, and Savage, 1985).

4. In passing, I cannot help reflecting that the interpretation of events given above suggests that the fortuitous timing of (1) Competition and Credit Control with the subsequent sharp increase in the demand for nominal *and* real £M3, (2) the episode of wage indexation during 1973–4, and (3) the oil shock and the decision to accommodate it meant a massive rise in £M3 followed two years later by massive inflation. Since this statistical artefact *dominates* all changes in £M3 and inflation between 1950 and 1980, it induced a quite false confidence by 1980 in the close relation between £M3 and inflation, a relation that has subsequently been exposed as invalid in the form in which it was then propounded.

5. The Appendix presents a rigorous treatment of this issue.

6. The very incomplete assessment implied by the debt/GDP ratio finds a parallel in private equity markets, where companies are sometimes judged by their *P/E* ratio. Sophisticated financial analysts now recognize the deficiencies of this indicator: it would be nice if discussion of the public sector were equally informed.

7. In an economy growing at rate n, equity and efficiency suggest it is preferable to plan not a constant consumption stream but a stream also rising at rate n, in which case the rule would be $C = (R - n)NW$. If one wishes to model the dependence of income tax revenue on interest rates, one can replace R by $R(1 - t)$ in the above formulae.

8. These simplifying assumptions may all be challenged. For example, since *nominal* interest income attracts income tax, the real tax take will tend to rise with inflation. Similarly, to the extent that bank deposits do not pay competitive interest rates, higher inflation and nominal interest rates will raise bank profits and thus corporation tax revenues.

9. Full inflation adjustment during a period in which inflation was expected to fall might be inappropriate since one would wish to make allowance for the (smallish) reduction in the inflation tax which would then ensue. However, a proper forward-looking indicator of solvency would deal with this issue automatically.

10. Callaghan's speech to the 1976 Labour Party Conference took as its theme the assertion that demand expansion would lead only to inflation, not to real output growth.

11. Critics of the policy might point out, with some justification, that Keynesian recessions hit investment and future supply capacity. This cost must be subtracted from any productivity or efficiency gains arising from removing the full employment guarantee.

References

Allsopp, C. J. and Mayes, D. G. (1985), in D. Morris (ed.), *The Economic System in the UK*, Chapters 12 and 13. Oxford: University Press.

Artis, M. and Currie, D. (1981), in W. A. Eltis and P. J. N. Sinclair (eds), *The Money Supply and the Exchange Rate*, Oxford: University Press.

Barro, R. J. (1974), 'Are Government Bonds Net Wealth?' *Journal of Political Economy*, 82, 1095–1118.

Biswas, R., Johns, C. and Savage, D. (1985), 'The Measurement of Fiscal Stance', *National Institute Economic Review*, 113, 50–65.

Blanchard, O. J. (1985), 'Debts, Deficits, and Finite Horizons', *Journal of Political Economy*, 93, 223–47.

Britton, A. J. C. (1986), 'Can Fiscal Expansion Cut Unemployment?' *National Institute Economic Review*, 115, 83–99.

Brown, C. V. (1980), *Taxation and the Incentive to Work*. Oxford: University Press.

Bruno, M. (1986), 'Sharp Disinflation Strategy: Israel 1985', *Economic Policy*, 2, 379–403.

Buiter, W. H. (1980), 'The Macroeconomics of Dr Pangloss', *Economic Journal*, 90, 34–50.

—— (1985), 'A Guide to Public Sector Debt and Deficits', *Economic Policy*, 1, 13–70.

—— and Miller, M. (1981), in W. A. Eltis and P. J. N. Sinclair (eds.), *The Money Supply and the Exchange Rate*. Oxford: University Press.

—— (1983), 'The Macroeconomic Consequences of a Change in Regime: The UK under Mrs Thatcher', *Brookings Papers on Economic Activity*, 2.

Burns, T. and Budd, A. (1979), 'The Role of the PSBR in Controlling the Money Supply', OECD, *Economic Outlook*, November, 26–30.

Cohen, D. (1985), 'How to Evaluate the Solvency of an Indebted Nation', *Economic Policy*, 1, 139–56.

—— and Sachs, J. (1984), 'Growth and External Debt under Risk of Debt Repudiation'. Washington DC: World Bank.

Davidson, J. *et al.* (1978), 'Econometric Modelling of the Aggregate Time Series Relationship between Consumers' Expenditure and Income in the UK', *Economic Journal*, 68, 661–92.

Devereux, M. and Morris, C. N. (1983), 'The Pattern of Revenue Receipts from North Sea Oil', *Fiscal Studies*, 4, 14–24.

Fforde, J. (1983), 'Setting Monetary Objectives', *Bank of England Quarterly Bulletin*, 23, 200–8.

Flemming, J. S. (1973), 'The Consumption Function when Capital Markets are Imperfect: the Permanent Income Hypothesis Reconsidered', *Oxford Economic Papers*, 25, 160–72.

Friedman, B. M. (1985), 'The Effect of Large Government Deficits on Interest Rates and Equity Returns', *Oxford Review of Economic Policy*, 1, 58–71.

Hendry, D. F. (1983), 'Econometric Modelling: The "Consumption Function" in Retrospect', *Scottish Journal of Political Economy*, 30, 193–220.

Hills, J. (1984), 'Public Assets and Liabilities and the Presentation of Budgetary Policy', in M. Ashworth, J. Hills, and C. N. Morris (eds.), *Public Finances in Perspective*. London: Institute for Fiscal Studies.

Kaldor, N. (1971), 'Conflicts in National Economic Objectives', *Economic Journal*, 81, 1–16.

King, M. A. (1985), 'Tax Reform in the UK and in the US', *Economic Policy*, 1, 219–30.

—— and Fullerton, D. (1984) *The Taxation of Income From Capital: A Comparative Study of the United States, United Kingdom, Sweden, and West Germany*. Chicago: University of Chicago Press.

Kydland, F. E. and Prescott, E. C. (1977), 'Rules Rather than Discretion: The Inconsistency of Optimal Plans', *Journal of Political Economy*, 85, 473–93.

Layard, P. R. G. *et al.* (1984), 'The Case for Unsustainable Growth', Centre for European Policy Studies, Economic Paper no. 31.

—— and Nickell, S. J. (1985), 'The Causes of British Unemployment', *National Institute Economic Review*, 111, 60–85.

Miller, M. H. (1982), 'Inflation-adjusting the Public Sector Financial Deficit', in J. A. Kay (ed.), *The 1982 Budget*. Oxford: Basil Blackwell.

—— (1985), 'Measuring the Stance of Fiscal Policy', *Oxford Review of Economic Policy*, 1, 44–57.

—— and Babbs, S. (1983), 'The True Cost of Debt Service and the Public Sector Financial Deficit'. Bank of England, mimeo.

Muellbauer, J. and Mendis, L. (1983), 'Employment Functions and Productivity Change: Has there been a British Productivity Breakthrough?' Centre for Economic Policy Research Discussion Paper. no. 32.

Muller, P. and R. W. R. Price, (1984), 'Structural Budget Indicators and the Interpretation of Fiscal Policy Stance in OECD Economies', *OECD Economic Studies*, 3, 27–72.

Odling-Smee, J. and Riley, C. (1985), 'Approaches to the PSBR', *National Institute Economic Review*, 113, 65–80.

Patterson, K. D. (1986), 'The Stability of Some Annual Consumption Functions', *Oxford Economic Papers*, 38, 1–30.

Pissarides, C. (1986), 'Unemployment and Vacancies in the UK: Facts, Theory, and Policy', *Economic Policy*, 1(3), 499–548.

Sargent, J. R. and Scott, M. Fg. (1986), 'Investment Incentives', *Midland Bank Review*, Spring.

Sargent, T. J. (1981), 'Stopping Moderate Inflations: The Methods of Poincare and Thatcher', mimeo.

—— and Wallace, N. (1981), 'Some Unpleasant Monetarist Arithmetic', *Quarterly Review*, Federal Reserve Bank of Minneapolis, Fall, 1–17.

Tobin, J. (1961), 'Money Capital, and Other Stores of Value', *American Economic Review*, 51, Papers and Proceedings, 26–34.

—— (1969), 'A General Equilibrium Approach to Monetary Theory', *Journal of Money, Credit, and Banking*, 1, 15–29.

Yarrow, G. (1986), 'Privatisation in Theory and Practice', *Economic Policy*, 2, 323–64.

CHAPTER 3

The Impact of North Sea Oil

Charles Bean

London School of Economics

1. A Review of the Facts

The last decade or so has seen major changes in the structure of the British economy. The decline in manufacturing has continued apace, while the discovery and exploitation of oil in the North Sea has meant that the United Kingdom has moved from a position of total dependence on imported oil, through self-sufficiency, to become a significant net exporter. This growing importance of oil production has occurred against the background of the two oil price hikes of 1973–4 and 1979 which have had major implications not only for the United Kingdom but also for its trading partners. To many people, the accelerated demise of the traditional manufacturing industries, and the associated rise in unemployment, is at least partly a result of the emergence of the United Kingdom as an oil producer. Indeed, some commentators even go so far as to see the discovery of vast oil reserves in the North Sea as a curse rather than a blessing. Is this view valid, or would Britain's economic performance have been even worse without oil? In this chapter I shall seek to answer this and the associated question of whether successive governments have used the proceeds from the North Sea wisely.

In 1975 the United Kingdom was almost totally dependent on imported oil. However, exploration in the previous decade had revealed significant reserves of oil under the continental shelf. At pre-1974 prices, many North Sea fields were barely profitable. The cost of importing a barrel of oil in 1970 was a little over £3 (in 1980 prices), while the average cost of North Sea oil production was just under £5 a barrel (again, at 1980 prices). The quadrupling of oil prices in 1974–5 suddenly raised the value of these reserves, conferring significant rents on their owners and making the exploitation of marginal fields a profitable proposition. By 1985 production had risen to almost a billion barrels per annum, and the United Kingdom had become the fourth-largest producer in the non-communist world after the United States, Saudi Arabia, and Mexico (see Table 3.1). British production represented $4\frac{1}{2}$ per cent of total world output and 6 per cent of free world output. From total dependence on imported oil ten years earlier, the United Kingdom had become a significant net exporter.

The global importance of the United Kingdom as an oil producer is mirrored domestically in the growing significance of oil as a share of national

I am grateful to my discussants John Odling-Smee and Marcus Miller, and to Sweder Van Wijnbergen for helpful advice.

Table 3.1
Output of major oil producers, 1975–1985
(million barrels p.a.)

	1975	1980	1985
UK	12	603	953
USA	3,653	3,722	3,856
USSR	3,600	4,432	4,373
Saudia Arabia	2,583	3,624	1,236
Iran	1,853	537	797
Mexico	294	779	1,101
OPEC	9,923	9,838	5,848
World	20,162	23,059	20,781

Source: Petroleum Economist, various issues.

output. Table 3.2 shows that the gross value of oil production in the first half of the 1980s was around $6\frac{1}{2}$ per cent of national output. This rather overstates the importance of oil because extraction costs have not been deducted from the value of oil production. However, since marginal operating costs in 1985 were around a quarter of the output price (obviously it varies from field to field), the figures do not greatly overstate the significance of oil in the economy.

Table 3.2 includes a number of macroeconomic indicators as well as the real price of oil. The oil price is measured relative to the implicit GNP price deflator for the United States rather than the United Kingdom. Consequently, it largely abstracts from movements in the sterling exchange rate and gives a better idea of the exogenous relative price shock imparted to the British economy by the two oil price hikes of 1974 and 1979. Of course, the effects of the two price increases (and for that matter the more recent fall) may have been very different, because the first episode occurred while the United Kingdom was still an oil importer, whereas the second occurred when development and production were well underway and the United Kingdom had reached self-sufficiency.

Table 3.2 clearly illustrates the decline in manufacturing that occurred during the 1970s and early 1980s. Between 1973 and 1981 the size of the manufacturing sector fell by nearly a fifth, while national income shows a modest rise over the same period. Much of this decline is concentrated over the period 1978–81, during which there was a marked appreciation of both the nominal exchange rate (between 1978 and 1980 the effective exchange rate rose 18 per cent) and the real exchange rate (defined as the relative price of domestic to foreign output and measured by relative producer prices in Table 3.2). This period of marked decline in the manufacturing sector coincides with the coming onstream of the major North Sea oil fields and the

Table 3.2

Oil production prices, and selected macroeconomic indicators, 1973–1985

	GDP at factor cost (1980 prices, 1980 = 100)	Gross oil production (1980 prices, as % of GDP)	Real oil price[a] (1980 = 100)	Mfg. output (1980 = 100)	Retail price inflation (%)	UK unemployment, (%)	Real exchange rate[b] (1980 = 100)
1973	94.6	—	15.9	114.2	9.1	2.4	72.9
1974	93.0	—	52.9	112.7	16.0	2.4	72.8
1975	92.0	0.0	52.9	105.0	24.2	3.7	76.0
1976	94.4	0.5	54.0	106.9	16.5	5.0	71.4
1977	96.9	1.6	55.0	109.0	15.9	5.3	76.0
1978	99.8	1.8	52.5	109.7	8.3	5.2	78.6
1979	102.4	2.7	63.9	109.5	13.3	4.8	87.3
1980	100.0	3.7	100.0	100.0	18.1	6.0	100.0
1981	98.6	4.9	103.3	94.0	11.9	9.3	100.8
1982	100.4	6.2	100.4	94.2	8.7	10.9	97.7
1983	103.7	6.3	84.6	96.9	4.6	11.9	91.0
1984	106.4	7.2	79.3	100.7	5.0	12.4	87.7
1985	109.9	6.7	75.4	103.6	6.1	12.9	90.0

[a]Relative to price of US output.
[b]Relative producer prices.

Sources: Central Statistical Office, *Economic Trends Annual Supplement 1986*; *Petroleum Economist*; and International Monetary Fund, *International Financial Statistics*.

second oil price shock. However, it also happens to coincide with the adoption of contractionary fiscal and monetary policies by the newly elected Conservative government under Mrs Thatcher, aimed at combating inflation and reducing the size of the public sector. A question I shall address in Section 3 is the extent to which the 1979–81 recession in general, and the demise in manufacturing in particular, can be attributed to North Sea oil or to the counterinflationary macroeconomic policies that were followed.

As already noted, the increase in real oil prices that occurred in the last decade or so has conferred considerable rents on the owners of the reserves. In practice, the government has appropriated most of these rents from the oil companies, enabling it to increase government spending and/or reduce taxes (possibly at a later date, if they are used to reduce government borrowing). The system of taxation on North Sea oil revenues is itself extremely complicated.

Table 3.3 provides estimates of the tax revenue attributable to oil. First, the oil companies pay mainstream corporation tax, and a proportion of this is due to their operations in the North Sea. Only recently has this become significant. Second, there is petroleum revenue tax (PRT). This is calculated on a field-by-field basis and is the chief source of revenue to the Exchequer. Third, the government collects royalties. Finally, a supplementary duty on petroleum was introduced in the 1981 Budget for a two-year period. During the two most recent fiscal years, tax receipts directly attributable to oil amounted to around 8 per cent of total tax receipts. However, the recent fall in oil prices (to under $10 a barrel at the time of writing) will, if maintained, significantly reduce the future tax yield from oil. A fall of $1 in the price of a barrel is estimated to reduce tax revenues by a little under £0.5 billion. On the basis of a forecast price of only $15 per barrel, a little over half the 1985 price of $28 a barrel, the government expects tax revenues of only £6 billion in 1986–7 and £4 billion in 1987–8 (1986 *Financial Statement and Budget Report*). There is, of course, considerable uncertainty about the future price of oil and therefore also about the forecast of tax revenues from this source, and a recovery of the price to $20 a barrel or more would significantly boost the Exchequer finances. All this highlights the very significant contribution of oil to the Exchequer during the first half of the 1980s.

Finally, Table 3.4 presents some information on the impact of oil on the balance of payments. The first column shows quite clearly the shift in the contribution of oil to the visible trade balance.[1] The first oil price shock led to a significant deterioration in this part of the trade balance, but this was gradually reversed. Net oil exports in 1984 amounted to no less than 2½ per cent of national income. However, this is not the only direct effect of oil on the balance of payments. Development in the North Sea has required the importation of capital equipment (especially for oil rigs); a significant fraction of the investment in the North Sea has been financed by inflows of foreign capital; and profits remitted abroad by foreign companies operating in the area will appear as a debit in the invisibles account. Table 3.4 includes such items in parentheses. While these adjustments would affect the composition of

Charles Bean

Table 3.3
Oil and the public finances

	Corp'n tax (£b)	Petrol. rev. tax (£b)	Royalties (£b)	Suppl. petrol. duty (£b)	Total £b	Total % of receipts	PSBR (£b)	Nat. debt (% of GDP)
1977/8	0.0	—	0.2	—	0.2	0.4	5.6	52.0
1978/9	0.1	0.2	0.3	—	0.6	0.9	9.2	53.3
1979/80	0.2	1.4	0.6	—	2.3	2.9	10.0	50.8
1980/1	0.3	2.4	1.0	—	3.7	3.9	12.7	47.8
1981/2	0.7	2.4	1.4	2.0	6.5	5.8	8.6	51.9
1982/3	0.5	3.3	1.6	2.4	7.8	6.4	8.9	50.1
1983/4	0.9	6.0	1.9	—	8.8	6.9	9.7	49.5
1984/5	2.4	7.2	2.4	—	12.0	8.7	10.1	51.1
1985/6	3.0	6.4	2.1	—	11.5	7.7	6.8	51.7
1986/7[a]	2.7	2.4	1.0	—	6.1	3.9	7.1	—

[a]Forecast.

Sources: Central Statistical Office, *Inland Revenue Statistics and Financial Statistics;* H.M. Treasury, *Financial Statement and Budget Report.*

Table 3.4
Oil and balance of payments, 1973–1984
(£ billion)

	Visible trade		Invisibles	Capital account
	Oil	Non-oil		
1973	−0.9	−1.7	1.6	0.1
		(−0.1)	(−0.1)	(0.1)
1974	−3.4	−2.0	2.0	1.5
		(−0.1)	(−0.2)	(0.2)
1975	−3.1	−0.2	1.8	0.2
		(−0.3)	(−0.5)	(0.9)
1976	−3.9	0.0	3.0	−3.0
		(−0.5)	(−0.7)	(1.1)
1977	−2.8	0.5	2.2	4.2
		(−0.5)	(−1.3)	(1.5)
1978	−2.0	0.5	2.5	−4.1
		(−0.2)	(−1.8)	(0.7)
1979	−0.7	−2.7	2.7	1.9
		(−0.2)	(−1.8)	(0.7)
1980	0.3	1.1	1.7	−1.5
		(−0.1)	(−2.7)	(0.8)
1981	3.1	0.3	3.2	−7.0
		(−0.4)	(−2.9)	(1.6)
1982	4.6	−2.3	2.3	−3.2
		(−0.5)	(−3.3)	(1.0)
1983	7.0	−7.8	4.0	−4.9
		(−0.4)	(−3.6)	(1.3)
1984	7.1	−11.2	5.0	−3.3
		(−0.3)	(−3.6)	(0.0)

Note:
Figures in brackets give contribution arising from oil-related activities, e.g. imports of rigs.

Source: Central Statistical Office, *UK Balance of Payments.*

the balance of payments, they do not materially affect the overall picture. Of course, these figures do not allow for the *indirect* effect of oil on the balance of payments through induced changes in activity and prices in the rest of the economy.

2. Theory

There is a considerable literature on the macroeconomic implications of a natural resource discovery.[2] The central question is whether such a discovery necessarily implies a contraction of other exporting and import-competing industries—the so-called 'Dutch disease', after the Dutch experience with natural gas. A subsidiary issue is the extent to which government policy measures are required to supplement or offset the resulting endogenous structural change in the economy. In discussing theoretical issues, it is helpful first to consider the 'long-run' implications, i.e., when there is full employment of both labour and capital. Once the underlying post-oil equilibrium of the economy has been identified, the process of adjustment to that equilibrium can be discussed.

Much of the theoretical discussion revolves around the distinction between oil, other non-oil tradable goods, and goods that are not internationally tradable. In reality, there is no clear dividing line between tradables and non-tradables because whether a good is tradable or not will depend on the international price differential relative to transport costs. However, it is a convenient fiction to assume that there are some goods that are intrinsically non-tradable. For succinctness, I shall henceforth refer to non-oil tradables and non-tradables as 'manufacturing' and 'services', respectively. Of course, there are many services that are traded internationally, and some manufactures that are not, but the appellations are convenient and should not cause confusion.

Equilibrium Implications

There are two primary channels through which the discovery of oil, or any other natural resource, can affect the economy. The first of these is through a 'spending' effect. The increased wealth arising from the oil discovery increases the demand for consumer goods (assuming they are normal), including the output of the services sector. Provided the country is reasonably small, the price of manufactures is determined largely or wholly by conditions in world rather than domestic markets. In that case, the price of services relative to manufactures[3] will rise. If domestic and foreign manufactures are not perfect substitutes, the price of domestically produced manufactures will also be bid up relative to the price of foreign manufactures; i.e., the terms of trade improve. This increased demand for services, and the consequent appreciation of the real exchange rate and shift of resources out of manufacturing and into services, is at the heart of most analyses of the 'Dutch disease'.

However, the second channel can sometimes lead to effects that offset or even reverse the first. This is the 'resource' effect, whereby an increased or reduced demand for factors of production leads to changes in factor rewards and a consequent change in supply in different parts of the economy. The magnitude and direction of this effect depend critically on the mobility of labour and capital and on the capital intensity of the industries involved. In the case of the United Kingdom and North Sea oil, the most appropriate assumption is that oil extraction is highly capital-intensive and therefore draws a minimal quantity of labour from other sectors, while the necessary capital (oil rigs) can be financed largely from abroad. In the polar case of a small country and perfect international capital mobility, the price of manufactures and the rate of profit are fixed by the rest of the world. If labour is the only other factor of production (and there is perfect competition and the production technologies exhibit constant returns to scale), this will also fix both the wage and the price of services. Thus the real exchange rate remains unchanged. The effect of the oil discovery is simply to increase the output of services through the income effect on the demand for services while manufacturing output contracts as employment in services expands.

Of course, this particular case of perfect capital mobility is extreme, along with many of the other underlying assumptions. However, it underscores the fact that a large appreciation of the real exchange rate is not a *necessary* consequence of the discovery of a natural resource. A degree of international capital mobility will tend to limit any appreciation of the real exchange rate, although it by no means obviates the need for resources to move out of the manufacturing sector and into the services (and oil) sectors. De-industrialization will still occur.

While a contraction of the manufacturing sector is a likely consequence of an oil discovery, this should not necessarily be a cause for concern. There is no reason to value driving motor cars more highly than watching plays, and the shift in the structure of production is the only way that the economy can benefit from the increased wealth occasioned by the oil discovery. However, this is not always the impression one would get from the media and even from certain parts of the economics profession. There are two main reasons for this.

The first cause for concern arises because oil is an exhaustible resource. While estimates of recoverable reserves vary, most commentators suggest that production is currently at or near its peak, and they predict a gradual tailing-off of production over the coming decades. The United Kingdom is forecast to become a net importer of oil again sometime in the next decade. One must then ask the question, What happens when the oil runs out? The answer depends critically on how the oil revenues are spent. If the revenues are dissipated in current consumption,[4] then the process of de-industrialization must eventually be reversed. However, once export markets have been lost they may be very difficult to re-enter. Similarly, the labour force may no longer possess the requisite skills if British manufacturers are to compete successfully on world markets. Thus, the *temporary* de-industrialization of the economy owing to oil may have *permanent* effects on the international competitiveness of British industry. This is often referred to as a 'hysteresis' effect.

Some of the oil revenues may, however, be saved rather than spent. To the extent that they are invested in either productive capital at home or financial assets overseas, all that is involved is a change in the asset composition of the wealth of the nation. In the case where the country consumes only the *annuity value* of the oil wealth, i.e. the permanent income, then spending patterns will not need to be reversed when the oil is exhausted, and the pro-industrialization phase need not occur. (The de-industralization will also be less pronounced.) We shall return to these issues in our discussion of policy in Section 4.

The second cause for concern stems from short-term adjustment problems. Although the economy may, as a whole, be better off as a result of the discovery of oil, some parts of the population, for example workers in manufacturing, may be made worse off in the absence of suitable redistributive taxes and subsidies by the government. This is especially likely in the short run when factors are not free to move between sectors or when markets do not clear. These short run problems of dynamic adjustment are the concern of the next sub-section.

Short-run Adjustment

Much of the 'Dutch disease' literature has focused on the problem of dynamic adjustment, with the most notable contributions being those of Eastwood and Venables (1982), Buiter and Miller (1981b), and Neary and Van Wijnbergen (1984). Eastwood and Venables examine the implications of a resource discovery—modelled as an exogenous windfall of foreign exchange—in the context of the celebrated 'overshooting' model of Dornbusch (1976). In this model there is only a single domestically produced good, which could be thought of as either a manufactured good which is an imperfect substitute for foreign manufactures, or a composite commodity comprising domestic manufactures and services. (In the rest of this section I shall adhere to the first interpretation.) There is perfect capital mobility, and operators in the exchange market are risk-neutral and are endowed with rational expectations so that uncovered interest parity holds. By contrast, there is sluggish adjustment of nominal wages and prices.

Eastwood and Venables were concerned to answer the question, Can the discovery of oil in such a framework lead to a domestic recession during the adjustment period? Their answer was no, unless there was a lag between the discovery and the increased demand it would engender. If there were no lag, the increased demand would require a deterioration in competitiveness to restore equilibrium in the goods market. With a fixed supply of money, this is brought about purely by a fall in the price of foreign goods in terms of domestic currency, i.e., by an appreciation of the nominal exchange rate, leaving the quantity of real-money balances (in terms of domestic output) unchanged. Since the price of domestic output is unaltered, adjustment is instantaneous and no recession is necessary.[5] However, if there was a lag between the oil discovery and increased spending, agents in the foreign exchange market, realizing the long-run implications of the discovery, would purchase domestic currency now, causing an immediate appreciation of the nominal exchange rate in advance of the increased spending. Thus there would be a deterioration in competitiveness and a temporary recession until domestic spending did increase.

The workings of the model are illustrated in Figure 3.1. The goods market equilibrium schedule (*GG*) shows the combinations of prices and competitiveness at which the demand for domestic (non-oil) output is equal to the fixed supply. It is upward-sloping, because a higher price level implies a lower stock of real-money balances and therefore a higher interest rate, which must be offset by greater competitiveness if the demand for domestic output is to remain equal to supply. Above the *GG* schedule there is an excess supply of goods and prices are falling. The interest rate equalization schedule (*RR*) shows the combinations of prices and competitiveness such that domestic and foreign real interest rates are equalized. It is also upward-sloping (and flatter than *GG*), because a higher price level again raises (nominal) interest rates which must be offset by higher inflation if the real interest rate is to remain unchanged. This is brought about by increased competitiveness, which generates an excess demand for domestic output. Above the *RR* schedule, domestic real interest rates exceed foreign real interest rates, and a real appreciation (deterioration in competitiveness) must be anticipated if investors are to be willing to hold both domestic and foreign assets simultaneously.

If the oil discovery affects only the demand for goods, then the new equilibrium requires an unchanged price level but a lower level of competitiveness. Without any spending lag, the economy jumps straight from

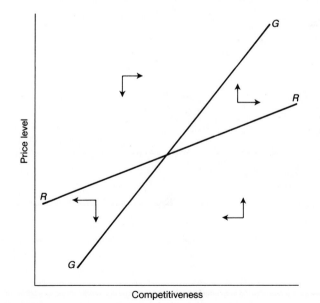

Fig. 3.1 The Dornbusch–Eastwood–Venables model.

the original equilibrium, point *A* in Figure 3.2, to the new equilibrium, point *D*. With a spending lag there is an immediate appreciation to point *B*, a recession between point *B* and point *C*, followed by a boom between *C* and *D* when the oil revenues finally accrue to consumers. If the oil revenue is itself a temporary phenomenon, the path would look something like the dashed line *EFGA*.

Buiter and Miller, and Neary and Van Wijnbergen, both highlighted the fragility of the conclusion that, absent a spending lag, there would be no recession. If the increase in oil wealth also increases the demand for real-money balances, then, with a non-accommodatory monetary policy, the domestic price level will have to fall to accommodate the increased demand. There must therefore be a recession along the transition path. Further, the exchange rate overshoots, with the initial appreciation being followed by a period of depreciation. In terms of Figure 3.2, the new post-oil equilibrium would be at *H* with an associated adjustment path *KH*.

These results clearly depend on the presence of both nominal rigidities and a non-accommodatory monetary policy. It is possible to avoid a recession (boom) by pursuing a suitably expansionary (contractionary) policy. Targets for £M3 were introduced in 1976 and at first were set only for the coming year. Now £M3 is an aggregate whose susceptibility to control through the *level* of interest rates (which is what matters in the model just discussed) is questionable.[6] Thus, the relevance of the model to at least the pre-1979 period is open to question. Since the introduction of the Medium Term Financial

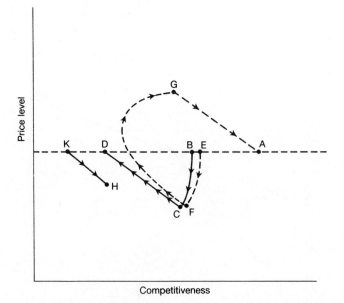

Fig. 3.2 Transition paths with an oil discovery.

Strategy in 1980, target growth rates for the money supply have generally been set three years ahead (although the target ranges for the second and third years have been frequently revised in the light of developments). Furthermore, although £M3 has remained an aggregate of interest, attention has also been focused on the narrow aggregates. Thus, the assumption of a non-accommodating monetary policy has been rather more appropriate since the inception of the Medium Term Financial Strategy.

Another reason for questioning the robustness of these results is the prominent role played by the assumption of sluggish *nominal* price adjustment. While there is, no doubt, nominal inertia, especially in wages, over the short term, its importance in the medium term is more questionable. Bean, Layard, and Nickell (1986) report annual wage equations for 18 OECD countries and find relatively little evidence of nominal inertia. This finding has been corroborated by Newell and Symons (1986), again using annual data, who argue that the nominal inertia in wage adjustment found by previous investigators is a consequence of the misspecification of terms-of-trade effects on wage behaviour. Does this imply that there can be no transition problem? The answer is no, because although nominal wage rigidity may be relatively short-lived, there is ample evidence that European economies in general and the United Kingdom in particular exhibit a considerable degree of *real* wage rigidity (see e.g. Branson and Rotemberg, 1980).

Let us return to the three-good world of the preceding section. If real (consumption) wages are rigid, then, for a given stock of productive capital, total employment in the economy could either rise or fall. The oil discovery produces an appreciation of the real exchange rate (because of the spending effect), which at given consumption wages lowers the product wage in terms of services and raises it in terms of manufactures. Thus, total employment rises if and only if the increase in the level of employment in the services (and oil) sector(s) outweighs the fall in the manufacturing sector. While the effects of nominal inertia can be avoided by pursuing a suitable accommodatory monetary policy, the presence of sluggish real-wage adjustment presents a much more difficult policy problem. Furthermore, provided the financial markets are forward-looking, the existence of a spending lag is likely to exacerbate any recessionary tendencies in the interregnum between discovery and exploitation. For further analysis of this issue see Bean (1986).

Empirical Evidence on the Spending Lag

Because the existence of a spending lag is such an important question in discussing the short-run effects of North Sea oil, I shall briefly present some empirical evidence on the issue. It is intimately related to the Barro–Ricardo debt neutrality (or 'ultra-rationality') proposition, which postulates that the time profile of the government's taxation programme is irrelevant.[7] A bond-financed tax cut today implies a higher level of taxes in the future. Consumers realizing this will increase their savings in order to pay the future tax bill. If capital markets are perfect, so that the government and consumers can borrow and lend on the same terms, consumption today will be unchanged. Barro's contribution (Barro, 1974) lay in demonstrating the formal validity of the proposition even if the beneficiaries of the tax cut were not around to pay the increase in future taxes, provided that they cared about the welfare of their offspring and suitably adjusted their bequests. Since it was widely believed that the oil rents, which as we saw in Section 1 have largely accrued to the government, would be returned in the form of lower taxes elsewhere rather than increased government expenditure, the existence of a spending lag rests on a denial of the validity of the Barro–Ricardo debt neutrality hypothesis.

There are, of course, many reasons why one would not expect it to hold. It requires an extraordinary amount of foresight by consumers to 'pierce the government veil' in this manner; capital markets are imperfect; and consumers may not be altruistic or may be uncertain about their date of death (Blanchard, 1985). However, it is important to know if it is at least even approximately true, and the existence or otherwise of a spending lag with respect to North Sea oil provides additional evidence on the issue.

A proper test of the debt neutrality proposition requires modelling expectations of future incomes, taxes, and government spending.[8] Here I take a more broad-brush approach by estimating a conventional reduced-form consumption function:

$$C_t = \alpha(L)C_{t-1} + \beta(L)Y_t + \gamma(L)S_t + \delta A_t^P + \varepsilon A_t^G + \zeta O_t + \eta r_t + \theta R_t + \kappa \qquad (3.1)$$

where C_t = real consumption expenditures
Y_t = real private non-property income, net of tax
S_t = the real (current) government surplus
A_t^P = real private wealth (including physical assets)
A_t^G = real government wealth (excluding oil)
O_t = the real value of North Sea oil
r_t = the real short interest rate
R_t = the nominal short interest rate

The estimate of oil wealth is obtained by valuing the (mean) estimate of possible reserves in licensed fields (as published in *UK Energy Statistics*) at the existing sterling oil price. This ignores extraction costs, and therefore somewhat overstates the oil rents accruing to the United Kingdom. However, the estimate of reserves also ignores possible reserves in as-yet-unexplored parts of United Kingdom waters and to that extent understates oil wealth. Definitions of all the variables are given in Appendix 1. $\alpha(L)$, $\beta(L)$, and $\gamma(L)$ are distributed lags. Under the debt neutrality hypothesis, we might expect that $\beta(L) = \gamma(L)$ and $\delta = \varepsilon = \zeta$. Even if the debt neutrality hypothesis is true, we might find $\beta(L) \neq \gamma(L)$ if the government surplus, S_t, is helpful for predicting future values of 'comprehensive income', $(Y_t + S_t)$. This can, however, be tested. We might also be interested in testing a conventional 'naive' model in which $\gamma(L) = \varepsilon = \zeta = 0$. Note, however, that $\gamma(L) \neq 0$ does not necessarily imply that there is an element of ultrarationality present, because the government surplus may be helpful in predicting future private income, Y_t. Again, this is testable.

Equation (3.1) was estimated on annual data 1958–84 by instrumental variables treating current Y_t, S_t, r_t, and R_t as endogenous.[9] Initially we allowed for one lag each of consumption, private income, and the government surplus on the right-hand side, but these were jointly insignificant. Table 3.5 reports a version of (3.1) omitting these under the rubric 'general model', as well as estimates of the 'ultra-rational' and 'naive' models. Since the measure of oil wealth is less than perfect, oil and non-oil wealth are not constrained to have the same coefficient in the 'ultra-rational' model. Because consumers may not normally internalize the government budget constraint, but may have rationally forecast a lower tax burden as a result of North Sea oil, oil wealth has been retained as a separate variable in the 'naive' model.

At first sight the 'ultra-rational' model does not fare too badly with a highly significant coefficient on oil wealth (its expected value would be around the real rate of interest, i.e. 0.02). The coefficient on other wealth is incorrectly signed but rather poorly defined, and there is quite a significant real interest rate effect. However, the fit of this model is considerably worse than that of the general model, and a formal test easily rejects the 'ultra-rational' model $(\chi^2(2) = 12.38)$, largely because the coefficients on private income and the government surplus are quite different $(t = 7.51)$. As noted, this could be because the government deficit is useful in predicting future 'comprehensive' income, but a Granger-test of the predictive power of the deficit does not support this explanation $(F(2, 22) = 0.90)$.

The 'naive' model does considerably better against the general model $(\chi^2(2) = 5.09)$, but there is some evidence from the estimates of the general model that there is a role for the government surplus which attracts a t-statistic of 2.72. Here, however, there is also evidence that the government surplus is useful for predicting future private income. (The Granger-test yields a test statistic of $F(2, 22) = 2.56$.) Thus, the general model is consistent with the absence of 'ultra-rationality' but with a degree of forward-looking behaviour by agents. The rather significant *nominal* interest rate is suggestive of credit rationing and the effects of changes in the mortgage rate on cash flow (see Jackman and Sutton, 1982) but could also indicate an inflation effect of some sort. Although oil wealth does at least attract a positive sign, the coefficient is less than a quarter of its size in the 'ultra-rational' model. There is therefore little evidence to suggest that private spending rose in advance of the reduction in the tax burden permitted by North Sea oil (relative to what would otherwise have been the case).

Charles Bean

Table 3.5
Tests of Barro–Ricardo debt neutrality

Independent variables	General model	'Ultra-rational' model	'Naive' model
Constant	9.372 (2.2)	21.381 (4.48)	9.213 (3.61)
Non-property income (Y)	0.913 (12.57)	0.777 (7.79)	0.879 (25.10)
Government current exhaustive surplus (S)	0.256 (2.72)		—
Private net wealth (A^P)	0.0062 (0.69)	−0.777 (0.04)	0.183 (3.93)
Government net wealth (A^G)	−0.0097 (0.61)		—
Oil wealth (O)	0.0066 (1.23)	0.0314 (5.00)	−0.0037 (0.98)
Real interest rate (r)	0.026 (0.23)	−0.448 (2.84)	0.211 (2.11)
Nominal interest rate (R)	−0.464 (3.65)	−0.281 (1.24)	−0.492 (3.40)
Standard error (as % of mean)	0.734	1.452	0.874
D.W. statistic	2.56	1.72	1.95
Instrument validity	$\chi^2(5)=2.98$	$\chi^2(7)=15.36$	$\chi^2(7)=8.07$

(i) Test that the surplus, S, Granger-causes private income, Y: $F(2, 22)=2.56$.
(ii) Test that the surplus, S, Granger-causes comprehensive income, $Y+S$: $F(2, 22)=0.90$.

Notes:
t-statistics in parentheses. Instrument validity test is Sargan's (1964) test of orthogonality of the error with the instruments. (See note 9 for list of these.)

3. A Quantitative Assessment

There has been a large number of studies attempting to quantify the impact on the British economy of North Sea oil and/or changes in the price of oil. These include Atkinson *et al.* (1983), Beenstock *et al.* (1981), Bond and Knobl (1982), Byatt *et al.* (1982), Forsyth and Kay (1980), McGuirk (1983), Powell and Horton (1985), and Spencer (1984). While the estimates of these authors often vary quite widely, the differences are often superficial rather than substantial and result from choosing a different counterfactual.

It bears emphasis that the question, What is the effect of North Sea oil on the economy?, is virtually meaningless because it is incompletely specified. First, the discovery of North Sea oil coincided roughly with the first oil price shock. Without oil, the United Kingdom would probably have needed to divert *more* resources to manufacturing in order to pay for the more expensive oil. Thus, while the discovery of North Sea oil may entail a smaller manufacturing sector *relative to an economy without oil*, it need not imply a change in the historical trend when taken in conjuction with the increased price of oil. Thus we must be careful to specify the reference point against which comparison is made.

Second, the policy environment must be clearly specified. How would fiscal and monetary policy have differed if the economy were without oil? Should the nominal money supply or interest rates be held constant? Should the budget deficit be allowed to vary, or should government spending and/or taxes be allowed to vary to maintain the deficit constant? Also, if expectations are forward-looking, as in the model considered below, the description of the stance of monetary and fiscal policy, and other exogenous variables for that matter, must apply not only to the current period but to all future dates as well. Temporary and permanent shocks consequently will have very different effects, and different assumptions will generally yield different results.

Some Personal Estimates

I first report the results of numerical simulations using a small macroeconomic model developed at the Centre for Labour Economics. This differs from many of the conventional macroeconomic forecasting models in possessing a reasonably coherent and consistent theoretical structure, particularly with respect to supply behaviour, and in distinguishing certain expectational variables explicitly. It is most easily thought of as a more developed, two-sector version of the 'overshooting' model of Dornbusch (1976) and Buiter–Miller (1981b), with forward-looking behaviour in asset markets and both nominal and real-wage inertia.

It is not possible to give a detailed description of the structure of every equation of the model and of the empirical estimates because of a lack of space. These are fully reported in Bean *et al.* (1985). However, Appendix 2 lists the equations of the log-linearized version of the model used here.

Since there are two distinct questions of interest, two different simulations are reported in Tables 3.6 and 3.7, respectively. Table 3.6 is a counterfactual experiment designed to answer the question, How would the structure of the British economy have differed without oil? That is, oil production is set to zero in the alternative scenerio, but the *historical* path of the oil price is retained. This could be thought of as a 'pure Dutch disease' simulation. Table 3.7 is a

Table 3.6
Effects of North Sea oil, 1974–1984
(percentage changes)

	1974	1975	1976	1977	1978	1979	1980	1981	1982	1983	1984
Manufacturing output	0.4	0.4	0.3	0.4	0.4	0.5	3.5	2.1	2.2	2.1	2.0
Services output	0.4	0.4	0.5	0.7	0.8	1.0	3.6	4.4	4.9	4.8	4.7
Manufacturing employment	0.2	0.3	0.0	-0.1	-0.3	-0.3	0.9	-1.1	-1.3	-1.5	-1.5
Services employment	0.2	0.2	0.4	0.6	0.7	0.7	2.1	2.9	3.0	2.8	2.8
Consumer price inflation	-0.6	-0.1	0.1	0.3	0.2	0.2	-2.5	0.8	0.9	0.7	0.6
Nominal exchange rate	0.3	0.0	0.5	1.3	1.9	2.6	6.6	8.2	9.9	10.7	10.8
Real exchange rate	1.1	0.8	1.2	1.8	2.2	2.6	10.0	10.9	11.8	11.9	11.8

Table 3.7
Effects of North Sea oil and oil price shocks, 1974–1984
(percentage changes)

	1974	1975	1976	1977	1978	1979	1980	1981	1982	1983	1984
Manufacturing output	-0.8	-3.4	-2.3	-2.0	-2.0	-1.9	0.2	-2.5	-1.8	-1.9	-2.0
Services output	-2.0	-1.4	-1.5	-1.4	-1.3	-1.2	0.0	0.8	1.2	1.2	1.2
Manufacturing employment	1.0	-2.0	-0.5	-0.1	-0.1	-0.2	1.3	-1.8	-1.4	-1.7	-1.7
Services employment	-1.0	-0.5	-0.8	-0.7	-0.6	-0.5	0.3	1.0	1.2	1.1	1.1
Consumer price inflation	1.2	-1.1	-1.2	-1.0	-0.8	-0.7	-1.9	-0.5	0.0	-0.1	-0.1
Nominal exchange rate	6.2	7.0	7.4	8.4	9.5	10.6	22.7	23.4	24.3	24.6	25.0
Real exchange rate	8.2	7.7	7.1	7.2	7.4	7.9	19.3	19.5	20.4	20.7	20.7

historical exercise designed to answer the question, How did the discovery of oil *and* the increase in oil prices affect the structure of the economy? In this simulation, not only is production set to zero in the alternative scenario, but real oil prices are also assumed to remain at their 1973 levels. The following assumptions have been made throughout: each of the two oil price shocks were unanticipated and are regarded as permanent, the volume of reserves and production was correctly evaluated (the value varies with the oil price and the exchange rate) but is assumed to be zero prior to the first oil price shock; real government spending and tax rates are kept constant (so the budget deficit and debt sales vary endogenously); monetary policy is non-accommodatory (despite the reservations expressed above); and effects on world activity and world interest rates are ignored.

The 'pure Dutch disease' simulation (Table 3.6) shows that the real exchange rate would have been 10–12 per cent lower in the first half of the 1980s without oil. In spite of this, manufacturing output would have been about 2 per cent lower and services output about 5 per cent lower. Thus, the presence of oil *per se* does not seem to imply that the manufacturing sector need actually contract, only that it benefits less from oil than the services sector. The expansion in activity with oil is a consequence of the decrease in raw material costs and the reduction in wage pressure brought about by the appreciation of the exchange rate. In spite of this, manufacturing employment still falls, because of substitution towards more energy-intensive production techniques, although overall employment increases. The spending lag effect is not sufficiently strong to push the economy into a recession in the second half of the 1970s, but the effect on demand clearly builds up slowly.[10]

Turning to the second simulation (Table 3.7) incorporating the two oil price shocks as well, we see that the increase in oil prices significantly depresses output, but to a lesser extent employment, compared with the previous simulation. The net effect is to produce a significant generalized recession in the pre-1980 interregnum and the classic 'Dutch disease' phenomenon of a contraction in manufacturing output and employment and an expansion of services output and employment in the exploitation period following the second oil price shock. The most interesting feature of the results is perhaps the 13 per cent appreciation of the nominal exchange rate (11 per cent real), which occurs in 1980 in the wake of the second oil price shock.[11] This compares with an actual 18 per cent appreciation of the effective nominal exchange rate between 1978 and 1980, and suggests that oil may play a significant role in explaining the behaviour of the exchange rate around the start of the decade.

While this simulation displays many of the features to be expected from the theoretical discussion, and which are qualitatively present in Table 3.2, clearly it cannot fully explain the magnitude of the collapse in manufacturing output and the horrendous rise in unemployment. A popular alternative explanation for the post-1979 recession is the contractionary fiscal, and especially monetary, policies pursued by the Thatcher government (see Buiter and

Miller, 1981a). In the Dornbusch-style model of Section 2, (permanent) changes in fiscal policy have no effect on demand, merely producing an offsetting movement in the exchange rate. However, such a conclusion no longer holds once tax rates are allowed to affect the supply side of the economy, for example the behaviour of wage bargainers. On the monetary side, a reduction in the rate of monetary growth will, given sluggish wage and price adjustment, produce a fall in real balances, a rise in domestic interest rates, and an (over-)appreciation of the exchange rate. The resulting loss in competitiveness leads to a recession which then provokes a moderation in inflation until equilibrium is restored.

To see if either fiscal or monetary policy can explain the post-1979 recession, I have conducted two further simulations. The first concerns fiscal policy and evaluates the effects of the switch from direct to indirect taxation contained in the 1979 Budget (a three-point cut in the standard rate of income tax and an increase in VAT from 8 to 15 per cent) coupled with a 1 per cent reduction in government expenditure in the first year and 2 per cent thereafter, relative to the status quo. (*Ex post*, this is a rather generous interpretation of government policy with respect to public expenditure.) The consequence is a fall of around $\frac{1}{2}-\frac{3}{4}$ per cent in employment, but concentrated entirely in services, and an *improvement* in competitiveness of 4 per cent.

The second experiment is a simulated monetary contraction in which the growth rate of the money stock is progressively reduced by 1 per cent per annum for five years. This produces an appreciation of the real exchange rate of around 8 per cent and a decline in manufacturing employment of around 1 per cent by the second year. However, it is more than compensated for by an expansion in services employment, and total output actually rises significantly. This happens because there is insufficient nominal inertia present to prevent *nominal* interest rates from actually falling, which stimulates consumption. (See the empirical results in Section 2 above.) This is not quite the end of the story, however, because a *combination* of an exogenous wage push and a non-accommodating monetary policy could yield a scenario similar to that portrayed in Table 3.2. Whether one chooses to describe the consequent unemployment as the result of the aggressive behaviour of wage bargainers or an excessively tight monetary policy seems to be partly a matter of semantics.[12] I conclude from these simulations that North Sea oil plays a significant, but by no means exclusive, role in explaining the appreciation of sterling in 1979–80 and the demise of manufacturing.

Other Studies

A number of studies of the impact of oil on the British economy were cited at the start of this section. Some of these rely on simulations of complete macroeconometric models, while others simply evaluate the change in the exchange rate necessary to restore balance of payments equilibrium using plausible estimates of export and import price elasticities.

Forsyth and Kay (1980), in one of the earliest attempts at quantification, compared the 'pre-oil' 1976 economy and the 'post-oil' 1980 one. The whole analysis is conducted at 1980 prices. They calculated that a 20–25 per cent appreciation of the real exchange rate, and a 15 per cent improvement in the terms of trade, would be necessary to restore current account equilibrium. They also estimated this would be associated with a 6 per cent contraction in manufacturing output. The closest analogue of this conceptual experiment is provided by a comparison of 1980 or 1981 in Table 3.6 with the zero base. Forsyth and Kay's estimates seem to be rather larger.

Byatt *et al.* (1982) argue that there are a number of factors that lead Forsyth and Kay to overstate the impact of oil, including their neglect of the capital account and their choice of price elasticities. They also emphasize that Forsyth and Kay's estimates say nothing about the required changes in industrial structure because account must also be taken of the effects of the simultaneous rise in oil prices. They suggest that, taking *both* effects together, a historical rise in the real exchange rate of only 10–15 per cent between 1978 and 1981 could be expected, and that the contraction in manufacturing would be much less than suggested by Forsyth and Kay. Comparing this with with Table 3.7, we see that this is very much in the same ball park as our 12 per cent estimate.

McGuirk (1983) calculates the effect of oil price changes on the external balance of the major industrial countries and then uses the IMF MERM price and income elasticities to calculate the exchange rate changes required to restore equilibrium. She concludes that an appreciation of the sterling–dollar exchange rate of 12 per cent would have been required between 1972 and 1978, while the equivalent figure for the period 1972–80, i.e. including the second oil price shock, is 17 per cent. (In terms of the effective exchange rate, the corresponding numbers are 12 and 23 per cent.) These numbers are of the same order of magnitude as those contained in Table 3.7, though nothing is said about the impact on output and employment.

Turning now to simulations using complete macroeconometric models, Beenstock *et al.* (1981) report estimates of an exchange rate equation containing direct effects from oil and simulations of a small model in which their equation is embedded. They suggest that North Sea oil had raised the real value of sterling by about 14 per cent by mid-1980, but there are no details given about the associated output and employment effects.

Bond and Knobl (1982) construct a small annual macroeconomic model specifically to look at the effects of North Sea oil. Their exchange rate system also includes direct effects from oil. They attribute more than half of the 45 per cent appreciation of the real exchange rate (measured here by relative unit labour costs) between 1977 and 1981 to the existence of North Sea oil and the rise in oil prices. Real income would have been $3\frac{3}{8}$ per cent higher and manufacturing output $3\frac{3}{4}$ per cent higher in the absence of the second oil price shock. A similar experiment on our model produces an increase in relative labour costs of only 12 per cent, a *rise* in real income of $1\frac{1}{4}$ per cent, and a fall in manufacturing output of only about $\frac{1}{4}$ per cent as a result of the second oil price shock.

Atkinson *et al.* (1983) use the National Institute model, which also includes an exchange rate equation containing direct oil effects. Making the same assumptions about fiscal policy employed on p. 81 above, but holding real interest rates constant, they conduct a simulation similar to Table 3.6 in which oil production is set to zero. They calculate that the exchange rate would have been 12 per cent lower, non-oil output $2\frac{1}{4}$ per cent lower, manufacturing output $5\frac{3}{4}$ per cent lower, and unemployment over $\frac{1}{2}$ million higher by 1981 without oil. The corresponding figures in Table 3.6 are 8 per cent, $3\frac{3}{4}$ per cent, 2 per cent, and 300,000. Thus, in both simulations, both total non-oil and manufacturing output are lower without oil. What is surprising about the Atkinson *et al.* results is that they suggest that the manufacturing sector would have been *relatively* worse of without oil, which seems rather implausible.

Spencer (1984) reports the results of simulations using the Treasury model. However, he replaces the model's usual exchange rate equation by the uncovered interest parity condition and assumes rational expectations in financial markets, which is in the spirit of both the theoretical discussion of Section 2 and the model of Appendix 2. He simulates the effect of the announcement in 1974 of a new discovery equivalent to 10 per cent of the full production of North Sea oil. Monetary policy is non-accommodating, and the real oil price is held at its 1974 value. Spencer finds that the nominal exchange rate appreciates 2 per cent by 1981 (half of this coming after 1977) and unemployment falls 30,000 by 1982. This is a rather large change in the exchange rate since it implies that North Sea oil, valued at 1974 prices, could have been expected to produce an exchange rate appreciation of 20 per cent and a fall in unemployment of 300,000. However, the appreciation of the real exchange (relative labour costs) is only about 9 per cent. Our model produces an appreciation of the nominal exchange rate of just under 4 per cent, an increase in relative labour costs of $4\frac{1}{2}$ per cent, and a rise in employment of 100,000 under the same assumptions.

Finally, Powell and Horton (1985) report the results of simulations using a later version of the Treasury model which does not incorporate forward-looking behaviour in exchange markets. They evaluate the effects of a 10 per cent fall in oil prices assuming a non-accommodating monetary policy, constant nominal government spending, and a small increase in world activity. By the second year the exchange rate has depreciated by $1\frac{3}{4}$ per cent and GDP is $\frac{1}{4}$ per cent higher. (No split between manufacturing and services is provided.) A similar simulation on our model produces a depreciation of $1\frac{1}{4}$ per cent and virtually no change in activity.

This discussion suggests that the estimates reported in Tables 3.6 and 3.7 are of the same order of magnitude as those reported by other researchers. If anything, the responses are a little on the low side. However, before passing on to a discussion of policy, one cautionary note should be sounded. A different approach to evaluating the effects of North Sea oil is provided by the work of Sheffrin and Russell (1984), who utilize an 'event-study' methodology, which entails identifying announcements of major oil finds and analysing exchange rate movements in the immediate aftermath. They are unable to identify any significant relationship between such announcements and exchange rate movements. This suggests that it may have taken a considerable time for the exchange markets to adjust to the discovery of oil. However, it does not rule out a very rapid response to movements in the price of oil, and a casual reading of the financial press indicates that the exchange rate is indeed very sensitive to movements in the oil price.

4. Policy

There are two aspects of policy that I want to consider. The first of these relates to adjustment problems, both in the short term while production builds up and in the long term, when the oil runs out. We have already seen that the discovery of oil has necessitated a shift of resources from manufacturing and into services. If factor markets worked well, this would not be a particular cause for concern. However, it seems that this is not the case, especially in respect of the labour market. As a result, the real appreciation and decline in manufacturing inevitably imposes costs on those who work in this sector while those in the services sector benefit. Of itself, this does not necessitate measures to prevent the appreciation and maintain the competitiveness of manufacturing. Rather, policies should be targeted directly at the cause of the market failure. It is beyond the scope of this chapter to address the reasons why the labour market fails to function efficiently—that is discussed elsewhere in this volume—but there is some presumption that the appropriate policy measures are those that improve the mobility of labour either between regions or between occupations, rather than intervention to depress the exchange rate or subsidies to manufacturing.

It is the long term, however, that tends to cause most worries. When the oil is exhausted the process of de-industrialization may have to be reversed as resources are switched from services back to manufacturing to pay for renewed oil imports (but see below). There is a widespread belief that, once export markets have been lost, they may be very difficult to re-enter, and that the workforce will lose the skill necessary to make British industry competitive. This sort of 'hysteresis' argument underlies the case for intervention to prevent the demise of manufacturing in the first place. However, matters are not quite as simple as they may seem. To begin with, if the costs of re-entering markets are correctly internalized by firms, then no policy intervention is required. Only if there are externalities, or if firms are unduly myopic, is there likely to be a case for intervention. Van Wijnbergen (1984a) analyses the particular case where there is 'learning-by-doing' that occurs only in manufacturing (see Kaldor, 1966), and which accrues to the industry in general rather than the firm in particular. There is thus apparently a case for subsidizing manufacturing. However, Van Wijnbergen shows that the discovery of oil could lead to a *fall* in the optimal subsidy to manufacturing if the proceeds from oil can be invested on the international capital market. The moral is that such arguments need to be looked at very carefully.

The second aspect of policy that I wish to address relates to the optimal intertemporal distribution of the gains from oil. It is worth enumerating first a general principle: the discovery of oil in the North Sea is a windfall gain to the United Kingdom, and there is a presumption that the benefits should accrue to all generations, and not simply to those alive at the time the oil is extracted. Note that this does not imply that the rate of oil extraction should be drastically reduced to ensure a continuing flow throughout the next century and beyond. So long as the population or the government has access to international capital markets, the depletion of one asset (oil) can be matched by the building up of others (claims on the rest of the world), or else by increased capital formation at home. There is no need for consumption to be matched to extraction, and naive balanced budget or PSBR targets are unlikely to help matters much. Extraction policy, about which we have said little, is quite independent of spending decisions. Indeed, the extraction policy followed by the oil companies—pump it out as quickly as possible—seems to have been a good decision in the light of the recent decline in oil prices, and probably not far from the social optimum. In this case the market seems to have worked quite well.

If consumers internalize the government budget identity, then the time profile of any reduction in the burden of non-oil taxes by the government will be immaterial.[13] However, the results of Section 2 (pp. 77–8) did not support the idea that private spending rose when the oil was discovered rather than extracted. There is thus an argument for suggesting that the government should have lowered the tax burden in advance of the receipt of the oil revenues. Odling-Smee and Riley (1985) calculate that 'permanent revenue' from North Sea oil—i.e., the level of consumption that could be maintained indefinitely if the proceeds were appropriately reinvested—is around £3 billion at current prices, or around 1 per cent of GDP. A tax cut of this order of magnitude would therefore have been warranted in the middle of the 1970s. There is little evidence that fiscal policy was indeed relaxed in this manner, but an unequivocal denial that fiscal policy responded in the appropriate way requires specifying the counterfactual of what would have happened in the absence of oil. Maybe fiscal policy would have been even tighter, in which case policy did indeed move in the right direction.

Perhaps more important than the issue of spending in the interregnum between discovery and exploitation is the question of how the benefits of oil are to be shared with future generations. First, note that the existence of a spending lag on consumption does not necessarily imply that the responsibility for managing the current proceeds from the North Sea falls to the government. Consumers may have been unable to increase their spending in advance of the oil revenues being made available to them because of borrowing constraints. However, that does not prevent them from *saving* when disposable income is transitorily high. Thus, a policy of cutting other taxes now and leaving the private sector to make its own decisions regarding the intertemporal allocation of spending could well be optimal. However, I prefer an interpretation of the results of Section 2 in which consumers are unduly myopic or do not care sufficiently about future generations, and are thus unlikely to save as much of the proceeds from oil as is socially desirable. In that case, government action to invest the surplus of oil revenues over and above the £3 billion or so 'permanent revenue' from the North Sea is called for.

There are three ways this surplus could be reinvested. First, the government could invest directly in domestic productive capital. Many socialists see North Sea oil as a heaven-sent opportunity for modernizing British industry (e.g. Barker, 1981). However, a case for concentrating investment of the surplus revenues in British industry must rest on the existence of market failures, and there is precious little evidence that British firms have been unable to undertake otherwise profitable investments because of a lack of capital. Rather, the evidence seems to suggest that firms are discouraged from investing in projects that might be profitable abroad because of their low expected rate of return. In addition, the record of successive governments in picking 'winners' is not very good. Rather, the bodies responsible for allocating government funds for industry seem to have been prone to capture by interest groups and the funds themselves channelled towards declining industries.

The second strategy is to accumulate foreign assets—either financial or real—which will provide a flow of income to the United Kingdom after the oil is exhausted. The notion of investing abroad rather than in domestic productive capital would be anathema to many people, but from the point of view of maximizing social welfare there are good grounds for investing the surplus revenues where they yield the maximum return, even if that happens to be in US government debt or Japanese car factories.

Finally the government, instead of accumulating assets, could reduce its liabilities, i.e. reduce its level of debt sales. As a consequence, the future tax burden would be reduced, permitting a higher level of consumption; and by reducing government claims on savings, private investment is also likely to be enhanced. Whether this strategy is preferred to the first two depends on whether the government or the private sector is better at making the appropriate allocative decisions. The present administration, of course, is somewhat suspicious of the ability of the public sector in this matter, and has at least shown an unwillingness to let the debt burden rise in spite of the depth of the recession (see Table 3.3).

I conclude that there are reasonably strong grounds for government intervention in the process of redistributing the gains from North Sea oil across succeeding generations through increased net investment of one form or another during the years of peak production. Such a policy would also have the effect of moderating the appreciation of the real exchange rate (and the consequent contraction in manufacturing) through increasing imports of capital goods or producing a new outflow of financial capital. To this extent it would lessen fears about 're-entry' problems after the oil is exhausted. Indeed, as pointed out in Section 2, if the government were to invest all but the annuity value of the oil, no such problems would occur. Whether policy has in fact been framed with such an objective in mind[14] is, however, much harder to answer definitively since it requires knowledge of what policy would have been in the *absence* of oil. Consequently one must remain somewhat agnostic about whether successive governments have indeed used the proceeds from the North Sea wisely.

5. Conclusions

The findings of this chapter may be summarized as follows.

1. The discovery of North Sea oil and the simultaneous increase in real oil prices have significantly increased the wealth of the United Kingdom—the 'permanent income' equivalent has been calculated at around 1 per cent of GDP. Manufacturing output has declined both absolutely and as a share of GDP since 1973, and the real exchange rate has appreciated.

2. Theoretical considerations suggest that the two phenomena may be connected. A windfall of foreign exchange (in the form of oil) can be expected to lead to an expansion of the services sector and a decline in manufacturing, and generally to produce an appreciation of the real exchange rate.

3. Numerical simulations suggest that without oil the real exchange rate would have been about 12 per cent lower in the first half of the 1980s, but that manufacturing output would actually have been lower rather than higher. However, the oil price shocks also imparted a contractionary stimulus to the economy. The net effect of North Sea oil and the oil price shocks was to reduce manufacturing output by 2 per cent and raise services output by $1\frac{1}{4}$ per cent. Oil played a significant, but by no means exclusive, role in the appreciation of sterling in 1979–80.

4. Evidence suggests that during the 1970s consumers did not increase their expenditure in anticipation of the reduction in taxes that North Sea oil would permit. A debt-financed tax cut by the government was called for to reduce any recessionary tendencies in the interregnum before exploitation.

5. Intergenerational equity suggests that surplus oil revenues above the 'permanent income' equivalent of North Sea oil should be invested rather than consumed. There is a prima facie case that the surplus revenues should be invested where they offer the greatest return. Such a strategy would also limit

the contraction of the manufacturing sector and would eliminate any re-entry problems arising from 'hysteresis' effects.

APPENDIX 1: DATA USED FOR TESTS OF DEBT NEUTRALITY

All data are annual.

A^P Real private wealth. Calculated as personal sector net wealth (beginning of period) deflated by the consumer price deflator. *Sources:* Central Statistical Office *Economic Trends* (1971) for pre-1966 data, and various issues of *Economic Trends* and Financial Statistics for post-1966 data.

A^G Real government wealth. Public sector net capital stock minus the national debt deflated by consumer price index. *Sources:* CSO *National Income and Expenditure Blue Book* and *Financial Statistics.*

C Real consumers' expenditure (£ m, 1980 prices). *Source:* CSO *Economic Trends Annual Supplement.*

O Estimate of value of oil reserves. Calculated by taking mean estimated remaining reserves in licensed fields (*Source: Energy Statistics*) times the sterling price of oil (*Source: International Financial Statistics*), deflated by consumer price index.

R Three-month Treasury bill rate. *Source: International Financial Statistics.*

r Real short-term interest rate. Calculated as $\{(1 + R/100)P/P_{+1}\} - 1$ where P is the consumer price index (*Source: Economic Trends Annual Supplement*).

S Current account surplus of the public sector, excluding debt interest payments and profits of public corporations, deflated by consumer price index. *Source: National Income and Expenditure Blue Book.*

Y Real private disposable non-property income. Calculated as real personal disposable income times personal income excluding profit and interest income, divided by total personal income. *Source: National Income and Expenditure Blue Book.*

APPENDIX 2: LISTING OF THE MACROECONOMIC MODEL

The equations of the log-linearised model are as follows.

$$pm = 0.19pe + 0.08pn + 0.73(wm + ty) + 0.17(ym - km_{-1}) \quad \text{(A3.1a)}$$

$$pn = 0.12pe + 0.6pm + 0.28(wn + ty) + 0.27(yn - kn_{-1}) \quad \text{(A3.1b)}$$

$$ym = 0.57c + 0.2g + 0.83(km - km_{-1}) + 2.06(kn - kn_{-1})$$
$$+ 0.295(p* + e - pm)_{-1} - 0.133sm_{-1} \tag{A3.2a}$$

$$yn = 0.664c + 0.232g + 0.962(km - km_{-1}) + 2.38(kn - kn_{-1})$$
$$+ 0.133(p* + e - pm) + 0.376(pm - pn) - 0.072sn_{-1} \tag{A3.2b}$$

$$(lm - ym) = 0.19pe + 0.08pn - 0.27(wm + ty) + 0.17(ym - km_{-1}) \tag{A3.3a}$$

$$(ln - yn) = 0.06pe + 0.32pm - 0.38(wn + ty) + 0.14(yn - kn_{-1}) \tag{A3.3b}$$

$$km = km_{-1} + 0.018E_{-1}qm \tag{A3.4a}$$

$$kn = kn_{-1} + 0.0122qn + 0.0125E_{-1}qn \tag{A3.4b}$$

$$sm = 0.974ym + 0.394sm_{-1} \tag{A3.5a}$$

$$sn = 0.543yn + 0.667sn_{-1} \tag{A3.5b}$$

$$Eqm_{+1} = i + pc - pc_{+1} + 1.05qm - 0.2ym + km - 0.929km_{-1} \tag{A3.6a}$$

$$Eqn_{+1} = i + pc - pc_{+1} + 1.05qn - 0.374yn + kn - 0.925kn_{-1} \tag{A3.6b}$$

$$wm = 0.73wm_{-1} - 0.21wm_{-2} + 0.79pc - 0.31pc_{-1} + 1.4l \tag{A3.7a}$$

$$wn = 1.1wn_{-1} - 0.5wn_{-2} + 0.5pc - 0.1pc_{-1} + 1.2l \tag{A3.7b}$$

$$c = 0.94yp + 0.06a_{-1} - 0.45i \tag{A3.8}$$

$$a = a_{-1} + 0.7i_{-1} - (pc - pc_{-1}) + 0.21(yp - c) + 0.09(qm - qm_{-1})$$
$$+ 0.21(qn - qn_{-1}) - 0.7(i^L - i^L_{-1}) \tag{A3.9}$$

$$ws = 0.58ws_{-1} + 0.3(wm - pc) + 0.7(wn - pc) - 0.174(wm - pc)_{-1}$$
$$- 0.406(wn - pc)_{-1} + 0.42l_{-1} \tag{A3.10}$$

$$cg = 0.087(wm - pc) + 0.203(wn - pc) + 0.29rr - 0.94l \tag{A3.11}$$

$$yp = 0.82ws + 0.18cg + \eta(xo + e - pc) \tag{A3.12}$$

$$Ee_{+1} = e + i - i* \tag{A3.13}$$

$$Ei^L_{+1} = 1.1i^L - 0.1i \tag{A3.14}$$

$$m - pc = 0.24y + 0.48(m - pc)_{-1} - 1.3i \qquad (A3.15)$$

$$y = 0.3ym + 0.7yn \qquad (A3.16)$$

$$l = 0.3lm + 0.7ln \qquad (A3.17)$$

$$pe = 0.32(pr + e) + 0.16(po + e) + 0.16pm + 0.36pm \qquad (A3.18)$$

$$pc = 0.35pm + 0.55pn + 0.1(p^* + e) + tx \qquad (A3.19)$$

An *m* after a letter denotes a manufacturing variable while an *n* after a variable denotes a non-manufacturing variable. The variables are:

a = real private wealth at end of period
c = real private consumption
cg = real current grants
e = nominal dollar exchange rate (price of foreign currency)
g = real government spending
i = nominal short-term interest rate
i^L = nominal long-term interest rate
ki = capital stock at end of period ($i = m, n$)
li = employment ($i = m, n$)
l = total employment
m = nominal money stock
pi = price of output ($i = m, n$)
p^* = price of foreign manufactures (dollars)
po = price of oil (dollars)
pr = price of non-oil raw materials (dollars)
pe = price of material inputs
pc = consumer price index
qi = Tobin's Q ($i = m, n$)
rr = replacement ratio
si = stock of inventories at end of period ($i = m, n$)
tx = expenditure tax rate
ty = income tax rate (including employers contributions)
wi = post-tax nominal wage ($i = m, n$)
ws = real post-tax wages and salaries
xo = value of oil rents (dollars)
yi = output ($i = m, n$)
y = total (non-oil) output
yp = private post-tax non-property income

Equations (A3.1), (A3.2), (A3.3), (A3.4), and (A3.5) determine prices, output, employment, the capital stock, and inventories in each sector. Equations (A3.6) are arbitrage relationships determining stock prices, while (A3.7) determine wages. Equation (A3.8) is the consumption function, and (A3.9) determines the level of real wealth as a function of stock prices, interest rates, and savings. Equations (A3.10), (A3.11), and (A3.12) determine wages and salaries, current grants, and hence personal disposable income. The coefficient $\eta = 0.037$ when the UK is considered to be an oil producer and $\eta = 0$ when the UK is considered not to be an oil producer. Equation (A3.13) is the uncovered interest parity condition, (A3.14) is the arbitrage condition for long bonds, and (A3.15) is a conventional demand-for-money function. Equations (A3.16)–(A3.19) are quasi-identities determining total output and employment, and the price of inputs and consumer prices. All variables are in logarithms except the interest rates and Tobin's Q.

The model is solved assuming rational expectations (myopic perfect foresight) of future asset prices (of which there are four: the exchange rate, the long-term interest rate, and the stock market valuation of manufacturing and non-manufacturing capital), using the numerical algorithm of Blanchard and Kahn (1980) as implemented by Buiter and Dunn (1982). In addition to the four non-predetermined asset prices already mentioned, there are 21 predetermined state variables in the system.

Notes

1. This is a net figure. North Sea oil is generally of high quality and much of it is exported. In return, a substantial quantity of lower-quality hydrocarbons are imported.
2. A by no mean exhaustive list would include Bruno and Sachs (1982), Buiter and Purvis (1982), Cassing and Warr (1985), Corden (1981, 1984), Corden and Neary (1982), Eastwood and Venables (1982), Forsyth and Kay (1980), Neary and Van Wijnbergen (1984), and Van Wijnbergen (1984a, 1984b) as well as the papers in Neary and Van Wijnbergen (1986).
3. The theoretical literature often refers to this as the real exchange rate rather than the relative price of domestic to foreign output. If the country is small so that the terms of trade in manufactures is fixed, then two measures will move together.
4. This could take the form of increased consumption of leisure (unemployment) as well as, or instead of, increased consumption of goods.
5. The model is as follows:

$$m - p = \alpha \bar{y} - \beta i \qquad \text{(Demand for money)}$$

$$y = -\gamma r + \delta(e - p) + \eta(x + e - p) \quad \text{(Demand for goods)}$$

$$\dot{p} = \lambda(y - \bar{y}) \qquad \text{(Phillips curve)}$$

$$\dot{e} = i - i^* \qquad \text{(Uncovered interest parity)}$$

where m is the money stock, p is the price of domestic output, y is the demand for domestic output, $\bar{y}$ is the fixed supply of domestic output, e is the price of foreign exchange, i is the nominal interest rate, r is the real interest rate, and x is the value of the oil discovery in foreign exchange. All variables are in logarithms except the interest rates, and the price level is predetermined. In fact, this is rather simpler than the Eastwood–Venables model, in which the demand for money depends on consumer prices rather than output price. In their model, there is actually a *boom* along the transition path.

6. The marginal assets in £M3 are interest-bearing bank deposits, so that the appropriate opportunity cost variable is not the level of interest rates, but the return offered on these marginal assets relative to the return on competing assets.

7. We are considering 'pure' fiscal policy here, in which the time profile of the money supply is unchanged. Of course, if the tax cut is ultimately financed by money creation, there may be real effects.

8. Under the life-cycle permanent income hypothesis,

$$\text{Consumption} = f \left[\begin{array}{l} \text{Private net wealth} \\ + \text{present value of non-property income} \\ - \text{present value of taxes} \end{array} \right] \quad \text{(i)}$$

where the form of the function $f(\cdot)$ depends on interest rates and the nature of preferences.

The government's solvency constraint requires that (see Buiter, 1985)

$$\begin{array}{l} \text{Present value of exhaustive} = \\ \text{government spending} \end{array} \left[\begin{array}{l} \text{Government net wealth} \\ + \text{present value of taxes} \\ + \text{present value of public sector} \\ \quad \text{capital formation program} \end{array} \right] \quad \text{(ii)}$$

where government net wealth comprises the stock of capital owned by the public sector, including the value of natural resouces net of extraction costs, less outstanding debt.

If the private sector retionally calculates the future taxes implied by the government spending programme, it follows that

$$\text{Consumption} = f \left[\begin{array}{l} \text{Total net wealth} \\ + \text{present value of non-property income} \\ + \text{present value of public sector capital} \\ \quad \text{formation programme} \\ - \text{present value of exhaustive government spending} \end{array} \right] \quad \text{(iii)}$$

where total net wealth is the sum of private and public sector net wealth. To carry out a test of the debt neutrality proposition, we need to test that (iii) performs at least as well as (i), or any other specification of the consumption function. For other evidence see Blinder and Deaton, 1985; Van Wijnbergen, 1985; and the survey by Seater, 1985.)

9. The additional instruments are lagged private non-property income and the lagged government surplus, world GDP, government spending, private investment, lagged real and nominal interest rates, and the current US nominal short interest rate.

10. Note that the *value* of North Sea oil production changed abruptly in 1980 because of the second oil price shock. It is this that produces the large movements in that year in Table 3.6.

11. It may seem surprising that introducing oil price effects on the rest of the economy produces a *greater* appreciation of the exchange rate. In most of the other models discussed below, an increase in oil prices would lead to a current account deterioration and an exchange rate depreciation, holding the value of North Sea oil constant. The disparity stems from different assumptions about the degree of capital mobility (and the specification of fiscal policy). In this model the capital

account is all-important in determining the behaviour of the exchange rate, whereas in the other models the current account plays a more important role.

12. One way of describing this scenario would be as the announcement of an 'incredible' reduction in the rate of monetary growth. Such an interpretation of the British experience has been provided by Sargent (1986).

13. Assuming that only lump-sum taxes are varied. There will, of course, be incentive effects from variations in distortionary taxes.

14. Note that the simulations in Section 3 assume that all revenues are remitted to consumers in the form of lower taxes now.

References

Atkinson, F. J., Brooks, S. J., and Hall, S. G. F. (1983), 'The Economic Effects of North Sea Oil', *National Institute Economic Review*, no. 104, 38–44.

Barker, T. (1981), 'De-industrialisation, North Sea Oil, and an Investment Strategy for the United Kingdom', in T. Barker and V. Brailovsky (eds.), *Oil or Industry?* London: Academic Press.

Barro, R. J. (1974), 'Are Government Bonds Net Wealth?', *Journal of Political Economy*, 82, 1095–117.

Bean, C. R. (1986), 'Real Wage Rigidity and the Effects of an Oil Discovery', London School of Economics Centre for Labour Economics, Working Paper no. 877.

——, Dinenis, E., and Probyn, C. (1985), 'A Small Macroeconomic Model', London School of Economics Centre for Labour Economics, Working Paper no. 794.

——, Layard, P. R. G., and Nickell, S. J. (1986), 'The Rise in Unemployment: A Multi-Country Study', *Economica* (Special Issue), 53, S1–S22.

Beenstock, M., Budd, A., and Warburton, P. (1981), 'Monetary Policy, Expectations and Real Exchange Rate Dynamics', in W. Eltis and P. Sinclair (eds.), *The Money Supply and the Exchange Rate*. Oxford: University Press.

Blanchard, O. J. (1985), 'Debt, Deficits, and Finite Horizons', *Journal of Political Economy*, 93, 223–47.

—— and Kahn, C. H. (1980), 'The Solution of Linear Difference Models under Rational Expectations', *Econometrica*, 48, 1305–11.

Blinder, A. S. and Deaton, A. S. (1985), 'The Time Series Consumption Function Revisited', *Brookings Papers on Economic Activity*, 2, 465–522.

Bond, M. E. and Knobl, A. (1982), 'Some Implications of North Sea Oil for the UK Economy', *IMF Staff Papers*, 29, 363–97.

Branson, W. and Rotemberg, J. (1980), 'International Adjustment with Wage Rigidities', *European Economic Review*, 13, 309–32.

Bruno, M. and Sachs, J. (1982), 'Energy and Resource Allocation: A Dynamic Model of the Dutch Disease', *Review of Economic Studies*, 49, 845–59.

Buiter, W. H. (1985), 'A Guide to Public Sector Debt and Deficits', *Economic Policy*, 1, 13–60.

—— and Dunn, R. (1982), 'A Program for Solving and Simulating Discrete Time Linear Rational Expectations Models', London School of Economics Centre for Labour Economics, Discussion Paper no. 127.

—— and Miller, M. H. (1981a), 'The Thatcher Experiment: The First Two Years', *Brookings Papers on Economic Activity*, 2, 315–80.

—— and Miller, M. H. (1981b), 'Monetary Policy and International Competitiveness: The Problem of Adjustment', in W. A. Eltis and P. J. N. Sinclair (eds.), *The Money Supply and the Exchange Rate*. Oxford: University Press.

—— and Purvis, D. D. (1982), 'Oil, Disinflation, and Export Competitiveness: A Model of the Dutch Disease', in J. Bhandari and B. Putnam (eds.), *Economic Interdependence and Flexible Exchange Rates*. Cambridge, Mass.: MIT Press.

Byatt, I. C. R., Hartley, N., Lomax, J. R., Powell, S., and Spencer, P. D. (1982), 'North Sea Oil and Structural Adjustment', Government Economic Service, Working Paper no. 54.

Cassing, J. H. and Warr, P. G. (1985), 'The Distributional Impact of a Resource Boom', *Journal of International Economics*, 18, 301–20.

Corden, W. M. (1981), 'The Exchange Rate, Monetary Policy and North Sea Oil: The Economic Theory of the Squeeze on Tradeables', *Oxford Economic Papers*, 33, 23–46.

—— (1984), 'Booming Sector and Dutch Disease Economics: Survey and Consolidation', *Oxford Economic Papers*, 36, 369–80.

—— and Neary, J. P. (1982), 'Booming Sector and De-industrialisation in a Small Open Economy', *Economic Journal*, 92, 825–48.

Dornbusch, R. (1976), 'Expectations and Exchange Rate Dynamics', *Journal of Political Economy*, 84, 1161–76.

Eastwood, R. K. and Venables, A. J. (1982), 'The Macroeconomic Implications of a Resource Discovery in an Open Economy', *Economic Journal*, 92, 285–99.

Forsyth, P. J. and Kay, J. A. (1980), 'The Economic Implications of North Sea Oil Revenues', *Fiscal Studies*, 1(3), 1–28.

Jackman, R. and Sutton, J. (1982), 'Imperfect Capital Markets and the Monetarist Black Box: Liquidity Constraints, Inflation, and the Asymmetric Effects of Interest Rate Policy', *Economic Journal*, 92, 108–28.

Kaldor, N. (1966), *Causes of the Slow Rate of Growth of the United Kingdom*. Cambridge: University Press.

McGuirk, A. K. (1983), 'Oil Price Changes and Real Exchange Rate Movements among Industrial Countries', *IMF Staff Papers*, 30, 843–84.

Neary, J. P. and Van Wijnbergen, S. (1984), 'Can Higher Oil Revenues Lead to a Recession? A Comment on Eastwood and Venables', *Economic Journal*, 94, 390–5.

—— (eds.) (1986), *Natural Resources and the Macroeconomy*. Oxford: Basil Blackwell.

Newell, A. and Symons, J. S. V. (1986), 'The Phillips Curve is a Real Wage Equation', London School of Economics Centre for Labour Economics, Working Paper no. 838.

Odling-Smee, J. and Riley, C. (1985), 'Approaches to the PSBR', *National Institute Economic Review*, 113, 65–80.

Powell, S. and Horton, G. (1985), 'The Economic Effects of Lower Oil Prices', Government Economic Service, Working Paper no. 76.

Sargan, J. D. (1964), 'Wages and Prices in the United Kingdom: A Study in Econometric Methodology', in P. E. Hart, G. Mills, and J. K. Whitaker (eds.), *Econometric Analysis for Economic Planning*. London: Butterworth.

Sargent, T. J. (1986), 'Stopping Moderate Inflations: The Methods of Poincare and Thatcher', in T. J. Sargent, *Rational Expectations and Inflation*. New York: Harper and Row.

Seater, J. J. (1985), 'Does Government Debt Matter? A Review', *Journal of Monetary Economics*, 16, 121–32.

Sheffrin, S. M. and Russell, T. (1984), 'Sterling and Oil Discoveries', *Journal of International Money and Finance*, 3, 311–26.

Spencer, P. D. (1984), 'The Effect of Oil Discoveries on the British Economy: Theoretical Ambiguities and the Consistent Expectations Simulation Approach', *Economic Journal*, 94, 633–44.

Van Wijnbergen, S. (1984a), 'Inflation, Employment, and the Dutch Disease in Oil Exporting Countries: A Short-Run Disequilibrium Analysis', *Quarterly Journal of Economics*, 94, 633–44.
—— (1984b), 'The "Dutch Disease": A Disease After All?' *Economic Journal*, 94, 41–55.
—— (1985), 'Interdependence Revisited: A Developing Countries Perspective on Macroeconomic Management and Trade Policy in the Industrial World', *Economic Policy*, 1, 81–114.

CHAPTER 4

The Impact of EEC Membership

Francesco Giavazzi

University of Venice

1. Introduction

In the early 1970s, when Britain was negotiating its entry into the European Economic Community (EEC), there were three items on the agenda.

1. There were the conditions under which Britain would join the customs union, and in particular the sign and the magnitude of the transfers between Britain and the countries that were already part of the union. This item was never really resolved: after 13 years, it is still the major source of disagreement between Britain and its partners. The disagreement centres on the two most evident costs of British membership: its contributions to the EEC budget, and the price of agricultural imports from the EEC. The two issues are closely related, since the EEC budget is appropriated almost entirely by the programmes designed to protect European agriculture.

2. There was the EEC request that Britain take steps to remove all barriers to international capital flows. British foreign exchange controls, established by the 1947 Exchange Control Act, had been very strict throughout the entire postwar period. They limited, with a varying degree of severity, direct investment, portfolio investment, and trade finance. Although the Treaty of Rome is explicit on the question of the liberalization of financial markets, the EEC request that Britain abolish exchange controls could not be very forceful, since at the time most EEC countries had some form of exchange controls. In fact, Britain was the first (in 1979) and only EEC country to remove all exchange controls.

3. There were the two 1970 Werner Reports (EEC 1970), which set forth the objective of achieving monetary unification among the EEC member countries by 1980. Although controversial, the issue of monetary unification at the time required no more than an agreement in principle. And in 1972—following the negotiation on the treaties of accession—Britain signed, in concert with all other member countries, the conclusions of the Werner report. The issue, however, became more pressing after the establishment of the European Monetary System (EMS) in 1979: the EEC is now putting pressure on Britain to join the exchange rate mechanism of the EMS.

A first version of this paper was presented at the Conference on the British Economy, Chelwood Gate, Sussex, 18–21 May 1986.

I am grateful to Barbara Gamba for research assistance; to Alasdair Smith, Chistopher Allsopp, Alan Winters, Andrea Boltho, Marco Pagano, and the editors of this volume for very helpful comments; and to Stefano Vona and Salvatore Rebecchini for helping me with the data.

This chapter reviews the impact of EEC membership on the British economy. Section 2 considers the welfare effects of the customs union: Britain's losses stem mainly from a worsening of the terms of trade owing to the shift in agricultural imports from low-cost Commonwealth producers to the EEC, and thus from the agricultural policy of the Community. Section 3 reviews the Common Agricultural Policy and the resource flows it induces within the EEC. The effects of EEC membership on the pattern of British trade in manufactured goods are analysed in Section 4. Section 5 examines the 1979 abolition of exchange controls; the issue of financial liberalization versus financial protectionism is important because the experience of the European Monetary System to date seems to suggests that exchange controls are a necessary condition for partnership in the EMS. Finally, Section 6 reviews the different aspects of the EMS choice: the role of capital controls, the relative weight of the dollar and the EMS currencies in sterling's effective exchange rate, fluctuations in the dollar and their effect on the exchange rate between the pound and the Deutschmark, sterling and the price of oil, and the width of the EMS fluctuation band.

2. The Welfare Effects of the Customs Union

Joining a customs union typically entails both welfare gains and welfare losses. The gains follow from the removal of tariff barriers *vis à vis* other members of the union; the losses arise from the (newly imposed) common external tariff.

A simple way to estimate the balance of these gains and losses is to consider the individuals who live in the country that joins the union and to calculate the amount of money they would need to be able to buy, at the post-union set of prices, the same bundle of goods which they were buying before. The difference between this amount of money and the country's national income, calculated assuming pre-union production levels and post-union prices, determines the transfer (positive or negative) needed to ensure that no one is worse off after the country has joined the union. The transfer is equal to the value of the country's pre-union trade bundle evaluated at post-union prices.[1]

This calculation assumes that no substitution in production or consumption takes place as a result of the change in relative prices that occurs following entry into the union. A country receiving such a transfer is therefore ensured non-negative welfare gains after joining the union, *even if* the composition of production and consumption remain at their pre-entry levels. To the extent that production levels and consumption bundles adjust to the new set of prices, the higher profits and the income savings thus generated will translate into net welfare gains for the country that has entered into the customs union.

Earl Grinols has performed this set of calculations for the UK over the period 1973–80.[2] He concludes that, if no substitution had taken place in consumption and in production, Britain could have maintained the pre-entry level of welfare only if it had received a transfer from its new partners. The required transfer is as large as 4 per cent of UK gross domestic product in 1974, and averages 2.3 per cent of GDP over the entire period. If Britain had received such a compensation, whatever substitution took place in consumption and in production would have generated a net welfare gain. But these gains are hard to estimate. On the production side, one has to correct for factors such as North Sea oil, growth, and technical change; the estimates of the gains from substitution in consumption vary with the assumptions about the utility function. Grinols's estimates of the gains from substitution range between 1 and 1.5 per cent of GDP per year over the years 1973–80.

In the years 1973–80, the actual net transfers between Britain and its European partners net out to about zero. Thus, if in those years there had been no substitution in production and in consumption, by joining the EEC Britain would have suffered a loss of income of around 2.3 per cent of GDP per year. Estimates of the substitution that actually took place in production and in consumption suggest that, by the end of the 1970s, this may have reduced the loss to about half of that.

Britain's loss stems mainly from the worsening terms of trade owing to the shift in agricultural imports from low-cost Commonwealth suppliers to the EEC, and thus from the agricultural policy of the Community. In essence, the Common Agricultural Policy (CAP) is a system designed to support the income of European farmers through a complicated network of regulations, involving the fixing of prices way above world market prices, variable levies on agricultural products imported from outside the EEC, and the granting of export subsidies enabling certain EEC commodities to compete in world markets.[3]

Britain, however, was supporting its farmers even before joining the EEC. The Agricultural Acts of 1949 and 1957 provided for the support of British farmers by a system of 'deficiency payments' which involved direct payments from the government to farmers. The system operated as follows. No tariffs or other restrictions were imposed on agricultural imports, and UK market prices were determined by world prices. British farmers were granted a subsidy consisting of the difference between the guaranteed price and the market price. Support prices in Britain were, however, lower than in the EEC. In 1968 the ratios of EEC to UK support prices were: wheat, 1.24; barley, 1.22; oats, 1.13; cattle, 1.24; pigs, 1.0; milk, 1.08; sugar beet, 1.00 (see Josling, 1971).

There are two major differences between the two systems. The first is the visibility of the subsidy. With deficiency payments the subsidy to farmers is direct and clearly visible, because it is financed out of taxpayers' money. Under the CAP consumers are still subsidizing farmers, but the subsidy is much less visible because it takes place through higher food prices. The second difference is that the CAP induces large resource flows across countries: the issue of who gains and who loses from the CAP is addressed in the next section.

3. Who Gains and Who Loses from the Agricultural Policy of the EEC

The CAP gives rise to two types of transfers: a Europe-wide transfer from consumers to farmers, and transfers across countries. The latter arise because the size of the agricultural sector and the goods in which each country specializes differ within the EEC. The countries that benefit from the CAP are the net exporters of agricultural products, with a large proportion of employment in agriculture, and those that specialize in the production of goods constantly in excess supply—mostly dairy products. Britain, a net importer with a small agricultural sector, is bound to lose.[4]

The welfare cost of the CAP stems from the deadweight losses that occur in the redistribution of income from consumers to producers: losses to consumers from the reduction in demand for agricultural products relative to such demand at world prices, additional costs incurred by producers of output which would not be competitive at world prices, and the direct costs associated with intervention to support agricultural prices (purchases, storage, and export refunds).

In two revealing studies of the agricultural policy of the Community, Morris (1980; Morris and Dilnot 1982) estimates that in 1978 the deadweight loss amounted to 0.4 per cent of the Community gross domestic product (GDP). Resource transfers across countries were also quite large, ranging from a loss of 1 per cent of GDP for Italy to a gain of 3 per cent for Ireland. Table 4.1 reports Morris's estimates of the cost to consumers, the subsidy to farmers,

Table 4.1

The effects of the EEC Common Agricultural Policy:
Resource flows in 1978 relative to free trade in agriculture and no subsidies to farmers

	Consumers' loss + taxpayers' contrib'n to EEC agricult. budget (£/person)	Producers' gain per person in agriculture (£/person)	Net change in resources (% of GDP)
Ireland	66.8	1700	3.24
Denmark	81.6	3200	1.15
Netherlands	87.4	4900	0.31
France	74.5	1800	−0.12
Belgium	93.2	5100	−0.50
Germany	93.4	2400	−0.53
UK	45.0	1700	−0.86
Italy	68.1	700	−1.26
EUR-9	71.2	1700	−0.41

Source: Morris (1980, p. 29).

and the change in resources as a percentage of each country's GDP. In contrast to the gains and losses discussed in the previous section, the estimates in this table compare the situation as it was in 1978 with one of free trade in agricultural products and no subsidies to farmers. In the case of the UK, therefore, this is not a comparison between the situation before and after accession, as it overlooks the system of deficiency payments that existed before 1973.

Three factors determine whether a country is a gainer or a loser in the CAP.

1. Consider first a country that is a net exporter of an agricultural product whose price is set above the world market price. In such a country, producers of that commodity receive a subsidy not only from consumers at home, but also from consumers in the rest of the EEC. Thus, the country overall gains.

Table 4.2 gives an example of how to estimate who gains and who loses from this source of inter-country transfers.[5] The first two columns show the ratio of the price guarenteed to European farmers (the intervention price) to the EEC import price net of tariff: this ratio determines the minimum subsidy to producers.[6] The second two columns show the ratio of the market price (in the UK) of each commodity to the EEC import price net of tariff (the world price): this ratio determines the loss of consumers. Finally, the last two columns show the degree of self-sufficiency of the three European countries that are the largest net exporters and the UK. The case of beef, for example suggests why Ireland is a big gainer from the CAP. In the years 1981–5 the price of beef in the EEC was almost twice as high as the import price net of tariff in Rotterdam, and Irish farmers produce over five times as much beef as the Irish consume.

2. Consider next a commodity which, at the price set by the EEC, turns out to be in excess supply throughout Europe. Producers of such a commodity receive a subsidy not only from consumers (for the amount that is sold on the market), but also from the EEC, which buys up the excess supply, stores it, and often sells it at a loss on world markets. These expenditures account for 70 per cent of the EEC budget. Contributions to this budget, however, are roughly proportional to each country's GDP.[7] Thus, a country that is a large producer of a commodity that is constantly in excess supply in Europe as a whole will gain.

Table 4.3 gives an example of how to estimate who gains and who loses from this second source of transfers. The first two columns show the Europe-wide degree of self-sufficiency in each product. As shown in the next two columns, EEC expenditure on agriculture is concentrated on dairy products whose excess supply is bigger. The last column in the table shows the largest producers of each commodity, and thus the likely gainers.

3. A third source of inter-country transfers originates from the fact that food prices are set in ECUs for the whole Community, but are then translated into individual currencies using artificial exchange rates ('green rates') which are usually different from market exchange rates. The reason for this divergence is that when, for example, the Deutschmark is revalued relative to the ECU,

Table 4.2
Data by commodity

Commodity	Ratio of intervention price to EEC import price net of tariff[a]		Ratio of UK market price to EEC import price net of tariff[a]		Degree of self-sufficiency (production as % of domestic consumption)	
	1976–81	1981–5	1976–81	1981–5	1976–80	1981–4
Wheat (soft)	1.1–1.4	0.9–1.1	1–1.3	1.1–1.3	FR 194 DK 134 GY 103 UK 68	FR 200 DK 123 GY 103 UK 102
Maize	1.2–1.6	1–1.3	1.5–1.9	1.3–1.6	FR 125 UK 0	FR 154 UK 0
Sugar	1.6	2.0	1.9	2.4[b]	BLUX 226 FR 200 DK 191 UK 40	BLUX 262 FR 226 DK 209 UK 55

Butter	1.4	1.2	1.2	1.3	NL 378 IRL 307 DK 259 UK 41	NL 443 IRL 302 DK 229 UK 62
Beef	1.7	2.0	1.6	1.8[c]	IRL 616 DK 323 NL 132 UK 77	IRL 543 DK 386 NL 156 UK 83

[a] Where two ratios appear, they correspond to the minimum and the maximum import price observed during the year.

[b] The EEC does not publish the market price of sugar. This is the ratio of the entry price to the import price and thus corresponds to the tariff rate.

[c] This market price is the average market price in the EEC.

Sources: EC, *Yearbook of Agricultural Statistics*, and *Annual Report on Agriculture*, various issues for all data but import prices. Import prices: *wheat*: soft red winter II, import price c.i.f. Rotterdam (EEC, *Agricultural Markets* (*AM*)); *beef*: EEC import price c.i.f. Rotterdam (EEC, *AM*); *sugar*: raw sugar, import price c.i.f. London (World Bank: *Commodities Trends and Price*); *maize*: yellow corn III, import price c.i.f. Rotterdam (EEC, *AM*); *butter*: import price c.i.f. London of New Zealand butter (Data Resources Inc.)

Table 4.3
Data by commodity

Commodity	EEC-wide deg. of self-suff. (%) 1976–80	1981–3	Expend. on each commodity as % of total EEC expend. on agric.[a] 1976–80	1981–4	Major producers (% of total EEC production) 1978–84
Milk	116	376			GY 23
			43.3	28.6	FR 23
					UK 14
Butter	116	128			NL 12
Wheat	111	124	12.8	14.1	FR 38
					IT 18
					UK 16
					GY 12
Beef	98	103	7.8	11.8	FR 29
					GY 22
					UK 13
Sugar	119	141	7.5	8.5	FR 28
					GY 25
					IT 12
					UK 10

[a]Expenditure of the Guarantee Section of the European Agricultural Guidance and Guarantee Fund (EAGGF).

Sources: EEC: *Yearbook of Agricultural Statistics; Agricultural Production in the Community*, various issues.

German farmers resist a reduction in the support price expressed in Deutschmarks; when it is devalued, German consumers resist an increase in the price of food. As a result, the ECU prices of agricultural products keep being converted into national currencies at the old exchange rate. This system, however, creates a potential for the arbitrage of goods, which the EEC eliminates by letting prices be determined by the market exchange rate and then compensating producers for the lower price they receive.

Consider, for example, a realignment of the European Monetary System in which the Deutschmark (DM) appreciates and the lira depreciates, both relative to the ECU. At the new market exchange rates the DM price of agricultural products should fall and their lira price should increase. The latter, however, remains unchanged, and German farmers, when they export to Italy, receive a compensating transfer from the EEC. This transfer corresponds to the difference between the price paid by Italian consumers and the pre-realignment DM price. Thus, any time a German farmer exports to Italy, he receives some money from the EEC: part of it is a subsidy to the German farmer, and part of it is a subsidy to the Italian consumer who is paying 'too little' for the food imported from Germany.

Who gains and who loses from this complicated system of visible and invisible transfers across countries and within countries is hard to tell. Table 4.4 shows the net visible transfers (payments in and out of the EEC budget) for the period 1980–4 and the divergence between market exchange rates and 'green rates'.

Table 4.4

The Effects of the EEC Common Agricutural Policy: Resource flows originating from the divergence between market exchange rates and 'Green Rates', 1980–1984
(millions of ECU)

Germany	+ 492
France	− 173
Italy	+ 129
Netherlands	+ 862
Belgium–Lux.	+ 54
UK	+ 111
Ireland	+ 1
Denmark	+ 62

Memorandum item: Divergence between Market exchange rates and 'Green Rates'
(ave. % differences; a positive sign indicates that the Green Rate is undervalued relative to the market rate)

	June 74–Dec. 78 (%)	Jan. 79–June 83 (%)
Germany	+ 10.5	+ 8.9
France	− 9.7	− 4.1
Italy	− 12.0	− 4.2
Netherlands	+ 9.8	+ 3.5
Belgium–Lux.	+ 2.3	− 0.9
Ireland	− 13.0	0.0
Denmark	0.0	0.0

		Jan.–Oct. 79	Nov. 79–June 83
UK	− 26.3	− 18	+ 6.2

Source: Gazzetta Ufficiale delle Comunita' Europee, Various issues.

Summary

The analysis of the effects of the CAP suggests that, by joining the EEC, Britain suffered a welfare loss both relative to its situation before accession and relative to free trade in agricultural products. Britain's loss, however, is not a problem specific to that country. The CAP is a system that redistributes income in Europe both within countries and across countries. As this section has shown, it does so at a very high cost, and according to criteria that it is difficult to rationalize. The EEC is now considering dismantling the CAP and introducing a system of deficiency payments. The major change would be that the whole system of intra-country and inter-country transfers would then become visible.

4. The EEC and UK Trade in Manufactures

In this section we ask the question, To what extent has entrance into the EEC changed the pattern of British trade in manufactures? When the UK joined the EEC, the six original members (Germany, France, Italy, Belgium, Luxembourg, and the Netherlands) had just completed the elimination of customs duties and quantitative restrictions on trade among themselves. Between 1958 and 1970, the share of imports from partner countries in total domestic expenditure on manufactures had increased roughly two and a half times (from 4.8 to 12.4 per cent), while the share of imports from non-member countries had increased by one-third (from 6.4 to 8.7 per cent). The expansion of intra-EEC trade had resulted largely from the increase in intra-industry trade in manufacturing; trade diversion had been relatively small and concentrated in agriculture.[8]

Table 4.5 shows the degree to which the customs union has opened up the British market to European products and vice versa during the first ten years of EEC membership. The first part of the table reports the share of UK manufactured imports from the EEC and the rest of the world in total domestic expenditure on manufactures at constant prices. The lower part of the table reports the market shares of UK manufactures in Europe. After a five-year transition period, trade barriers between Britain and the EEC were completely removed in 1978. During the transition period (1973–8) imports from the EEC increased their market share in the UK by almost 70 per cent, while the share of imports from the rest of the world remained virtually unchanged. Over the same period, British firms increased their market shares on the Continent by 60 per cent in Germany, 30 per cent in France, and 40 per cent in Italy.

The performance of British manufactures in Europe is even more remarkable between 1977–8 and 1982–3, a period of extraordinary real appreciation of the pound. In the UK the effects of the loss of competitiveness and of the complete removal of tariff barriers versus the Continent interact: the

Table 4.5
The performance of UK manufactures

	1972/3	1977/8	1982/3
Import penetration[a] (%) in the UK of manufactures from:			
EEC	2.9	4.9	7.9
Rest of the world	6.3	6.8	9.0
UK manufactures as % of total domestic sales in:[b]			
Germany	0.5	0.8	0.9
France	1.0	1.4	1.6
Italy	0.7	0.9	1.1

[a]Manufactured imports from each area as % of total domestic sales in the UK at constant prices.
[b]Manufactured imports from the UK as % of total domestic sales in each country at constant prices.

Source: calculations based on data on bilateral trade flows at constant prices from EEC, VOLIMEX Databank.

market share of European imports increases by 60 per cent and the share of imports from the rest of the world by 30 per cent. In Europe, however, the market shares of UK manufactures grow 17 per cent in Germany and Italy and 10 per cent in France, thus suggesting that the abolition of tariff barriers may have offset the competitiveness loss.

Although suggestive of the consequences of entry into the EEC, the data in Table 4.5 do not tell us the extent to which our observations are the trade creation and trade diversion effects of integration. The increase in British trade with the EEC had already started in the late 1960s, and some argue that EEC membership did little to accelerate this process.

In two recent papers, Alan Winters (1984, 1985) estimates the trade creation and trade diversion effects of EEC membership on UK manufactures. His results are an improvement upon the numerous empirical studies that have attempted to estimate the impact of EEC membership on UK trade,[9] because he explicitly takes into account the interaction between imports and domestic demand, as well as the possibility that the demand function for manufactures is non-homothetic[10]. Winters's results are reported in Tables 4.6 and 4.7. Between 1972 and 1979, the domestic producers' loss of market share in the UK that can be ascribed to entry into the EEC is estimated at 12.7 per cent. As expected, all EEC countries increase their market shares in the UK, but so also do the United States, Japan, and Switzerland, an indication of external trade creation. Evidence of trade diversion is weak and is limited to Canada and

Table 4.6
Change in shares of the UK market
due to accession. Manufactures: 1979
relative to 1972[a]

	%
Germany	3.9
France	2.0
Italy	1.4
Be-Lux	1.8
Netherlands	1.4
USA	1.2
Japan	0.8
Switzerland	0.6
Canada	−0.2
Sweden	−0.1
UK	−12.7
	0

[a]Estimates of the change in the share
of manufactures produced by each
country in total UK sales, which can
be ascribed to entry into the EEC.

Source: Winters (1984).

Sweden. The effect of integration on UK market shares in the EEC (reported in Table 4.7) is positive, as expected.

Summary

Converting the shares reported in Tables 4.6 and 4.7 into percentages of trade flows indicates that entry into the EEC has had a substantial effect on UK exports to Europe, accounting for up to 50 per cent of actual exports in 1979. The effect on UK imports from Europe, however, is larger: in 1979 it accounts for up to 60–70 per cent of imports. Thus, the message of these estimates is that accession substantially increased Britain's manufacturing exports to Europe, but not by as much as it increased British imports from Europe.

5. The Effects of the 1979 Abolition of Exchange Controls

When Britain joined the EEC, a wide variety of foreign exchange regulations was keeping the UK financial system isolated from the international financial markets. Direct investment overseas was strictly regulated. Portfolio invest-

Table 4.7
Changes in UK producers' shares in each market due to
accession. Manufactures: 1979 relative to 1972[a]
(percentages)

GY	FR	IT	USA	JP	UK
0.8	0.3	0.8	−0.16	−0.08	−12.7

[a]Estimates of the change in market share of UK
manufactures in total manufactures sales in each country,
which can be ascribed to entry into the EEC.

Source: Winters (1984, 1985).

ment was not forbidden, but foreign exchange for this purpose could be obtained only out of external liquidations in the 'investment currency' market. The City of London, which had a long history in providing financing for foreign trade on a world-wide basis, was restricted in its ability to honour its traditions. UK resident banks were forbidden from providing sterling financing for third-party trade, that is, trade not involving the UK. This constraint diminished the role of sterling as an international currency. The growth of London as a financial centre was all in the form of dollar-denominated transactions, which were not regulated by the UK authorities. All these restrictions were swept away in October 1979.[11]

Besides allowing portfolio readjustments,[12] the liberalization had two important effects. It eliminated any divergence between onshore and offshore interest rates, i.e., between interest rates in the UK and interest rates on sterling-denominated deposits overseas. As shown in Figure 4.1, between 1974 and October 1979 the prohibition on international arbitrage operations stabilized domestic interest rates relative to offshore rates. After October 1979 deviations from covered interest arbitrage practically disappeared.

There is also some evidence that the abolition of exchange controls promoted the use of sterling in international financial markets. Table 4.8 shows estimates of the size of the offshore market in sterling, and of the flow of new international bond issues denominated in sterling. There is some evidence that the liberalization reversed the long-term decline in the international role of sterling.[13]

6. Sterling and the European Monetary System

There are two major arguments put forward by those who hold that the time has come for Britian to make the final step towards full integration with Europe by joining the EMS. The first is that the EMS has so far provided an

Francesco Giavazzi

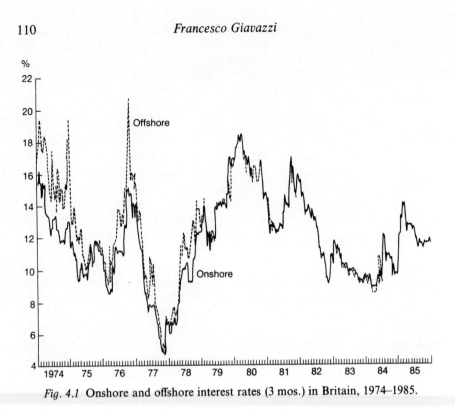

Fig. 4.1 Onshore and offshore interest rates (3 mos.) in Britain, 1974–1985.

Table 4.8
The use of sterling in international financial markets
(percentage share)

	1978	1983	1985
Size of offshore market demominated in sterling:[a]			
Assets	1.2	1.2	1.9
Liabilities	1.4	1.3	2.0
Sterling-denominated international bond issues:[b]	0.7	3.6	4.0

[a]% of total external assets and liabilities of banks reporting to the Bank for International Settlements. (*Source:* BIS, *International Banking Developments*, various issues).
[b]% of total bond issues. (*Source:* Morgan Guaranty Trust, *World Financial Markets*, various issues).

environment of substantial exchange rate stability for its members:

the parity grid has stabilized EMS cross rates and in the process provided a considerable degree of stability to members' nominal effective rates, given the relatively large proportion of trade that the members conduct with one another. There is no parallel to the gyrations of the dollar, pound, and yen in the variations of the effective exchange rate of any EMS currency. Real exchange rates have also been stabilized, in large part by avoiding gyrations in nominal rates but also to some extent by a willingness to accommodate divergent inflation rates through periodic adjustments in central rates. [Artis *et al.* 1986, p. 21]

The second argument is that an exchange rate commitment is far more effective than the Medium Term Financial Strategy in affecting inflationary expectations, and that exchange rate targets are more credible inside the EMS (see Chapter 1):

the case for preferring cooperative management of the exchange rate in the context of the EMS to independent management rests upon the greater credibility of an international commitment to a functioning and successful mechanism as opposed to a unilateral declaration of intentions. Markets have come to expect that full EMS members take their commitments seriously . . . [and] any new member is likely to . . . benefit from this stock of credibility. [Artis *et al.* 1986, p. 20]

The benefits of credibility would come in the form of lower interst rates:

there is a fair presumption that the interest rates required to hold a given exchange rate might be lower—because of the credibility factor—under the EMS than they are at present without formally stated exchange rate objectives. [Brittan 1985]

The major argument against joining the EMS is that capital controls seem to be a necessary part of the system:

The anticipation of exchange rate realignments induces balance of payments crises, whenever monetary authorities try to minimize the volatility of short-term interest rates. In order to avoid undesired fluctuations in domestic short-term interest rates, strong currency countries can neutralize speculative attacks in various ways. In contrast, weak currency countries are not able to offset large reserve losses for prolonged periods of time, and therefore can only use capital controls to stabilize domestic interest rates. The evidence on the movements of offshore rates indeed confirms that expectations about EMS realignments could induce large changes in short-term interest rates in the absence of capital controls. The likelihood of large interest rate fluctuations is enhanced by the possibility that expectations of a realignment be self-fulfilling, and that speculative attacks take place in the absence of changes in 'fundamentals'. In the present system weak currency countries have to choose between the welfare losses associated with capital controls and the losses arising from the volatility of short-term interest rates, and, as the evidence shows, they overwhelmingly opt for the former. Thus capital controls appear to be an important feature of the EMS, which allows weak currency countries to take part in the exchange rate arrangement, without suffering from excessive domestic interest rate fluctuations. [Giavazzi and Giovannini 1986a, p. 473]

In the absence of capital controls, EMS membership is therefore likely to bring lower interest rates—because of the credibility argument—in periods of calm, when the probability of a realignment is low, but also occasional blips, when rates have to be sharply raised:

It introduces something of a sort of gearing effect. It probably gives you greater capacity to withstand, as it were, the ripples, but somewhat greater vulnerability to the waves, and it is a matter of judgement what is likely to be the incidence of ripples and waves.[14]

This section discusses the 'waves'. It is often said that if Britain joins the EMS two factors will occasionally put pressure on the exchange rate of sterling relative to its EMS partners, and thus force a realignment: fluctuations in the dollar, and fluctuations in the dollar price of oil. An exchange rate realignment, however, may also take place whenever European countries are hit by regional shocks, or if their macroeconomic structures differ: in such cases (as shown by Mundell's optimum currency area argument) international policy co-ordination and identical policy objectives are not sufficient conditions for fixed exchange rates to be an optimal arrangement. Before discussing the 'waves' and the role of capital controls, I review the argument that EMS membership would stabilize sterling's effective exchange rate.

The EMS and Sterling Effective Exchange Rate

The most widely adopted weighting scheme in the calculation of effective exchange rates is that of the IMF MERM weights.[15] Two sets of MERM weights are available, the first based on 1972 trade flows and the second using data relative to 1977.

Table 4.9 reports the two sets of weights for the four large European countries. I have considered the effective exchange rate relative to the ten major currencies, dividing them in four groups: the dollar area (US dollar and Canadian dollar), the EMS currencies (Deutschmark, French franc, Italian lira, Belgian franc, and Dutch guilder), the yen, and the pound.

Based on 1972 trade weights, pegging the pound to the dollar or to the EMS currencies would have been a matter of indifference from the standpoint of stabilizing the UK effective exchange rate. By 1977, however, the weight of the EMS currencies in sterling's effective exchange rate was up to 0.5 while the weight of the dollar was down to 0.33.[16] Thus, if Britain today decided to announce a bilateral exchange rate target, consideration of the effective exchange rate would clearly suggest pegging to the ECU rather than to the dollar.

The Dollar and the Deutschmark–Sterling Exchange Rate

Evidence from daily, monthly, and quarterly exchange rate changes confirms the common observation that fluctuations in intra-European exchange rates

Table 4.9
IMF MERM weights, 1972 and 1977

	EMS currencies	Dollar area	Yen	Pound
1972				
France	0.53	0.33	0.08	0.06
Italy	0.55	0.32	0.08	0.05
Germany	0.48	0.36	0.10	0.06
UK	0.43	0.43	0.14	—
1977				
France	0.53	0.30	0.12	0.05
Italy	0.55	0.26	0.13	0.06
Germany	0.50	0.28	0.16	0.06
UK	0.50	0.33	0.17	—

Source: Artus and Rhomberg (1973); Artus and McGuirk (1981).

are associated in a systematic way with the dollar. When the dollar is 'strong' on foreign exchange markets, the Deutschmark tends to be 'weak' *vis-à-vis* other European currencies. The results for sterling are reproduced in Table 4.10. The coefficients are estimates of the percentage depreciation (appreciation) of sterling relative to the DM for a 1 per cent depreciation (appreciation) of the effective dollar exchange rate. For example, between 1973 and 1979 a 1 per cent depreciation of the effective dollar index is associated, on average, with a 0.56 per cent depreciation of the pound relative to the DM, on a day-to-day basis.

What is it that brings about these co-movements of the dollar and the pound–DM rate? Giavazzi and Giovannini (1986a) show that a dynamic portfolio model, which explains exchange rate correlations in terms of co-movements of money and output growth rates in different countries, goes some way towards explaining the data. In the case of sterling, the 'theoretical' correlation produced by that model, using monthly data over the period March 1979–October 1985, is −0.47 (the actual coefficient being −0.24 in Table 4.10).[17]

These results point towards divergent monetary policy objectives—a money growth rate target in Germany and an effective exchange rate target in the UK—as the explanation of the observed co-movements of the sterling–DM rate with the dollar.

Oil and the Deutschmark–Sterling Exchange Rate

The role of sterling as a petro-currency is another often observed source of asymmetry in the movements of its exchange rate relative to the Deutschmark.

Table 4.10

The dollar and the bilateral DM–sterling exchange rate[a]

	1 June 1973–9 Mar. 1979 (pre-EMS)
Daily data	−0.56 (0.04)
Monthly data	−0.53 (0.16)
Quarterly data	−0.16 (0.28)
	12 Mar. 1979–15 Oct. 1985 (EMS)
Daily data	−0.17 (0.03)
Monthly data	−0.24 (0.10)
Quarterly data	−0.01 (0.24)

[a]Regression coefficients of % changes in the sterling price of one DM on % changes in the effective exchange rate of the dollar. A negative sign indicates that a dollar depreciation is associated with an appreciation of the DM relative to sterling. Regressions include a constant term; standard errors are in parentheses. The effective exchange rate of the dollar relative to the nine major currencies (Belgian franc, Canadian dollar, French franc, Deutschmark, Italian lira, yen, Dutch guilder, Swiss franc, and pound sterling) is built using GNP weights.

Source: Giavazzi and Giovannini (1986).

The regression coefficients reported in Table 4.11 confirm the common observation that a fall in the dollar price of oil is associated with a weakening in the value of the pound. I have divided the sample into two sub-periods: the effect on the sterling–DM exchange rate of a 1 per cent change in the dollar price of oil in the spot market is, on average, larger after January 1983, when the price of oil started to fall.

The Effects of Structural Asymmetries in a System of Centrally Managed Exchange Rates

The examples discussed above are by no means exhaustive of the factors that may put pressure on the exchange rate of sterling relative to the EMS currencies. They point, however, to two important sources of those exchange rate movements: policy asymmetries (different monetary policy objectives in the first example), and structural asymmetries (the role of North Sea oil in the second example). This section extends the discussion of structural asymmetries by reviewing Mundell's argument for optimum currency areas (see Mundell, 1968). The purpose is to show that, even when countries have

Table 4.11

Oil and the bilateral DM–sterling exchange
rate[a]

	Aug. 1980–Dec. 1983
Weekly data	−0.014 (0.007)
Monthly data	−0.007 (0.003)
	Jan. 1983–Dec. 1985
Weekly data	−0.024 (0.012)
Monthly data	−0.010 (0.007)

[a]Regression coefficients of % changes in the
sterling price of one DM on % changes in the
dollar price of oil. A negative sign indicates
that a fall in the dollar price of oil is
associated with an appreciation of the DM
relative to sterling. Regressions include a
constant term; standard errors are in paren-
thesis. The oil price is the dollar price of
British North Sea oil on the spot market.

identical objectives and monetary policy is decided upon co-operatively,
exchange rate realignments (provided they have real effects) can be the
optimal way to redistribute the costs of common disturbances if countries'
macroeconomic structures differ and production cannot be easily relocated.

To illustrate this point I consider a world of three countries:[18] 'America',
and two European countries (for simplicity I shall refer to them as 'Germany'
and 'Britain'). Each country produces a single good, and the three goods are
imperfect substitutes. The model is log-linear, and all variables are expressed
as deviations from their means.[19] Output is produced in each country using a
two-factor Cobb–Douglas technology with decreasing returns to scale. Inputs
to production are labour and materials. Under competition, the supply
functions in the three countries are:

$$q_i = -\sigma_1 (w_i - p_i) - \sigma_2(p_i^m - p_i) \qquad i = A, B, G \qquad (4.1)$$

where q_i, p_i, and w_i denote, respectively, output, the GDP deflator, and
nominal wages in country i ('America', 'Britain', and 'Germany'); nominal
wages in each country are predetermined and are set equal to 1 for
simplicity;[20] p_i^m is the domestic currency price of oil in country i; the world
price of oil is linked to a deflator where the weight of American goods is α and
the weights of the two European goods are β and $(1 - \alpha - \beta)$, respectively. The

domestic currency price of oil in the three countries is therefore

$$p_A^m = v - (1-\alpha)\eta_1 - (1-\alpha-\beta)\eta_2 + p_A \tag{4.2'}$$

$$p_G^m = v + \alpha\,\eta_1 - (1-\alpha-\beta)\eta_2 + p_G \tag{4.2''}$$

$$p_B^m = v + \alpha\eta_1 + (\alpha+\beta)\eta_2 + p_B \tag{4.2'''}$$

where $\eta_1 \equiv e_1 + p_A - p_G$ and $\eta_2 \equiv e_2 + p_G - p_B$ are, respectively, the terms of trade between Germany and America and between Britain and Germany; e_1 is the dollar–DM exchange rate and e_2 is the sterling–DM exchange rate; v is the 'real' price of materials. Subscripts A, B and G denote 'America', 'Britain', and 'Germany', respectively.

Demand for each good is a function of its price relative to the other two goods and of total spending in each country. Solving for q_A, q_B, and q_G, and assuming identical income and price elasticities in the three countries, demand for each good can be written as

$$q_A = -\delta\eta_1 - \delta(\eta_1 + \eta_2) \tag{4.3'}$$

$$q_G = \delta(\eta_1 - \eta_2) \tag{4.3''}$$

$$q_B = \delta\eta_2 + \delta(n_1 + \eta_2). \tag{4.3'''}$$

The model is closed, assuming money market equilibrium in each country.[21] Money demand equations are (assuming constant velocity)

$$m_i - p_i = q_i \qquad i = A, B, G. \tag{4.4}$$

I explicitly overlook the problems that may arise from non-cooperative behaviour in Europe,[22] assuming that European monetary policy is run by a central authority which sets the region-wide money supply $(m_G + m_B)$ and the intra-European exchange rate, e_2. Its objective is to minimize the region-wide square deviations of prices and output levels from equilibrium. It therefore minimizes

$$L = (q_G^2 + p_G^2) + (q_B^2 + p_B^2). \tag{4.5}$$

In this model, Europe may be hit by two types of exogenous shocks: a change in the real price of materials, v, and a change in the American money stock, m_A. So far, the only source of asymmetry in Europe may arise from equation (4.2), i.e., from the possibility that the weight of German goods in the deflator of the price of materials prices, β, differs from the weight of British goods $(1-\alpha-\beta)$. Following an exogenous change in v or in m_A, minimization of (4.5), subject to (4.1)–(4.4), leaves the intra-European exchange rate e_2 unchanged only if

$$\sigma_2(1-\sigma_1)(1-\alpha-2\beta) = 0. \tag{4.6}$$

This condition[23] is satisfied only if the two European goods have the same weight in the deflator of the price of materials.

A different source of structural asymmetry may arise from σ_2, the coefficient of materials in the supply function. In order to study the role of differences in σ_2, it is sufficient to reduce the model to the two European countries, assuming $\alpha = 0$. In this case, following an exogenous change in the real price of materials, the optimal response of the European monetary authority will leave the exchange rate unchanged only if

$$\sigma_{G2}(1 - 2\beta) + \beta(\sigma_{G2} - \sigma_{B2}) = 0 \qquad (4.7)$$

where σ_{G2} and σ_{B2} are, respectively, the coefficient of materials in the supply function of Germany and of Britain. Expression (4.7) is satisfied only if $\beta = \frac{1}{2}$, i.e., if the two goods have the same weight in the materials' price deflator, and if $\sigma_{G2} = \sigma_{B2}$, i.e., if there are no structural asymmetries.

These examples show that international policy co-ordination and identical macroeconomic objectives are not sufficient conditions for fixed exchange rates to be an optimal arrangement. In the examples discussed above, fixed exchange rates are suboptimal because the macroeconomic structures of countries differ, but the same is true if countries are hit by local disturbances. This suggests that the EMS could remain a system of fixed but adjustable parities even after European countries had agreed on common macroeconomic objectives and monetary and exchange rate policies were set co-operatively.

The Role of Capital Controls in the EMS

The EMS experience so far has been that, in 'weak currency' countries, the anticipation of a realignment induces a balance of payments crisis whenever monetary authorities try to stabilize domestic interest rates. Faced with the choice between the welfare losses associated with capital controls and the losses arising from the volatility of domestic interest rates, these countries have usually opted for the former.

In this section we look at the experience of capital controls in France and Italy: to what extent have these controls been able to insulate domestic interest rates in the wake of parity realignments? The question deserves attention because it is at the core of Britain's decision on whether or not to join the EMS.

The evidence on deviations from the condition of covered interest rate parity between the domestic money market and the Euromarket indicates that the exchange controls enforced in France and Italy are indeed effective in severing the link between offshore and onshore interest rates.[24] Table 4.12 reproduces the results presented in Giavazzi and Pagano (1985). That paper investigates the effectiveness of capital controls in severing the link between onshore and offshore interest rates in four EMS countries: two countries (France and Italy) in which very strict controls on capital movements are enforced, and two countries (Germany and the Netherlands) where international capital flows are almost entirely free. The degree of insulation of the

Table 4.12
Potential profits from covered arbitrage, 1982–1984

Direction[a]	27 Sep. 82–30 Aug. 84			27 Sep. 82–30 Mar. 83			1 Apr. 83–30 Aug. 84		
	Outwards $(R1>0)$	Inwards $(R2>o)$	Neither $(R1\leq0)$ $(R2\leq0)$	Outwards $(R1>0)$	Inwards $(R2>0)$	Neither $(R1\leq0)$ $(R2\leq0)$	Outwards $(R1>0)$	Inwards $(R2>0)$	Neither $(R1\leq0)$ $(R2\leq0)$
Italy									
Mean rate of return[b]	3.04	0.44	—	4.34	—		0.43	0.43	
(St. dev.)	(3.63)	(0.47)		(2.66)			(0.49)	(0.47)	
No. of days	173	33	261	120	2	5	53	31	256
Frequency (%)	37	7	56	95	1	4	16	9	75
France									
Mean rate of return[b]	3.99	—		9.55	—		1.55	—	
(St. dev.)	(5.37)			(6.55)			(1.25)		
No. of days	390	0	66	119	0	4	271	0	62
Frequency (%)	85	0	15	97	0	3	87	0	13

	12 Nov. 80–30 Aug. 84			12 Nov. 80–30 Mar. 83			1 Apr. 83–30 Aug. 84		
Germany									
Mean rate of return[b]	—	0.34		—	0.31		—	0.35	
(St. dev.)		(0.21)			(0.22)			(0.20)	
No. of days	0	441	22	0	113	14	0	328	8
Frequency (%)		95	5		89	11		98	2
Netherlands									
Mean rate of return[b]	—	0.14		—	0.11		—	0.15	
(St. dev.)		(0.12)			(0.10)			(0.13)	
No. of days	0	170	297	0	30	97	0	140	200
Frequency (%)		36	64		24	76		41	59
Italy									
Mean rate of return[b]		3.51	0.42		4.03	0.31		0.47	0.41
(St. dev.)		(4.37)	(0.52)		(4.20)	(0.43)		(0.54)	(0.50)
No. of days	336	572	41	102	493	4	234	79	37
Frequency (%)	36	60	4	17	82	1	68	22	10

[a] 'Direction' indicates the direction in which unexploited arbitrage profits are observed.

[b] The rates of return represent the instantaneous profits which could have been earned on each (costless and riskless) arbitrage operation in the absence of controls. R_1 and R_2 are defined in the text.

Source: Giavazzi and Pagano (1985).

domestic financial market from the international market is measured by looking at the deviations from the condition of covered arbitrage between the return on a deposit issued in the domestic market and denominated in the home currency and the covered return on a Eurodeposit of the same maturity. The results reported in the table are obtained using data that reflect the prices at which an investor can actually carry out the transactions required by the arbitrage operation.[25] The data are therefore capable of detecting the presence of unexploited profit opportunities.

For each country, the data set consists of daily observations on bid and offer prices quoted at 3 pm: Euro-rates and exchange rates are those quoted on the London market; domestic rates are money market rates in Paris, Frankfurt, Amsterdam, and Milan at the same time.[26] All interest rates are on three-month loans. The sample period is 27 September 1982–30 August 1984.

An arbitrage operation between the domestic money market and the Euromarket can take place in two opposite directions: either borrowing on the domestic market to buy covered Eurodollars,[27] or borrowing on the Euromarket to invest at home. Assuming that there are no transaction costs beyond the bid–offer spread, the profit to be earned in the first operation is

$$R1 = (1 + r_B^*)F_B/S_A - (1 + r_A)$$

while in the second case it is:

$$R2 = (1 + r_B)S_B/F_A - (1 + r_A^*)$$

where r and r^* are the domestic and the Eurodollar rates, respectively; the subscript A denotes the rate at which one can borrow (offer rate) and the subscript B the lending rate (bid rate); S is the spot exchange rate (price of one dollar in units of domestic currency); and F the forward rate—here the subscript A denotes the price at which one can *buy* dollars (spot or forward), and subscript B, the price at which one can *sell* dollars (spot or forward).

Notice that, although $R1$ and $R2$ have the the dimension of a rate of return (for example, 5 per cent), they represent the instantaneous profit to be earned on each (costless and riskless) arbitrage operation. In the absence of capital controls, these profits are potentially infinite and prices will move so as to eliminate any profit opportunity: in this case we should observe $R1 \leq 0$, $R2 \leq 0$. If controls on capital flows are biting, i.e., if they prevent profitable arbitrage operations, we should observe $R1 > 0$, $R2 \leq 0$: it would be profitable to borrow at home to buy Eurodollars and sell dollars forward. If, instead, controls were designed to prevent capital inflows, we should observe $R2 > 0$, $R1 \leq 0$, indicating that domestic residents are prevented from borrowing on the Euromarket.

But it could happen that, although capital controls are always formally in existence, we observe $R1 \leq 0$, $R2 \leq 0$ over substantial time intervals.[28] What this means is that over these intervals either the degree of mobility allowed by the controls is sufficient to exhaust all profit opportunities, or controls are very strict but the central bank intervenes to keep the onshore rate equal to the offshore rate.

The data described above have been used to build daily series of $R1$ and $R2$. The mean of the *positive* realizations of $R1$ measures the average profit of the arbitrage operations forbidden by the controls when these are biting. It also indicates the extent to which capital controls have on average kept the rate on domestic loans below the level it would have reached in the absence of controls (the covered Eurodollar bid rate) in the periods when they were biting.[29] Similarly, the mean of the positive realizations of $R2$ measures the extent to which the covered Eurodollar offer rate was below the domestic bid rate in periods when the controls were effective in preventing domestic residents from borrowing abroad. Finally, the frequency of the observations in which both $R1$ and $R2$ are negative indicates how often there were no profit opportunities in either direction.

The period 27 September 1982–30 August 1984 has been divided into two sub-periods: the first, which runs until 30 March 1983, includes one EMS realignment, on 22 March 1983. The second does not include any realignment and is characterized by a long period of calm within the EMS. The results for both France and Italy indicate that, with an unchanged capital controls regime, deviations from covered interest rate parity are larger before the dates of realignment. In both cases, almost every observation in the period before the realignment is characterized by $R1 > 0$, signalling that the controls were biting. The mean deviation of the domestic offer rate from the covered Eurodollar bid rate was 4.3 per cent in Italy, 9.6 per cent in France (expressed in annualized percentage rates of return). The wider deviation observed in the French case may depend upon the fact that the realignment of March 1983 was triggered by strong speculation against the French franc. Looking at Italy in the period of EMS calm, the most interesting finding is the number of observations when there were no potential arbitrage profits: 75 per cent of all observations in this period (256 days over a total of 340). In France we keep observing potential arbitrage profits also after the realignment, but their mean falls from almost 10 per cent to $1\frac{1}{2}$ per cent. This result, which suggests some effectiveness of capital controls also in periods of EMS calm, may depend upon the fact that in 1982–4 domestic interest rates in France were strictly controlled and therefore did not reflect actual market prices.

Domestic interest rates in Germany lie on the opposite side: throughout the whole period, it would have been profitable to borrow on the Euromarket and lend in the German money market. The mean deviation, however, is very small (0.33 per cent). This finding reflects the enforcement by the German monetary authorities of policies aimed at limiting capital inflows. Finally, the results for the Dutch guilder provide an example of how covered interest parity holds in the absence of capital controls. Throughout the entire period, most observations reveal the absence of potential arbitrage profits; when these appear (in the form of $R2 > 0$, as for Germany), their mean lies between 0.1 and 0.2 per cent.[30]

By severing the link between Euro-rates and domestic interest rates, capital controls also reduce the volatility of domestic rates. An alternative measure of the effectiveness of capital controls is thus the difference between the variance of offshore and onshore rates. Table 4.13 provides such a comparison for Italy and France. As expected, the variability of offshore rates falls dramatically in periods of EMS calm: for Italy it is almost identical to the variability of

Table 4.13
Variability of 'onshore' and 'offshore' interest rates

	12. Nov. 80–30 Aug. 84	12 Nov. 80–30 Mar. 83	1 Apr. 83–30 Aug. 84
Italy			
'Onshore'	1.8	1.3	1.1
'Offshore'	4.8	4.5	1.3
France			
'Onshore'	0.5	0.4	0.3
'Offshore'	5.2	6.3	1.4

Notes:
'Variability' is measured by the standard deviation. 'Onshore rate is the offer rate on the domestic money market (Italy: 'tasso pronti contro termine'). 'Offshore rate' is the bid rate on covered 3-month Euro-deposits.

Source: Giavazzi and Pagano (1985).

domestic rates. As noted above, the very low variability of domestic rates in France is probably a consequence of the fact that these rates were more tightly controlled.

This evidence clearly indicates that, in the case of Italy, capital controls are effective in severing the link between Euro-rates and domestic interest rates *only in the wake of EMS realignments*. During those periods they keep both the level and the variability of domestic rates below that of the corresponding Euro-rates. In periods of EMS calm, neither the mean nor the variability of domestic rates is very different from that of the corresponding Euro-rates. The results for France indicate some effectiveness of capital controls also in periods of EMS calm.

A visual summary of these results appears in Figures 4.2 and 4.3, which show onshore and offshore interest rates on French franc and lira-denominated deposits throughout the EMS period.

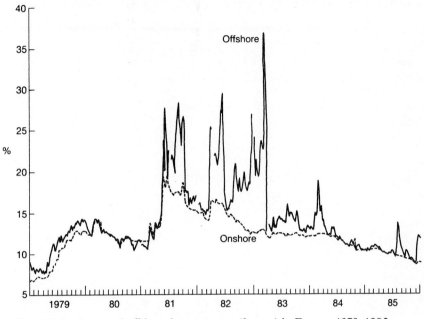

Fig. 4.2 Onshore and offshore interest rates (3 mos.) in France, 1979–1985.

The Width of the Band

It is often argued (e.g. Artis *et al.* 1986, p. 27) that a wider fluctuation band, by allowing an EMS currency to crawl upwards and downwards relative to its central parity, will dampen the fluctuation of interest rates in the anticipation of a realignment. In the current system, the width of the band is ±2.25 per cent for all currencies but the lira, which may fluctuate within a band more than twice as large (±6 per cent).

The wider the band, the smaller the jump in the spot exchange rate on the day of the realignment, because in between realignments the exchange rate may crawl slowly towards the top of the band. This is clearly shown in Figure 4.4, which compares the lira–DM and the French franc–DM exchange rates around the March 1983 realignment. On the day of the realignment the French franc jumps, but all that happens to the lira is that the band is shifted up, while the exchange rate—which had crawled smoothly towards the top of the band in the weeks preceding the realignment—does not move. With a wider band the expected capital loss on the day of the realignment should therefore be small, and thus should give rise to small interest rate fluctuations in the anticipation of the realignment.

Figure 4.3, however, shows that at the time of the 1983 realignment a wider

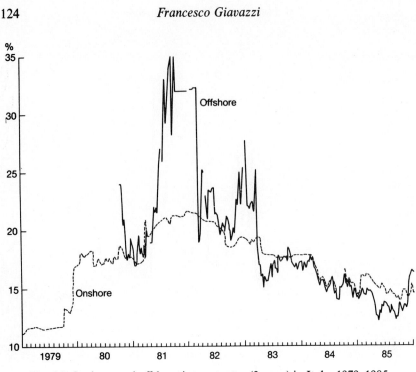

Fig. 4.3 Onshore and offshore interest rates (3 mos.) in Italy, 1979–1985.

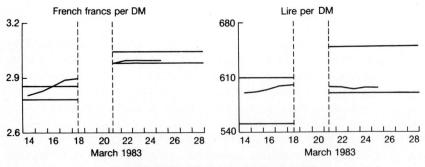

Fig. 4.4 EMS realignment of March 1983.

band has been insufficient to avoid large differentials between onshore and offshore interest rates on lira-denominated deposits. *This is because the market could not exclude the possibility that the realignment might change the central parity between the lira and the Deutschmark by more than 6 per cent, and thus cause a jump in the market exchange rate.*

The experience of the lira, therefore, indicates that a wider band, although it tends to dampen the fluctuation of interest rates around realignments, is not a way around the trade-off between exchange controls and interest rate volatility.[31]

The Term Structure of Interest Rates in the Anticipation of an EMS Realignment

Figure 4.5 shows onshore and offshore interest rates on French francs around the April 1986 realignment. The effect on interest rates of the uncertainty surrounding the time of the realignment is striking. Near the date of the realignment, when uncertainty regarding its exact timing vanishes, the term structure of offshore rates is downward-sloping: interest rates on shorter maturities are above interest rates on longer maturities because the capital loss arising from a given expected devaluation of the French franc is larger, the shorter the maturity of the deposit. But when there is a lot of uncertainty regarding the time of the realignment (as it is the case in the months of January and February), the term structure tilts up and down.[32]

Summary

So far, the EMS experience reminds us that the trade-off between exchange controls and volatility of domestic interest rates is unavoidable in a system of

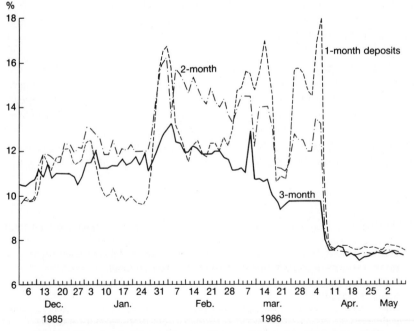

Fig. 4.5 Euromarket interest rates, France, December 1985–May 1986.

fixed but adjustable parities, and disappears only in a system of irrevocably fixed exchange rates.[33] This trade-off, however, may be more favourable than that between exchange rate volatility and interest rate volatility, which arises in a regime of purely floating exchange rates and which has characterized the recent experience of the UK.

7. Conclusions

To conclude, it may be helpful to repeat the main points of the paper.

1. The analysis of the effects of the CAP suggests that, by joining the EEC, Britain suffered a welfare loss both relative to its situation before accession, and relative to free trade in agricultural products. Britain's loss, however, is not a problem specific to that country. The CAP is a system that redistributes income in Europe both within countries and across countries. It does so at a very high cost, and according to criteria that it is difficult to rationalize. The EEC is now considering the dismantling of the CAP and the introduction of a system of deficiency payments. The major change would be that the whole system of intra-country and inter-country transfers would then become visible.

2. As regards manufactures, entry into the EEC has had a substantial effect on UK exports to Europe, accounting for up to 50 per cent of actual exports in 1979. The effect on UK imports from Europe, however, is larger: in 1979 it accounts for up to 60–70 per cent of imports. Thus, the message of these estimates is that accession increased substantially Britain's manufacturing exports to Europe, but not by as much as it increased British imports from Europe.

3. As regards Britain's possible entry into the European Monetary System, the trade-off between exchange controls and volatility of domestic interest rates is unavoidable in a system of fixed but adjustable parities, and disappears only in a system of irrevocably fixed exchange rates. This trade-off, however, may be more favourable than that between exchange-rate volatility and interest rate volatility, which arises in a regime of purely floating exchange rates and which has characterized the recent experience of the UK.

Notes

1. If this transfer is applied consistently to all countries, the enlargement of a customs union can lead to a welfare improvement for both the new and the old members because, as shown by Grinols (1984), the money needed to effect the transfer can be raised through a properly specified common external tariff.
2. For an early general equilibrium study of the effects of accession, see Miller and Spencer (1977).
3. The CAP has been rationalized in various ways: the strategic aspect of self-sufficiency, the protection of the traditional sector, price stabilization, etc.
4. In 1980–3 the share of agriculture in total GDP was 2.2 per cent in the UK, 3.7 per

cent on average in the rest of the EEC; the share of employment in agriculture was 2.5 per cent in the UK, 7.6 per cent in the EEC.

5. The commodities reported in Table 4.2 were selected because they are the only ones for which reliable estimates of the EEC import price net of tariff are available.

6. The subsidy may be larger because the EEC market price is in general above the intervention price. The actual subsidy lies in between the first two columns of Table 4.2.

7. Excluding tariff revenues, 70 per cent of EEC financing comes from a fraction of each country's revenue from value added taxes.

8. For an assessment of the early experience of European economic integration see Balassa (1975).

9. For a review of these studies see Mayes (1978), Morgan (1980), and Boltho (1984).

10. Homothetic demand and separability between imports and home-produced manufactures is assumed, for example, in Fetherston *et al.* (1979). Allowing for non-separability is important because substitution takes place not only among imports from different countries, but also between imports and domestic demand. Assuming separability excludes for example the possibility of observing external trade creation. The assumption on the income elasticity of demand is crucial in these studies because the effect of EEC membership is estimated by comparing actual trade flows with an estimate of what trade flows would have been in the absence of integration. To obtain an unbiased estimate of the effect of integration, it is thus important to allow for the possibility that demand functions are not homothetic and that therefore expenditure shares change as income grows.

11. For a description of the exchange controls in force at that time, and for an assessment of the effects of their abolition, see Chrystal (1985).

12. As noted by Chrystal (1985), it is impossible to say how much of the capital flows observed after October 1979 can be ascribed to the abolition of exchange controls: at the time of liberalization, the UK was in the midst of the transition from being a net oil importer to being a net oil exporter.

13. This is documented by Colchester (1986).

14. Answer by A. L. Coleby of the Bank of England in 'Minutes of Evidence to the Treasury and Civil Service Committee on the Financial and Economic Consequences of UK Membership of the European Communities', House of Commons, Session 1984–5, p. 39.

15. This is also the index used by the Bank of England. It is calculated as follows: consider for example the weight of the yen in the MERM index for the UK (0.14 in 1972). The effective exchange rate index is constructed so that a 1 per cent depreciation of the yen relative to the pound has the same effect on the UK trade balance as a uniform appreciation of the pound by 0.14 per cent.

16. The most recent set of MERM weights published by the IMF are the weights for 1977. The evidence on the shift in British trade flows after 1977 suggests that the tendency has been towards a further increase in the weight of the EMS currencies at the expense of the dollar.

17. The portfolio model has no power to explain the data before 1979. Between 1973 and 1979 the source of the observed correlation probably lies in the presence of capital controls in the UK. The role of capital controls in explaining the asymmetric movements of European exchange rates is discussed in Giavazzi and Giovannini (1986a).

18. This example is borrowed from Giavazzi and Giovannini (1986b).

19. A two-country version of this model is used by Canzoneri and Henderson (1986).

20. This is the only source of non-neutrality in the model, and it is the reason why exchange rate realignments have real effects.
21. Because the only asset held by residents of each country is the money of that country (i.e., there is no capital mobility), trade must always be balanced. This is ensured by the assumption that countries have the same propensity to import. The same assumption is made in Canzoneri and Henderson (1986).
22. If European monetary authorities do not co-operate, exchange rate realignments may take place even if countries are perfectly symmetric. This happens when they are hit by common supply shocks and the exchange rate system works asymmetrically with one currency playing the role of the nth currency. This possibility is relevant in the EMS because, although the system was explicitly designed to work symmetrically, its experience has been characterized by widespread asymmetries, with the Deutschmark effectively playing the role of the nth currency. For evidence see Micossi (1985) and Giavazzi and Giovannini (1987). The losses from lack of international co-ordination in a regime of managed exchange rates are studied in Giavazzi and Giovannini (1985).
23. Equations (4.6) and (4.7) below are derived assuming $\delta = \frac{1}{3}$.
24. The onshore rate is the return on a deposit issued, for example, in Paris and denominated in French francs; the offshore rate is the return on a deposit also denominated in French francs, but issued outside France, for example in London. A Difference between the two rates signals the presence of unexploited arbitrage profits, which can only be attributed to the active enforcement of capital controls.
25. This requires: (1) that the observations on spot and forward exchange rates and interest rates be simultaneous (same time of the day), because in an arbitrage operation short positions in foreign currency are instantaneously covered on the forward market; and (2) the use of both bid and offer prices, so that they reflect those actually faced by sellers and buyers, lenders and borrowers. Using bid and and offer prices, we take into account transaction costs, to the extent that these are reflected in the bid–offer spread. Brokerage fees and other charges may still account for a small portion of the observed unexploited profit opportunities. The results reported in the table are obtained using data that satisfy both of these requirements.
26. All the data used are from the Data Resources Inc. FACS Data Bank. Domestic money market rates are those quoted by the local branches of Bank of America.
27. Or any other Eurocurrency deposit. I refer to Eurodollars because this is the rate used in our tests. This rate was chosen because the Eurodollar market is the largest single market among all Eurocurrencies and is therefore unaffected by the problems that affect other Eurocurrency markets, such as the lira and the french franc, because of their thinness.
28. Neither $R1 = R2 = 0$, nor $R1 > 0$, $R2 > 0$ can ever be observed because of the transaction costs reflected in the bid–offer spread.
29. In a study of capital controls in Japan, Ito (1983) uses the *mean* of $R1$ to measure the intensity of controls. This measure, however, underestimates the deviation from covered interest rate arbitrage because, as we have seen, $R1$ may take negative values even in the presence of capital controls. This distortion is eliminated if we consider only the positive realizations of $R1$.
30. Notice that this result is stronger than the corresponding finding for Italy, despite the fact that there—in the second sub-period—we observe an even higher frequency of observations characterized by the absence of arbitrage opportunities. First, in the Dutch case it holds independently of the EMS regime (realignment or

no realignment). Second, the bid–offer spread on the spot and the forward market is smaller for the Dutch guilder than for the lira (typically, 0.5 per cent instead of 1.5 per cent for the lira in the period of EMS calm), hence reducing the region where the $R1 \leq 0$, $R2 \leq 0$ result may occur.

31. The experience of the lira thus seems to contradict the presumption of the Public Policy Centre Committee: '[If Britain joined the EMS] until the UK inflation rate slows down there is likely to be need of periodic parity realignments in order to prevent a progressive erosion of the British competitive position. However, provided that the market has confidence that these changes will be small and prompt, and will not involve discontinuous changes in market exchange rates over a realignment, there is no evident reason why this should significantly disrupt the market confidence in the predictability of future exchange rates on which the stabilizing character of capital flows is dependent' (Artis *et al*. 1986, pp. 8–9).

32. The term structure of interest rates on Euro-franc deposits in the months preceding the March 1983 realignment is studied by Collins (1984).

33. As noticed by Charles Goodhart (1986): 'While one may argue that comparison between Eurocurrency and domestic interest rates in the French and Italian case may have been exaggerated by the narrow nature of these markets, on the other hand a bi-polar EMS system with two huge, free capital markets would seem to encourage far larger surges of funds between London and Frankfurt than has ever been likely between Frankfurt and Milan or Paris.'

References

Artis, M. *et al*. (1986), 'The Need for an Exchange Rate Policy and the Option of Full UK Membership of the EMS'. London: Public Policy Centre.

Artus, J. and McGuirk, A. (1981), 'A Revised version of the Multilateral Exchange Rate Model', *IMF Staff Papers*.

Artus, J. and Rhomberg (1973), 'A Multilateral Exchange Rate Model', *IMF Staff Papers*.

Balassa, B. (1975), 'Trade Creation and Trade Diversion in the European Common Market: An Appraisal of the Evidence', in B. Balassa (ed.), *European Economic Integration*. Amsterdam: North-Holland.

Boltho, A. (1984), 'The European Economy', in D. Morris (ed.), *The Economic System of the UK*. Oxford: Oxford University Press.

Brittan, S. (1985), 'Now, alas, it is time to join the EMS', *Financial Times*, 14 November.

Canzoneri, M. B. and Henderson, D. W. (1986), 'Strategic Aspects of Macroeconomic Policymaking in Interdependent Economies'. Mimeo.

Chrystal, A. K. (1985), 'The Abolition of Exchange Controls in the UK: Are There Any Lessons for Other Countries?' *Euromobiliare Occasional Paper*, no. 1. Milan: Euromobiliare.

Colchester, N. (1986), 'A Heavyweight Sheds Pounds', *Financial Time*, 8 April.

Collins, S. (1984), 'Exchange Rate Expectations and Interest Parity During Credibility Crises: The French Franc, March 1983'. Harvard University, mimeo.

European Economic Commission (1970), Interim Report on the Establishment by Stages of Economic and Monetary Union, and Report of the Council and the Commission on the Realization by Stages of Economic and Monetary Union in the Community. Brussels: EEC.

Fetherston, M., Moore, B., and Rhodes, J. (1979), 'EEC Membership and UK Trade in Manufactures. *Cambridge Journal of Economics*, 3, 399–407.

Giavazzi, F. and Giovannini, A. (1985), 'Monetary Policy Interactions Under Managed Exchange Rates'. Mimeo.

—— (1986a), 'The EMS and the Dollar', *Economic Policy*, 2, 456–85.

—— (1986b), 'Exchange Rates and Prices in Europe', mimeo.

—— (1987), 'Is the EMS a Greater Deutschmark Area?', mimeo.

Giavazzi, F. and Pagano, M. (1985), 'Capital Controls and the European Monetary System', *Euromobiliare Occasional Papers*, no. 1. Milan: Euromobiliare.

Goodhart, C. (1986), 'Has the Time Come for the UK to Join the EMS?' *The Banker*, 136, 26–8.

Grinols, E. L. (1984), 'A Thorn in the Lion's Paw: Has Britain Paid Too Much for Common Market Membership?' *Journal of International Economics*, 16, 271–93.

Ito, T. (1983), 'Capital Controls and Covered Interest Rate Parity', National Bureau of Economic Research Working Paper no. 1187.

Josling, T. (1971), 'The Agricultural Burden: A Reappraisal', in J. Pinder (ed.), *The Economics of Europe*. London: Charles Knight.

Mayes, D. G. (1978), 'The Effects of Economic Integration on Trade', *Journal of Common Market Studies*, 17, 1–25.

Micossi, S. (1985), 'The Intervention and Financing Mechanisms of the EMS and the Role of the ECU', *Banca Nazionale del Lavoro Quarterly Review*, 155, 327–45.

Miller, M. H. and Spencer, J. E. (1977), 'The Static Economic Effects of the UK Joining the EEC: A General Equilibrium Approach', *Review of Economic Studies*, 136, 71–94.

Morgan, A. D. (1980), 'The Balance of Payments and British Membership of the European Community', in W. Wallace (ed.), *Britain in Europe*. London: Heinemann.

Morris, C. N. (1980), 'The Common Agricultural Policy', *Fiscal Studies*, 1(2), 17–35.

—— and Dilnot, A. W. (1982), 'The Distributional Effects of the Common Agricultural Policy', *Fiscal Studies*, 3(2), 92–101.

Mundell, R. A. (1968), *International Economics*, New York: Macmillan.

Winters, A. L. (1984), 'British Imports of Manufactures and the Common Market', *Oxford Economic Papers*, 36, 103–18.

—— (1985), 'Separability and the Modelling of International Economic Integration: UK Exports to Five Industrial Countries', *European Economic Review*, 27, 335–53.

CHAPTER 5

The Labour Market

Richard Layard and Stephen Nickell

London School of Economics and Oxford University

1. Introduction

The biggest single cause of our high unemployment is the failure of our jobs market, the weak link in our economy.

White Paper of March 1985, *Exployment, The Challenge for the Nation* (pp. 12–13)

Most people are dissatisfied with Britain's economic performance over the last 15 years, and many blame the institutions of the labour market. It is a natural argument, since our most obvious economic failure is the rise of unemployment.

But can one argue that unemployment has nearly trebled since 1979 because our labour market institutions have got so much worse? Clearly not. Up to 1979 our institutional arrangements did become a bit more rigid, but since then they have become a bit less so. So the rigidity argument cannot be of the form, 'Unemployment has risen because rigidity has risen.' It must be of the form, 'Unemployment has risen because the system has been subjected to deflationary shocks, and a rigid labour market has been unable to absorb them.' This will be the central theme of this chapter. We shall not discuss the deflationary shocks, which are the subject of other chapters in this book. Rather, we shall focus on the reaction in the labour market.

First (in Sections 2 and 3), we shall look at the labour market as an aggregate, and try to explain why unemployment has ratcheted upwards in the way shown in Figure 5.1 below. The central mystery is why, at present levels of unemployment, wage inflation is not falling. One approach is to focus on the impact of long-term unemployment on attachment to the labour force. According to this account, a sharp deflationary shock increases the number of long-term unemployed, many of whom effectively withdraw from the labour market. A rival, although related, interpretation focuses on the role of the unions. If unions are concerned mainly with 'insiders' and there is a contraction of employment, the unions become concerned with a smaller proportion of the labour force.

To discriminate between these two approaches, we shall deploy one of the

We are extremely grateful to Andy Murfin and Paul Kong for help with this paper. Jonathan Haskel kindly did the flows analysis of Tables 5.1 and 5.2. We are also grateful to David Stanton, Patrick Minford, and Graham Reid for helpful comments, and to the Economic and Social Research Council and the Esmee Fairbairn Charitable Trust for financial assistance. Data sources are available on request, and are as in Layard and Nickell (1986a) and Nickell (1986). A longer version of this paper is available on request (Layard and Nickell, 1986b); this contains further evidence on the matters discussed in Section 4 and also a full discussion of hours of work.

basic facts about the labour market: that unemployment has risen hugely while vacancies are now as high as they were in 1977–8. The fact that vacancies exist in that (limited) abundance argues in favour of the explanation in terms of workers' incentives to take work and firms' incentives to fill vacancies, as against explanations that focus solely on the role of unions in holding down the number of jobs, once this number has fallen.

A quite different explanation of unemployment focuses on structural issues and the rigidities in the structure of relative wages (rather than of the general wage level). In Section 4 we show how inflexible relative wages are in this country—whether by industry, region, age, or sex. This makes unemployment higher than it would otherwise be. But there is no evidence that these problems have worsened in a way that could explain the *rise* in unemployment.

Thus far, we have been concerned with employment (an input) rather than with output. But the test of the labour market is not only whether it can use the labour available, but whether it can use it to produce something. In Section 5 we therefore look at productivity. Sections 3–5 each end with a summary.

2. Aggregate Unemployment

Some Basic Facts

We shall begin with some basic facts. Unemployment has quadrupled since 1970 (see Figure 5.1). The most relevant series we have is for male unemployment, since measured female unemployment depends so much on women's varying entitlements to benefits. Male unemployment (on the official

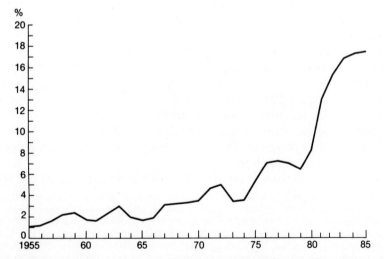

Fig. 5.1 Male unemployment rate, 1955–1985 (pre-1982 definition of unemployment).

pre-1982 definition)[1] has increased from 4 to 17 per cent—mainly though two huge steps, one in 1974–6 and the second in 1979–82. On the OECD's standardized definitions, male unemployment is now nearly twice as high in Britain as in France, Germany, Italy, or the United States.[2] And male employment is now lower here than it was in 1911.

The increase in unemployment has come about almost entirely through an increase in the duration of unemployment. As can be seen from Figure 5.2, the inflow into unemployment in recent years has been rather less than it was in the late 1960s, though about a fifth above its level in the late 1970s. There has been a huge build-up of long-term unemployed—that is, of those unemployed for over a year (see Figure 5.3). In fact, since 1981 short-term unemployment has actually fallen a bit, while long-term unemployment has soared.

Unemployment of this kind must be both inefficient and inequitable. It must be inefficient since it cannot reflect any necessary search or redeployment of labour and in fact causes huge depreciation of the stock of human capital. It must be inequitable since it reflects the concentration of the total man-weeks of unemployment in a very small proportion of the population. The number of men who become unemployed is roughly $2\frac{1}{2}$ million a year—only 16 per cent of the male workforce. But the stock of unemployed men is nearly $2\frac{1}{2}$ million. So those who do become unemployed can expected on average to remain so for roughly a year.

The rise in unemployment has not been matched by a commensurate fall in vacancies. Vacancies are indeed low (about two-thirds of their average level in

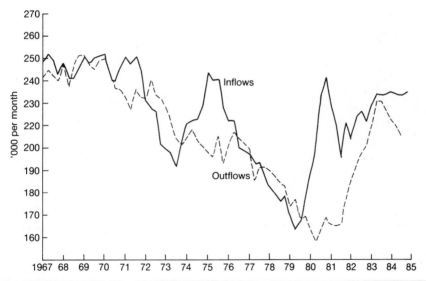

Fig. 5.2 Male unemployment inflows and outflows, 1967–1985 (pre-1982 definition of unemployment).

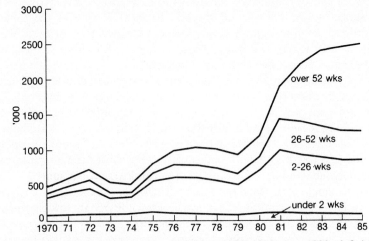

Fig. 5.3 Male unemployment by duration, 1970–1985 (pre-1982 definition of unemployment).

the 1960s), but they are at about the same level as in the economic troughs of 1958, 1963, and 1971–2 and above their level in 1976 (see Figure 5.4). The outward shift of the *u/v* curve is thus a basic puzzle which we have to explain.

While unemployment has risen, the labour force has not stood still. Indeed, it has risen continuously since 1971 (except in 1983), though much more

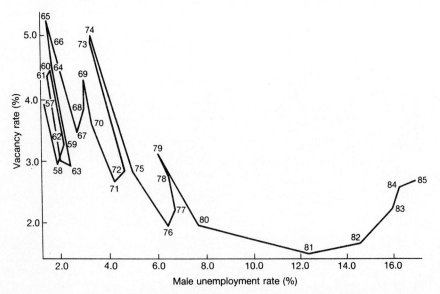

Fig. 5.4 Vacancies and male unemployment, 1957–1985.

Fig. 5.5 Rate of growth of hourly earnings of male manual workers, 1960–1985.

slowly than in the United States and Japan. The increase is entirely due to the rising number of women in the labour force. This reflects partly the size of the adult population, but also the increasing participation rate of women. By contrast, the participation rate of men has fallen, mainly owing to earlier retirement.

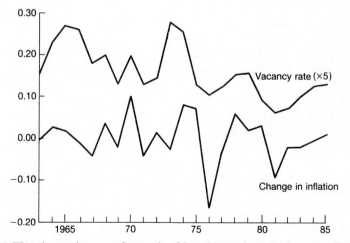

Fig. 5.6 The change in rate of growth of hourly earnings (male manual) and the vacancy rate (× 5), 1963–1985.

The mechanism by which labour supply affects employment is through its effects on wages. At some level of unemployment, wage inflation will be stable—increasing at lower unemployment and falling at higher unemployment. Figure 5.5 therefore shows the history of wage inflation, while Figure 5.6 shows changes in wage inflation against the level of vacancies. There is clearly some relationship.

A Labour Market Model

To explain the movement of unemployment, we shall present a simple model. This draws on earlier work (Layard and Nickell, 1986a), but simplifies it and extends it to focus on the apparent ratchet effect in the level of unemployment.

In the long run, unemployment is determined so that there is equality between

1. the 'feasible' real wage, implied by the pricing behaviour of firms, and
2. the 'target' real wage, implied by the wage-setting behaviour of wage-bargainers.

This is illustrated at point A in Figure 5.7.

Let us go behind the curves, starting with the price-setting relationship determining the 'feasible' real wage. We shall define prices (p) as the price of value added; i.e., at the level of the firm, final prices adjusted for changes in materials' prices, and at the level of the whole economy, for changes in the price of imports. Firms set their value added prices as a mark-up on hourly labour cost (w). But this mark-up will tend to rise if output is higher. Since output is related to employment via the production function, it follows that the real wage falls as employment rises, as in Figure 5.7. The mark-up falls if inflation is greater than expected ($p > p^e$), both because prices will not be adjusted enough upwards for the higher wages, and because firms will underestimate competitors' prices and keep their prices low to retain business.[3]

Wages in turn are set as a mark-up on expected prices. The mark-up increases as employment rises and is also affected by a whole host of wage pressure variables (z), to which we return later. If inflation is greater than expected the mark-up will fall, since, when prices turn out to be higher than expected, the real wage achieved will be lower than the real wage bargained for.

In the longer run, the growth of the capital stock will lead to productivity improvements, which, on the one hand, will lead firms to reduce their mark-up of prices on wages and, on the other hand, will lead firms and workers to bargain for a higher mark-up of wages on prices.[4] Thus, in static, log-linear form we have the following model:[5]

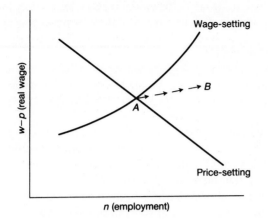

Fig. 5.7 The consequences of a positive demand shock.

Price setting: $p - w = \alpha_0 + \alpha_1(p - p^e) + \alpha_2(n - l) + \alpha_3(k - l),$
$$(\alpha_1 < 0, \; \alpha_2 \geqslant 0, \; \alpha_3 < 0) \tag{5.1}$$

Wage setting: $w - p = \beta_0 + \beta_1(p - p^e) + \beta_2(n - l) + \beta_3(k - l) + z,$
$$(\beta_1 < 0, \; \beta_2 > 0, \; \beta_3 > 0) \tag{5.2}$$

    where w = hourly labour cost (including employers' labour taxes)
           p = value added price
           k = capital stock
           l = labour force
           n = employment (note the unemployment rate $u = l - n$)
           z = 'wage pressure' (the influence of mismatch, employment
               protection, replacement ratio, union power, incomes policy,
               relative import prices, and employers' labour taxes)

There are many points worth noting about this framework. First, it is very general. For example, if $\alpha_1 = 0$ and $\alpha_2 = -\alpha_3$, then (5.1) becomes the standard labour demand equation for a competitive industry. Similarly, a restricted version of (5.2) yields a competitive labour supply equation. On the other hand, if $\alpha_2 = 0$ we have the pure mark-up or normal cost pricing model, where prices are unaffected by demand in the short run. Second, to complete a model of a closed economy, we may add the following equations:

Production function: $y - k = f(n - k)$ (5.3)

Aggregate demand: $y = y^d(x)$ (5.4)

where y = value added output
         x = exogenous determinants of real demand
So, given the resources of the economy as specified by k and l, the model will, in the short run, yield w, p, n, y for any given level of demand (x), price expectations (p^e), and wage pressure (z). In the longer term, when price

surprises are ruled out ($p = p^e$), the model reveals, for given z, the level of y, n, $w - p$, and y^d consistent with no surprises. If no surprises is synonymous with stable inflation, these levels correspond to the NAIRU (non-accelerating inflation rate of unemployment).

The great advantage of writing the model as we have done is that (5.1) and (5.2) alone will yield the no-surprise (or NAIRU) values of employment and the real wage, and are thus eminently suitable for analysing long-term unemployment trends.[6]

In order to see how the model operates, we consider, first, the consequences of an aggregate demand shock starting from a position of equilibrium ($p = p^e$). This is illustrated in Figure 5.7. An increase in real demand raises employment, and this tends to raise prices relative to wages in the price equation, and wages relative to prices in the wage equation. The only way in which these tendencies can be made consistent is via the positive price surprise brought about by a rise in inflation. This tends to offset the consequences of the rise in the level of activity on both sides of the market, leading us to a point such as B, which is below the wage line and above the price line. (Note that the effect of a positive price surprise is to raise the price-determined real wage.) So we have the standard result that a positive demand shock will raise employment, raise inflation, but have an indeterminate impact on the real wage. However, we can be more precise on this latter point in certain special cases. If the product market is competitive, then $\alpha_1 = 0$ and $\alpha_2 = -\alpha_3$ in equation (5.1), as we have already noted. Thus B must lie on the price line, which slopes downwards. The real wage must, therefore, fall. On the other hand, under strict normal cost pricing, $\alpha_2 = 0$ and the price line is horizontal. Under these circumstances the real wage must rise, since B must be above the horizontal price line.

Turning to the consequences of a supply shock, in Figure 5.8 we illustrate the outcome of a rise in wage pressure, z (a negative supply shock). If real demand remains fixed, then we move to a point such as B, with a fall in employment and positive price surprises generated by rising inflation. The real wage has risen, and we have the combination of inflation and 'classical' unemployment typical of such a shock. If the rise in wage pressure is permanent, real demand must fall if inflation is to be stabilized. This may happen either autonomously (via real balance effects, for example) or as a result of a conscious policy shift. In consequence, we move to a new equilibrium at C, with lower 'equilibrium' employment and a real wage that will be higher to the extent that prices are influenced by demand. In the extreme case of normal cost pricing, the price line is horizontal and the real wage will revert back to its original level. The additional unemployment will then apparently be entirely 'Keynesian', although it has, in fact, been brought about by the rise in wage pressure.

It is clear from this analysis that the wage pressure variables are the key to the long-run analysis of unemployment. It is also clear that focusing on the

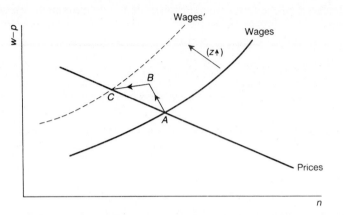

Fig. 5.8 The consequences of a rise in wage pressure.

real-wage outcome will not be very useful in trying to understand what is happening. The real wage that finally emerges has as much to do with the pricing policy of firms as with labour market activity.

Our next step is to attach some numbers to the fundamental model. Our equations are based on Nickell (1987). The dynamic versions of each equation are (annual data 1956–83):[7]

Prices: $p-w=\alpha_0-0.61\Delta^2w-0.51\Delta^2w_{-1}-0.253u+0.075\Delta u-0.338\Delta^2u-1.07(k-l)$. (5.1′)

Wages: $w-p=\beta_0-0.36\Delta^2p-0.104\log u+0.532u-1.174\Delta u-0.356\Delta^2u+1.07(k-l)+z$. (5.2′)

A number of points are worth noting. The price surprise terms are represented by Δ^2w in the price equation and Δ^2p in the wage equation. One of the key properties of the wage equation is the dependence of wages on $\log u$ as well as u. This has profound implications and we shall return to this point at a later stage. At the moment it suffices to say that a 1 percentage point rise in unemployment has a lesser impact on wages, the higher is its initial level. A final point concerns the role of the productivity variable $(k-l)$. The model imposes the restriction that increases in the stock of capital have no impact on unemployment *in the long run*. This is perfectly consistent with the data and implies that the long-run coefficient on $k-l$ is the same (in absolute value) in both price and wage equations. Were this not the case, the implication would be that firms and workers would be trying to extract, on a permanent basis, more or less than 100 per cent of the growth in trend productivity. Since this would imply either *permanently* rising or *permanently* falling unemployment at stable inflation, we decided to rule out this possibility—it seems inconsistent with the apparent consequences of two centuries of economic growth.

To understand the long-run determinants of unemployment, we can write equations (5.1′) and (5.2′) in their long-run form, expanding the wage equation around an unemployment rate of $\bar{u}$. This gives

Prices: $p - w = \alpha_0 - 0.253u - 1.07(k - l).$ (5.1″)

Wages: $w - p = \beta_0' - \left(\dfrac{0.104}{\bar{u}} - 0.532 \right) u + 1.07(k - l) + z.$ (5.2″)

The long-run level of unemployment is given by adding these equations to obtain

$$u = \left(0.253 + \frac{0.104}{\bar{u}} - 0.532 \right)^{-1} (z + \alpha_0 + \beta_0'). \qquad (5.5)$$

Thus, wage pressure (z) is crucial to our explanation of unemployment.[8] The next step, therefore, is to look at the movement of the wage pressure index—see Figure 5.9. (We shall discuss its constituent parts later.) As can be seen, it moves broadly in line with unemployment up to 1980, and any divergences are identified with increasing or decreasing inflation, as appropriate. However, since 1980 the index has risen little, with the years 1980–5 having wage pressure only 4 points higher than the 1974–80 average. The

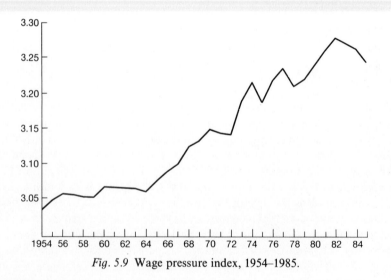

Fig. 5.9 Wage pressure index, 1954–1985.

Note: This is based on

$z = 0.068$ mismatch $+ 0.28$ replacement ratio $+ 0.49v$ log $(Pm/\bar{P})$
    $+ 0.29 \, \Delta \, (v \log (Pm/\bar{P})) + 0.030$ union power $+ 0.66t_1$.

$Pm/\bar{P}$ is the real price of imports, and t_1 is employers' labour tax rate. The mismatch variable has been smoothed to remove its cyclical component. v is the share of imports in GDP.

long-run NAIRU (for male unemployment) is now around 12 per cent; yet actual unemployment is much higher than this, with the 1981–5 average being nearly 10 points above the level for 1974–80. Thus, the index does not seem to explain how the high unemployment of the 1980s could be accompanied by such relatively small reductions in wage inflation.

The answer to the apparent paradox lies in the fact that the short-term NAIRU is not the same as the long-term NAIRU. This arises from the dynamics of the system and especially of the wage equation (5.2′). As the wage pressure equation makes clear, wage pressure is less not only when unemployment is higher but also when unemployment is rising. By the same token, wage pressure at a given level of unemployment is higher when unemployment is falling. Thus, suppose the wage equation is, for simplicity,

$$w - p = \beta_0 - \beta_2 \log u - \beta_3(u - u_{-1}) \qquad (5.6)$$

as compared with the long-run wage relationship

$$w - p = \beta_0 - \beta_2 \log u.$$

In Figure 5.10 we show the long-run NAIRU at point A as usual. But suppose last year's employment was at n_{-1}. The short-run wage pressure equation (5.6) is given by the dotted line and the short-run NAIRU is at B. This is the essence of our present difficulties. We have got to a very high level of unemployment, and reducing unemployment is always liable to produce increasing inflation.

What accounts for the long-lasting effect of past unemployment in the wage equation? The evidence suggests that it results from the effect of high unemployment on the numbers of the long-term unemployed. But in order to give all theories a run for their money, we need first to consider from basic principles how the unemployment situation might be expected to influence the degree of wage pressure.

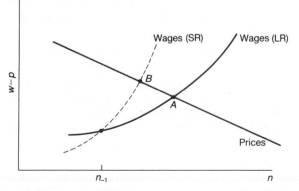

Fig. 5.10 Short-run NAIRU (at B) and long-run NAIRU (at A).

Unemployment and Wage Pressure

Two parties are involved in wage determination: firms and unions. Their relative importance differs in different parts of the economy.[9] Let us begin with firms. Firms, if they were free to choose wages, would set them at a level that would enable them to recruit, retain, and motivate workers. For recruitment purposes, they would choose lower wages, the more plentiful the supply of workers that they faced. Similar factors would affect the ability of firms to restrain quitting and to motivate workers, for workers are easier to retain and motivate, the more job market competition they would face if they themselves became unemployed.[10]

Thus, a key variable is the number of acceptable unemployed workers who are out there 'beating at the gates'. Since few unemployed workers (30 per cent) get re-employed in the industry of their previous job, we would expect that it was general (rather than industry-specific) unemployment that affected wage behaviour in each industry. And this turns out to be the case (see p. 161 below).

But the level of unemployment on its own does not adequately measure the number of acceptable workers beating at the gates. The composition of unemployment also matters. If a high proportion of the unemployed have been out of work for a long time, the employers may consider them undesirable as workers; equally, the workers themselves may be discouraged, and may have largely given up searching. Thus, long-term unemployment represents a less effective labour supply than short-term unemployment. So employers will be influenced both by the level of unemployment and by the proportion of the unemployed who are long-term unemployed (R). As we have seen this proportion has doubled since 1979, and we shall find that this is a major factor explaining the current degree of wage pressure.

But what about the union response to unemployment? Unions too will care about the numbers of workers 'beating at the gates'. For if wages are pushed too high, some union members will lose their jobs and end up in competition with other unemployed job-seekers.[11] So if general unemployment is high, and predominantly short-term, individual unions will be less inclined to push on wages and so risk unemployment for their members.

But unions will be concerned not only with the bleakness of the world outside, but also with the likelihood that their members will be ejected into it. So another key variable will be 'fear'—the fear of job loss. The extent of job loss will of course depend on the wages that each union selects. But this will in turn depend on how unfavourable a demand curve the union faces. The union may evaluate its demand curve largely in terms of, say, last year's job loss.[12] This could be proxied by last year's rate of inflow into unemployment (I) or by the change in unemployment.

One extreme view is in fact that wage behaviour depends *only* on the change in unemployment, and not at all on the level (Blanchard and Summers

1986).[13] This has been offered as an explanation of why wage inflation fell so much between 1980–1 and 1982–3, and so little since. The chief line of reasoning is that the unions care only about their members and set the wage so as to maintain the chances of their continued employment (see also Lindbeck and Snower 1984). If unemployment has been low and stable for some time, wage claims will be no higher than if unemployment has been high and stable for some time. For the unions are concerned only with ensuring the continued employment of those employed in the previous period, and this does not require a lower wage when unemployment is high. But when employment is falling, unions do moderate their behaviour in order to try to prevent employment falling further.

There are many obvious problems with this 'insider–outsider' line of argument. First, it provides no explanation of the fact that, over longish periods, the size of the labour force has a clear effect on the level of employment. This must involve some responsiveness of wages to the labour force, as well as to employment.[14] Second, given the huge level of annual turnover in enterprises, it is hard to understand why employment has not been steadily falling if wage-setting only takes account of surviving workers. Third, the theory fails to explain why it is general unemployment rather than industry-specific unemployment (or employment) that most clearly affects the wages in an industry (see p. 161 below).

But even so, it is important to investigate systematically the effect of flow variables like unemployment flows and the change in employment, as compared with the level of unemployment and the composition of unemployment by duration. This is done in Nickell (1986), and we shall summarize the results. The most successful equation is one that includes only the log of unemployment and the proportion of the unemployed out of work for over a year (R):[15]

$$w - p = \beta_0'' - 0.36\Delta^2 p - 0.104 \log u + 0.212 R + 1.07(k-l) + z. \quad (5.7)$$
$$\qquad\qquad (7.8) \qquad\qquad (3.7)$$

IV estimates 1956–83, s.e. $= 0.0114$.

When this equation was expanded to include the inflow of unemployment, we obtained a t-statistic of only 1.3 and the significance of the duration term increased. When the equation was expanded to include lagged employment terms, the coefficients were

$$n_{-1}: \quad 0.46 \ (2.2)$$

$$n_{-2}: \ -0.52 \ (2.1)$$

and the t-statistics on $\log u$ and R remained 5.7 and 4.1, respectively. However, this version of the equation fits very badly over the 1980s. So our conclusion is that the story based on the effects of long-duration unemployment is the most persuasive.

Before pursuing the implications of this, we should refer to one other issue: the impact of region-specific unemployment rates. It is often suggested that, since wage bargaining is undertaken nationally in so many sectors (e.g. the public sector) and companies (e.g., ICI and the four main motor car manufacturers), wages may be most strongly influenced by the tightness of the labour market in the most buoyant region—that is, the South-East. So we added to our standard equation a variable measuring the South-East's unemployment rate relative to the national average, expecting it to reduce wage pressure. It did so—but its t-statistic was only 0.7. This is not surprising, given that this variable has recently had a high value, and yet there has been little apparent reduction of wage pressure.

We are therefore ready to investigate how the duration of unemployment affects the dynamics of wage behaviour. The first step is to see how the proportion of unemployed out of work for over a year (R) is affected by the history of unemployment. The relevant equation is

$$R = 0.054 + 0.61R_{-1} - 2.41u + 5.58u_{-1} - 2.18u_{-2} \qquad (5.7')$$
$$\quad\;\; (2.1) \quad\; (3.7) \qquad (5.6) \quad\; (6.5) \qquad (2.4)$$

OLS estimation 1956–83, s.e. $= 0.023$, $\bar{R}^2 = 0.84$.

This equation makes very good sense. As unemployment rises, the long-term unemployed proportion falls initially, since historically increases in unemployment come about because the inflow rises. In the long run, however, the long-term proportion tends to rise with unemployment. If we now solve out for R and substitute into (5.7), we obtain, after some manipulation, equation (5.2'), which is how we obtained that equation in the first place (see Nickell 1986, equation (26)).

Interestingly, (5.2') is similar to what is obtained from the following directly estimated dynamic wage equation:

$$w - p = \beta_0 - 0.113 \log u + 0.425u - 0.803\Delta u + 1.07(k - l) + z \qquad (5.2''')$$
$$\qquad\quad\; (5.2) \qquad\qquad (1.03) \quad\; (1.9)$$

IV estimation 1956–83, s.e. $= 0.0125$, D.W. $= 1.81$.

This was our most successful dynamic wage equation (except for one that depended heavily on unemployment lagged three years). But the important point is that (5.2''') gives no behavioural insight into how the dynamics arise, whereas our two equations involving long-term unemployment, (5.7) and (5.7'), do just that.

We can now see how our model helps us to understand the movement of inflation. From (5.2') we can see that in the long run, if unemployment gets high enough (above 19 per cent), further unemployment fails to reduce wage pressure, because the proportion of long-term unemployed becomes so high (see Figure 5.11).

But what happens to the rate of change of nominal wages? As equations

(5.1′) and (5.2′) make clear, the rate of change of inflation is directly related to the difference between the target real wage and the feasible real wage (each measured in the absence of nominal inertia, i.e., with $\Delta^2 w = \Delta^2 p = 0$). To see this, we add (5.1′) to (5.2′) after first expanding (5.2′) around $\bar{u}$, setting $\Delta^2 w = \Delta^2 w_{-1} = \Delta^2 p$, and omitting $\Delta^2 u$. This gives us

$$\Delta^2 w = -0.68 \left\{ \left(\frac{0.104}{\bar{u}} - 0.279 \right) u + 1.10 \Delta u - z - \alpha_0 - \beta_0' \right\}$$

where the term in brackets is the gap between feasible and target wage. Using (5.5), this can be rewritten

$$\Delta^2 w = -0.68 \left\{ \left(\frac{0.104}{\bar{u}} - 0.279 \right) (u - u^*) + 1.10 \Delta u \right\}. \qquad (5.8)$$

Thus, as unemployment grows, the effect of higher unemployment on cutting inflation is reduced. This is exactly what we should expect by looking at Figure 5.11 and bearing in mind that the change in inflation is proportional to the distance between the two lines. This distance reaches its minimum when unemployment is 37 per cent, and if unemployment goes higher than this it

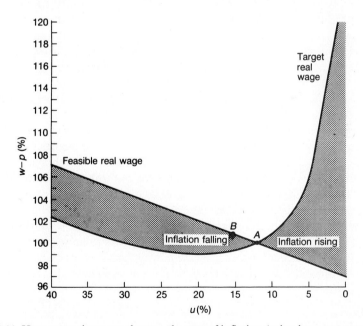

Fig. 5.11 How unemployment changes the rate of inflation (using long-run wage and price equations).

Note: This diagram is drawn to scale and corresponds to 1985. A is the long-run NAIRU: B is the short-run NAIRU when $u_{-1} = 17$ per cent; and $\Delta^2 w = 0.68$ (target real wage − feasible real wage).

starts to lose its power to reduce inflation. For beyond that point higher unemployment raises the target real wage more than it raises the feasible real wage. This observation is highly speculative since it lies way beyond the sample range, but it does raise the spectre that, if wage pressure became fierce enough, there might be no unemployment rate that could stabilize inflation.

More relevant to our present range of experience, the diagram shows clearly how the benefits of additional unemployment vary with the existing level of unemployment. If unemployment is low, more unemployment will have a marked effect on the change in inflation. But if unemployment is already high, the counterinflation gains from further unemployment are very limited. Thus the following table shows the (negative) effect on the change of inflation of 1 extra point of unemployment, starting from different levels of unemployment.

$\bar{u}$	Effect of 1 extra percentage point of unemployment on $(-\Delta^2 w)$
0.07	0.82%
0.12	0.39%
0.17	0.22%

(The values correspond to $0.68\ (0.104/\bar{u} - 0.279)$.) This indicates, for example, that a 1 point rise in unemployment from a base line of 7 per cent (i.e., 1979 male unemployment) will cause inflation to slow down at four times the speed of the slow-down induced by a similar rise in unemployment from a base-line of 17 per cent (i.e., 1985 male unemployment). However, this is a long-run effect. The Δu term in (5.8) reveals, for example, that, if we start from the current base-line of 17 per cent male unemployment and assume that this is 5 points above the long-run natural rate (our estimate is around 12 per cent), then any attempt to reduce unemployment down to this level at a rate of more than 2 percentage points per year will actually generate increasing inflation from the start. Even if unemployment is reduced at 1 percentage point per year, inflation will start to rise well before the natural rate is attained. This arises because of the way in which the duration structure of unemployment changes when unemployment declines. Falls in unemployment lead initially to a sharp reduction in the short-term unemployed. This withdrawal of a considerable proportion of the most active and desirable workers from the unemployed pool generates an increase in wage pressure which eases off only when the duration structure returns to normal and the major reduction in unemployment has come from the long-term end of the spectrum.

To summarize, therefore, once we take account of the fact that the long-term unemployed have only a minor impact on wages, we find that, in the long run, the inflation-reducing effects of extra unemployment decline rapidly as unemployment rises. For the same reason, the impact of changes in wage pressure on unemployment increases as the general level of unemployment goes up.

3. Influences on Wage Pressure

Having established the overall framework, we now need to look at the various wage pressure factors (z), which determine the long-run NAIRU. How far does each help us to explain the long rise in unemployment, and how does the duration of unemployment (as a more endogenous influence) fit into the story?

The wage pressure factors we shall investigate are (in order): the duration of unemployment, employment protection, mismatch, benefits, unions, incomes policy, taxes, and import prices.

The Duration of Unemployment and the u/v *Curve*

To think about the first four of these influences, we need to go behind the simplified model we have been using so far, and look at the flow of people through unemployment. This gives us a relationship between the unemployment rate (u), the vacancy rate (v), and a number of shift variables (x): $f(u, v, x) = 0$. We can also conceive of the structural wage equation lying behind (5.2) as including vacancies (as well as unemployment) as a determinant of wages. The wage equation (5.2) we have used so far is therefore a semi-reduced form in which vacancies have been substituted out, using $f(u, v, x) = 0$. It therefore includes all the variables (x) that affect the relationship of vacancies and unemployment. However, to check on our interpretation of the role of these variables in equation (5.2), we must look directly at the structural u/v relationship. Where does it come from, and what factors affect it?

The u/v curve reflects the process by which unemployed workers are matched to vacancies to generate a flow of hirings (or job-matches). One would expect that the number of hirings would depend positively on the number of vacancies that firms are willing to fill per period, and also on the number of unemployed people looking for work per period. It will be reduced by any mismatch (mm) between unemployment and vacancies. The intensity with which firms want to fill vacancies will vary according to how they view the quality of the unemployed and on such things as employment protection legislation and the like. So the vacancies that are relevant per period are some proportion (g) that firms wish to fill. Similarly, workers may vary in their intensity of search, depending on their past experience and on the level of unemployment benefits and the like. So the unemployed that are relevant per period are some proportion (c). This gives us our matching equation:

$$A = f(gV, cU, mm) \qquad (5.9)$$
$$+ \quad + \quad -$$

where A is the numbers leaving unemployment per period and U and V are the numbers of vacancies and unemployed.

We can now see clearly how the proportion of long-term unemployed (R) has its effect. For both g and c will decrease as the proportion R rises. Hence (for given flows) the u/v curve shifts out as the proportion of long-term unemployed goes up. This is exactly what Budd, Levine, and Smith (1985) have found.[16] The fact that long-term unemployment shows up in the structural u/v relationship adds greatly to our confidence that its effect in the semi-reduced form wage equation (5.7) is also valid.

To obtain the long-run u/v curve, we note that in a steady state the outflow from unemployment equals the inflow. This has been roughly true for the last few years and was also true in the late 1970s. In this case $A = S$, where S is the inflow to unemployment. This gives us

$$\frac{U}{N} = \frac{S/N}{A/U} \tag{5.10}$$

where S/N is the inflow into unemployment as a proportion of the employed, and A/U is the proportion of the unemployed who leave unemployment. The unemployment rate (relative to employment) is simply the ratio of these two proportions.

Which of these two proportions accounts for the huge rise in unemployment? A glance at Figure 5.2 shows that the increased inflow rate into unemployment (S/N) would have increased unemployment by only a fifth. The main, 'cause' of increased unemployment has been the halving in the outflow rate (A/U).

It is easy to see how the pile-up of long-term unemployment could help to explain this fall in the outflow rate (A/U). For the outflow rate is always very much lower for those who have been unemployed longer. As Figure 5.12 shows, for people who have been unemployed over four years it is now 4 per cent per quarter, compared with 41 per cent per quarter for those who have recently lost their jobs. Thus, when long-term unemployment piles up, the overall outflow rate falls, even if the duration-specific outflow rates remain constant. We can therefore examine the effect of the duration structure upon the outflow rate by constructing an index of the outflow rate as it would have been over time with the duration-specific outflow rates unchanging but with the duration structure of unemployment changing as it has. This is shown in Figure 5.13. The (fixed) duration-specific outflow rates are those for January 1984 (as shown in Figure 5.12).

As the index shows, the change in the duration structure of unemployment accounts for all of the fall in the overall outflow rate since early 1981. This is the period during which the proportion of long-term unemployed has continuously risen while (as Table 5.1 shows) the duration-specific outflow rates have changed little. Before 1981 there was no increase in the proportion of long-term unemployed, and the fall in the outflow rate was due entirely to the sharp fall in the duration-specific outflow rates (Table 5.2).

So what happened in the 1980s was this. The proportions of people leaving unemployment at each duration fell, but they fell by nothing like one-half (see Table 5.2). This, however, led to an increase in the proportion of the unemployed who were long-term unemployed. Because the outflow rates are

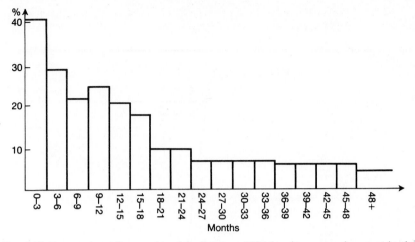

Fig. 5.12 Proportion of unemployed in January 1984 leaving unemployment in the next three months.

Table 5.1
Outflow from unemployment, 1981–1985

	% of unemployed in Jan. leaving in next 3 mos, by duration (mos) in Jan.									
	0–3	3–6	6–9	9–12	12–15	15–18	18–24	24–36	36–48	48+
1981	36.7	29.4	26.1	19.3	17.4	—	—	—	—	—
1982	40.4	31.4	23.9	21.8	18.7	24.4	18.9	—	—	—
1983	39.2	28.1	21.5	20.2	17.9	23.8	10.8	8.7	—	—
1984	41.1	29.7	22.2	25.3	21.4	18.7	10.4	7.8	6.0	4.3
1985	41.8	28.6	22.7	23.7	21.1	—	—	8.1	6.4	5.1

lower for the long-term unemployed than for those with shorter durations, an equiproportionate fall in all outflow rates leads to a more than proportionate fall in the average outflow rate.[17] If there were now a major economic recovery, the inflow into unemployment would fall sharply and so would short-term unemployment. But it is most unlikely that long-term unemployment would fall at all rapidly, unless specific measures were taken to encourage employers to hire the long-term unemployed.

Reverting to the u/v curve (5.9), Pissarides (1986) has shown that it exhibits constant returns to scale. We can therefore divide both sides by unemployment to get

$$\frac{A}{U} = f\left(g\,\frac{V}{U},\, c,\, mm\right)$$

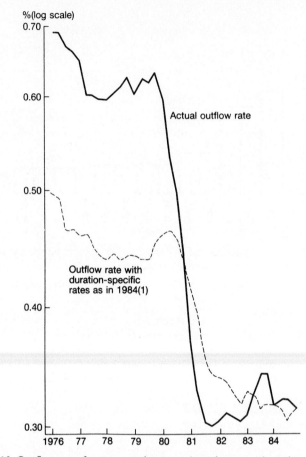

%(log scale)

Fig. 5.13 Outflow rate from unemployment (per three mos.), males, 1976–1984.

which can be substituted into (5.10) to get the long-run u/v curve. Clearly, a complete model would need an equation to explain the inflow rate (S/N). This was attempted in Nickell (1982) but is not reported here. An important factor affecting flows both into and out of unemployment is employment protection: our next factor affecting the u/v relationship.

Employment Protection

If the cost of firing workers increases, employers will become more leary about hiring. Thus the proportion (g) of vacancies they are willing to fill per period will fall. Of course, at the same time the number of firings will fall also. Since in equilibrium firings equal hirings (a), in equilibrium a also falls. What happens

Table 5.2
Outflow from unemployment, 1976–1985

| | % of unemployed in Jan. leaving in the next 3 mos, by duration (mos.) in January | | | |
	0–3	3–6	6–9	9+
1976	56.2	38.9	31.8	18.1
1977	56.0	41.4	35.1	20.1
1978	54.9	41.8	37.5	21.5
1979	56.6	41.0	35.0	16.6
1980	52.0	36.7	30.0	17.3
1981	36.7	29.4	26.1	13.9
1982	40.4	31.4	23.9	15.3
1983	39.2	28.1	21.5	13.8
1984	41.1	29.7	22.2	13.6
1985	41.8	28.6	22.7	12.1

to the u/v curve (and thus to equilibrium unemployment) depends on which of these effects dominates.

Let us begin with the facts about employment protection laws and then give evidence on their net effect. There have been three main changes. The Redundancy Payments Act 1965 introduced statutory payments when a worker is made redundant, a part of which is a direct cost to the employer. The Industrial Relations Act 1971 established legal rights against unfair dismissal (now covering all workers employed for over two years by the same employer). The Employment Protection Act 1975 extended the periods of notice required before termination.

Employment protection has been studied in some detail in Nickell (1979, 1982), with mixed results. The net impact on unemployment is unclear. As we have said, if it becomes more difficult or expensive for firms to reduce employment, this will reduce flows into unemployment. So employment protection must be a cause of the downward trend in inflow during the 1970s, But, by making employers more choosy in hiring, it will also reduce the outflow from unemployment. Both these effects were detected in Nickell (1982), but the net impact was in the direction of a reduction in unemployment. This result is, however, very tentative, since the variable used to capture the legislation (numbers of Industrial Tribunal cases) is clearly rather weak. Survey evidence is also ambiguous (see Jackman, Layard, and Pissarides 1984). The most recent survey by the CBI asked employers how (1) abolition or reduction of redundancy entitlements and (2) abolition or reduction of unfair dismissal rights would affect the number of their employees. The replies were

	Definitely increase employment	Possibly increase employment
Redundancy entitlements	5%	14%
Unfair dismissal rights	3%	7%

Thus, reverting to the u/v curve, it seems quite likely that employment protection has had little effect, reducing equilibrium a and g by roughly offsetting magnitudes.

Mismatch

Another variable affecting the location of the u/v curve is the mismatch (mm) between unemployment and vacancies. Other things equal, unemployment will tend to rise if the unemployed became less well matched to the vacancies available. We can therefore ask, Are structural factors an important part of the explanation for the rise in unemployment? This is a tough question. The first issue is, Which structural dimension matters most? Probably the most serious is the regional dimension. Hardly any of the unemployed find work in a different region from the one they worked in before. By contrast, two-thirds of men who became unemployed in autumn 1978 and found work within four months found it in a different industry (24 categories) or occupation (18 categories) from their previous job.

The next issue is how to measure mismatch. The most obvious concept of a good match is one where the ratio of unemployment to vacancies is the same in each region.[18] The incidence of structural unemployment could then be measured by the proportion of the unemployed who would have to be in a different region if perfect matching were secured. This is given by

$$mm = \tfrac{1}{2}\sum|u_i - v_i|$$

where u_i is the proportion of the unemployed in region i and v_i is the proportion of vacancies. This index is charted in Figure 5.14.[19] It shows that the degree of regional mismatch has been reduced.

This may seem surprising, for many people feel that the amount of structural unemployment has risen. However, both statements are true. When we measure regional mismatch we are trying to find an index that could have *caused* an increase in unemployment. When we measure the amount of structural unemployment, we measure the *number* of unemployed people who would have to shift regions in order to restore proportionality between unemployment and vacancies. This is given by

$$SU = mm(uL).$$

In recent years structural unemployment has risen because of the increase in unemployment, but not because of an increase in mismatch. Mismatch has

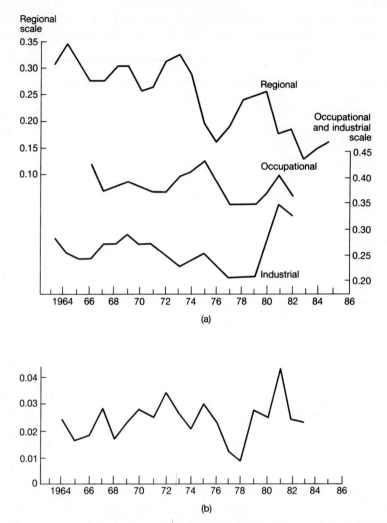

Fig. 5.14 (a) Mismatch indices, 1964–1985. (b) Index of change in the industrial composition of employment, 1964–1983.

fallen, because the proportional rise in unemployment rates has been less in the high-unemployment regions. Structural unemployment has risen, because the *absolute* rise in unemployment rates has been greater in the high-unemployment regions.[20] But to see that regional imbalance is not a *cause* of the shift of the aggregate u/v curve, we have only to note that the proportional increase in unemployment at given vacancies is on average higher *within* each region than it is for the national aggregate.[21]

Turning to other dimensions of mismatch, we find in Figure 5.14 no obvious trend in occupational mismatch (similarly calculated). As regards industrial mismatch, however, this was high in 1981 and 1982. This measure depends on classifying the unemployed by the industry of their last job, and unfortunately this analysis of the unemployed has now been discontinued, so we cannot tell how mismatch has been progressing recently in that dimension.

But it is important to form some view. Presumably, mismatch is increased by larger changes in the industrial structure of employment. Industrial structure did change quite sharply in 1981 and 1982, but this turbulence has now declined. To indicate this we show, in Figure 5.14, one half of the sum of the absolute changes in employment shares in each of 24 sectors.[22] There has been no major upward trend in this measure of turbulence since the early 1970s. In the econometric work reported earlier we used a simplified version of this index—namely, the absolute change in the share of unemployment falling within the 'production industries'. This suggested that since the 1960s increases in mismatch have raised wage pressure by 1 percentage point, implying a rise in unemployment of a little over 1 point.[23]

Our general conclusion is that increases in mismatch are not an important reason for the outward shift of the u/v curve. We also doubt whether employment protection is that important. So what could account for that part of the outward shift not explained by long-term unemployment?

Benefits

The obvious explanation is some aspect of the benefit system. Let us examine first the level of benefits. If, when productivity rises, benefits rise as much as wages, we should probably expect unemployment to remain unchanged. But if the replacement ratio (of benefits to net income in work) changed, we should expect unemployment to change. But the replacement ratio has changed little since the mid-1960s, though it has fluctuated considerably, rising by about 30 per cent between the late 1950s and the late 1960s.[24] So the replacement ratio cannot explain much of the increase in unemployment since 1970.

A more important factor may be the administration of benefits, and the application of the work test. There is good evidence that this was applied less strictly from the later 1960s onwards, even before the economic troubles of the 1970s (Layard 1986). Then during the 1970s the job centres became physically separated from the benefit offices, making it even more difficult to ensure that claimants were encouraged to seek work. Since 1982 claimants have not even been required to register at job centres. Casual impression also suggests that there have been profound changes in social attitudes to living on the dole—the most obvious of these being the attitudes of students. Thus, by a process of elimination, and on grounds of inherent plausibility, there is good reason to suppose that an important reason for the shift of the u/v curve has been changes in the intensity with which the unemployed seek work at given vacancies.

Jackman and Williams (1985) have used individual cross-section data to study the intensity of job search, as measured by the number of job applications; for men who became unemployed in autumn 1978 and were still unemployed four months later, the median number of applications was one per month. (The figure in the United States seems to be four times as high.) Application rates are lower for those made redundant than for those who quit. Since the unemployed now include a lower than usual proportion who quit, this might help to explain the outward shift of the u/v curve.

Jackman and Williams also find that application rates are affected by benefits. The effect of benefits on application rates is directly in line with the findings of Narendranathan, Nickell, and Stern (1985), who estimate the effect of benefits on job-finding using the same sample. The respective elasticities with respect to benefits were -0.25 and -0.40.[25] These elasticities are not high. They reflect the amount by which benefits displace the wage line in Figure 5.2 to the left. The total effect on unemployment should be slightly less than this. However, when we include the replacement ratio in our time-series wage equation, we estimate the total elasticity of unemployment with respect to benefits to be around 0.7 at the sample mean. Even this is not high. It implies that the 30 per cent rise in the replacement ratio between the late 1950s and the late 1960s increased unemployment by only about 20 per cent—or half a percentage point.

Finally, while we are considering the role of benefits, we must refer to a more indirect mechanism through which they may exert their influence. If benefits are available without time limit and without an effective work test, it is not surprising that, when employment is reduced by a major adverse shock, long-term unemployment develops with all the bad implications we have already discussed. A sensible solution seems to be the one advocated by Beveridge, that, after some time limit, public support for those without regular jobs should be provided through payment for work done (or training received) on a public programme.

Unions

We come now to a radically different way of viewing the labour market, in which unions play a crucial role. As we have already said, we do not believe that specifically union-oriented analysis throws much light on the rise in unemployment since 1979, since it cannot also explain the shift in the u/v curve (which is evidently closely related to the rise in unemployment).[26] However, the unions are an important feature of the scene, and we must attempt to clarify their impact.

We can begin with union membership. Almost half of all employees in employment are members (roughly 60 per cent of manual workers and 40 per cent of white-collar). The rates vary widely between sectors, as the following figures for 1979 show (Bain 1983, p. 11):

Manufacturing	
Manual	80%
White collar	44%
All	70%
Construction	37%
Private services	17%
Public sector	82%

About one-fifth of all workers are in closed shops, meaning that to hold the job they have to join the union.

But more important are the proportion of workers whose wages are determined by collective bargaining, whether or not they themselves are union members. Of full-time workers in 1978, the proportions 'covered' by collective agreements were 71 per cent of men and 68 per cent of women (New Earnings Survey for 1978). Most of the collective bargaining that matters is now with single employers, and the majority of that is at the plant level. Thus, if we confine ourselves to private sector employees, and ask what is the most important level of pay bargaining affecting their wages, the answers from the 1980 Workplace Industrial Relations Survey were as follows (Bain 1983, p. 144):

Single-employer bargains	
Plant level	30%
Firm level	18%
Multi-employer arrangements	
National or regional bargains	21%
Wages councils	5%
Management decisions	26%

For non-manual workers, management decision is more common, and national or regional bargains less common. Likewise, for smaller establishments, managerial decision is more common and firm-level bargaining less so. The general conclusion is that, although 80 per cent of unionists are now in the largest 22 unions, the pattern of bargaining is highly decentralized.

What are its effects? First, unions appear to raise the wages of manual male trade unionists by about 11 per cent above those of other similar workers. This estimate comes from Stewart (1983) and is based on individual data from the National Training Survey. According to Stewart (1985), trade unions have affected wages mainly where there is a closed shop, especially where a pre-entry closed shop (now outlawed) existed.

To get some feeling for how the union mark-up has changed over time, we have to use a different procedure, based on a cross-section of industries rather than individuals (Layard, Metcalf, and Nickell, 1978). The results of this, updated and scaled for consistency with Stewart, are shown in Figure 5.15. This shows that the mark-up has tended to rise over time. During the 1970s the

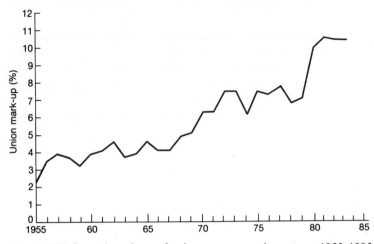

Fig. 5.15 Estimated mark-up of union over non-union wages, 1955–1985.

rise was accompanied by a rise in trade union membership and, at least up to 1973, can be taken as associated with autonomous wage-push (the end of deference and all that). Since 1980 union membership has fallen somewhat, even among employees. One might therefore be inclined to explain the high mark-up in the 1980s by the disinflation of 1981–3, since deflation typically causes a rise in the union mark-up (Lewis 1963). On the other hand, Batstone (1984) reports that shop steward organization and activity has not declined significantly since 1980, and today's high mark-up may therefore in part reflect continued militancy.

If this is the effect of unions on wages, What is their effect on employment?[27] The effect is indirect. For unions do not normally bargain over the level of employment in their enterprises (Oswald and Turnbull 1985; Oswald 1984). Bargaining does take place when redundancies are proposed, but experience of the last five years shows that unions' ability to affect the scale of redundancy is limited. (They do of course frequently ensure that there is maximum use of voluntary redundancy, and that compulsory redundancy follows the principle of 'last in–first out'.) Bargaining also takes place over manning levels, but this affects the ratio of employment to capital rather than the total level of employment. (Investment is not generally bargained over.) So bargains basically concern wages, and then employers determine employment subject to the wages that have been determined.

The outcome is unlikely to clear the market in the union sector. But what about the non-union sector? Will not this be market-clearing? Suppose it is. Then all unemployment will be voluntary. Jobs are always available in the non-union sector, and workers choose not to take them, either because they want a holiday, permanent or temporary (Minford 1985), or because it is more efficient to search for a union job while unemployed than while working in the non-union sector (Hall 1975).[28]

This model may be depicted as in Figure 5.16 (ignoring issues to do with search). A few points should be noted. First, the supply curve is rising as a function of the real wage in the competitive sector, given the level of real benefit. It is essential to recognize the diversity of human nature in this way, and misleading to say that wages in the competitive sector are determined at the level of benefit (plus or minus a fixed mark-up)—as though all workers

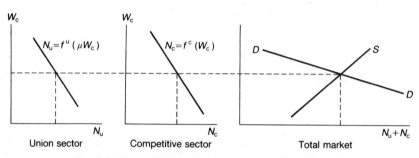

Fig. 5.16 A market-clearing model of the labour market.

were equally hard-working. According to our earlier estimate from Narendranathan *et al.* (1985), the elasticity of this supply curve is in fact only 0.1 (when unemployment is 10 per cent). The next point to note is that the demand for union labour depends on μW_c where μ is 1 plus the mark-up of the union over the non-union wage. Clearly, if μ rises, the aggregate labour demand curve *DD* moves to the left; competitive wages fall, and employment falls because fewer people are willing to work. This, in essence, is Minford's account of how unions destroy employment.

There is, however, one reason that makes it impossible to accept the model as a satisfactory stylization of the system. All the evidence suggests that even unskilled markets may fail to clear, and, even more important, that the degree to which they do clear varies sharply from period to period. This evidence comes from the answers of Confederation of British Industry employers to the question, Is your output likely to be limited in the next four months by shortages of (a) skilled labour, (b) other labour? The answers are graphed in Figure 5.17. They show how unhelpful is the assumption of continuous market-clearing. They also show that the less skilled occupations (which in Confederation of British Industry firms tend to be less unionized) have a particular excess supply of labour.[29]

If the market-clearing framework helps little, how can one conceive of the effect of union power upon employment? We adopt a simple synthetic approach. In some cases wages are set by firms, and *their* efficiency wages may

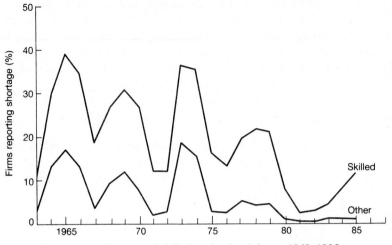

Fig. 5.17 Shortage of skilled and other labour, 1963–1985.

not be market-clearing. In other cases unions play a role in bargaining, and again their pushfulness will raise the degree of wage pressure. The final outcome (e.g. in Figure 5.7) is one where at prevailing wages more people are wanting work than there is work available. Most of them eventually get into work through the process of matching the unemployed to vacancies. Benefits slow down the speed of this matching and thus create wage pressure and reduce employment. Union power also creates wage pressure and reduces employment. In our estimates, the increase in the trade union mark-up since the 1960s has raised wage pressure by 3–4 percentage points and unemployment by 2–3 points.

Incomes Policy

A standard way to reduce wage pressure is through incomes policy. A glance at Figure 5.5 shows the powerful effect of the 1975–7 incomes policy on the rate of wage inflation. (In 1975–6 the £6 a week limit equalled 10 per cent of average pay, and in 1976–7 the limit was 5 per cent.) Wadhwani (1985) has traced these dynamic effects in a quarterly model. Our annual model has been less successful at picking them up.

Of course, after 1977 the policy began to break down,[30] making some rise in unemployment after 1979 quite likely. A major problem arose from the inability of unions to control their shop stewards. This made the TUC unwilling to endorse the policy formally after the first two years (even though it did not oppose it). Bruno and Sachs (1985) have suggested that countries responded best to the oil shock of 1973 if they had rather centralized wage bargaining, making possible 'corporatist' solutions (as in Austria and

Sweden). In more recent work with Bean (Bean *et al.* 1986), we have further explored this and shown that, among 17 OECD countries, the *more* centralized countries have 'target' real consumption wages that respond *more* strongly to unemployment and to falls in the 'feasible' real consumption wage. In the scale of corporativeness Britain ranks twelfth—near the bottom. This means that it is peculiarly vulnerable to supply shocks.

Taxes and Import Prices

A supply shock is anything that reduces the feasible real consumption wage at given employment. If we write w^* as the log of the wage (so that $w = w^* + t_1$ where t_1 is employers' labour taxes), then the log real consumption wage is

$$w^* - t_2 - (\bar{p} + t_3) + \text{constant}$$

where t_2 is the personal tax rate, t_3 is the indirect tax rate, and $\bar{p}$ is the log final output price. The relation of the latter to the price of value added (p) is given by

$$\bar{p} = p + v(p_m - p)$$

where p_m is the log price of imports and v the share of imports in GDP. Thus the log real consumption wage is

$$w - p - t_1 - t_2 - t_3 - v(p_m - p) + \text{constant}.$$

If $w - p$ remains constant, then the real consumption wage falls whenever there is a rise in taxes or in relative import prices. Thus, if taxes or relative import prices rise, and workers try to maintain their real consumption wage, they will push up $w - p$ and unemployment will have to rise to restore equilibrium. It is only if rises in taxes or relative import prices are voluntarily absorbed by workers that they do not generate wage pressure.

We estimate that all taxes except t_1 are voluntarily absorbed in the long run, but that employers' labour taxes and rises in relative import prices do increase unemployment. Since the 1960s, we tentatively estimate that labour taxes raised wage pressure by $1\frac{1}{2}$ points, and unemployment by between 1 and 2 points. The rise in relative import prices in the early 1970s raised wage pressure by $3\frac{1}{2}$ points and unemployment by 2 points, but developments in the 1980s have been more favourable, and we await their further course with bated breath.

It has often been suggested that the falls in productivity growth in the 1970s caused problems because they were resisted in wage demands. But we found no evidence that falls in productivity growth generated wage pressure.

Conclusion

Thus, to understand unemployment we have to understand the wage pressure generated at a given level of unemployment. This is now very high owing to the high proportion of long-term unemployed. Looking back over the last 15 years, wage pressure has increased partly because of union militancy, partly because of taxes, and partly because of easier social security. Mismatch has contributed little to the increase in unemployment. Even so, it is a serious problem, and we would be much better off if we had a better match between the structure of labour demand and supply. We turn now to this subject.

4. Relative Wage Rigidity and the Structure of Employment

In Section 3 we focused on the aggregate labour market, analysing its problems in terms of the inflexibility of the general level of real wages. In this section we look at the flexibility or otherwise of the relative wages of different groups, and ask how far this accounts for mismatch or other problems.

There are at least five dimensions of matching that are important: industry, region, skill, age, and sex.

Industry

We shall begin with industrial structure; for, even though many workers are not closely attached to industries, it is changes in industrial structure that primarily effect the fortunes of the different regions. The basic change in industrial structure has been the huge decline in manufacturing employment (Figure 5.18). This has certainly led to a migration of workers out of manufacturing, but to little change in relative wages.

These processes have been studied in detail by Pissarides (1978) and Pissarides and McMaster (1984a). Movement of workers between industries was found to respond to sector-specific vacancies and to relative wages, with both playing a roughly equal role in the redeployment of labour. But the role of wages is not particularly functional, since wages do not respond to sector-specific vacancies as much as to aggregate vacancies in the economy as a whole.[31]

Region

Turning to the more serious problem of regional inbalance, workers do tend to leave the high-unemployment regions (in net terms). But the movement is much less than it would be if we had a more flexible housing market (see for example Hughes and McCormick 1981). Moreover, the wage structure plays a small role in the adjustment process. It is remarkable how similar wages are in the different regions despite the huge differences in unemployment. This reflects the fact that relative wages react very weakly to unemployment differences (Pissarides and McMaster 1984b). In the upshot, if a region starts with 1 point of unemployment above the national average, it will experience 12 man-years of unemployment before all excess unemployment has been

Fig. 5.18 Manufacturing and non-manufacturing employees in employment, 1973–1986.

eliminated. Thus, to evaluate regional policy, one could compute the present value of a policy to create a lower productivity job in the region or permit the outmigration to occur towards higher-productivity regions.

Skill

One of the most basic facts about unemployment is that it is concentrated on manual workers, and nearly half of it on semi- and unskilled manual workers. In 1983 male unemployment rates were

Non-manual	5%
Skilled manual	12%
Semi- and unskilled manual	23%

Why is this?

There is no doubt that relative wages affect the relative demand for labour at different skill levels. Nissim (1984), working on certain engineering industries, estimated the Allen elasticity of substitution between skilled and semi-skilled workers at around $2\frac{1}{2}$ (s. e. = 0.3). This is crudely illustrated in Figure 5.19 (crudely because the Allen elasticity is not the same as a 'direct' elasticity).

Given the effect of wages on demand, low-wage differentials seem an

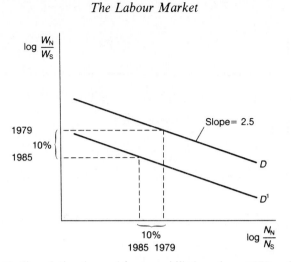

Fig. 5.19 The relative demand for non-skilled workers, 1979 and 1985.

obvious explanation of the unemployment of the less-skilled. Such differentials might be due to union preferences for equality,[32] or to employers' concepts of efficiency wages—or even of fair wages. Wages councils do not appear to be a major explanation, since only about $1\frac{1}{2}$ million workers are covered by them alone and not also by collective bargaining.

One cannot estimate how flexible skill differentials are with respect to relative unemployment rates, since there is no adequate time-series of unemployment rates by skill. However, the evidence of the Family Expenditure Survey suggests that unemployment rates for the less skilled have risen roughly in proportion to unemployment rates for the skilled (Micklewright 1983; see also General Household Survey). In other words, the proportional fall in employment has been twice as great for the less-skilled as for the skilled manual workers. At the same time, differentials have widened for men to an extraordinary degree (see Figure 5.20). Thus relative unskilled wages (say at the bottom decile) have fallen since 1979 by roughly 10 per cent relative to the mean. This is illustrated in Figure 5.19.

If both relative employment and relative wages have fallen, relative demand must have fallen substantially. With an elasticity of substitution of 2.5, relative demand must have fallen by around a third. This is a huge change. It must reflect partly increasing mechanization and partly the reduction of relative overmanning. But it brings into sharp focus the problems now facing the less skilled.

In such a situation there are two possible solutions. One is to improve the relative employment of the less skilled by subsidies to employers of less skilled labour (Layard 1985). This can reduce the NAIRU by matching demand more closely to supply. The other is to train the less skilled and thus reduce the

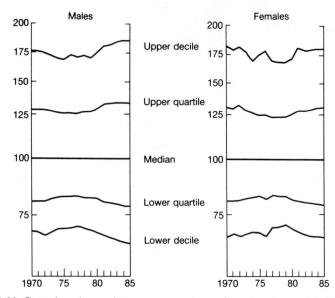

Fig. 5.20 Gross hourly earnings as a percentage of median (log scale), 1970–1985.

NAIRU by matching supply more closely to demand. In any normal optimization exercise, a bit of both would be indicated.

This brings us to the subject of training. If unemployment is due partly to rigid relative wages, the social returns to training are huge and greatly exceed the private returns (Johnson and Layard 1986). For suppose that at the NAIRU skilled labour was fully employed and unskilled was not. The social return to training an unskilled person to be skilled would be the marginal product of skilled labour (rather more if skilled labour and less-skilled are complementary so that more skilled labour raises the demand for the less-skilled). But what are the private returns to training—to the firm and the worker combined? They are the skilled wage minus the unskilled wage (after adjusting both for the probability of employment). When there is involuntary unemployment of the less skilled, there is thus a huge externality in the returns to training.

This provides a strong argument for state subsidization. Other arguments stem from imperfect capital markets (higher cost of capital for workers than firms), biased information, and so on. For these reasons, the Industrial Training Act 1964 set up a levy-grant system whereby firms paid a small percentage of payroll into a fund but were rebated if they spent an equivalent amount on training. As time went by, the system lost its marginal effect as the percentage of payroll was so low relative to the amount thaat firms were paying anyway. Yet despite this, firms were paying remarkably little. In consequence, the general view is that British workmen are less well trained than those in other European countries (Prais 1981). The government now organizes a two-year Youth Training Scheme which is open to all children who leave school at 16. But the second year of this has been introduced only this year, and it remains to be seen how effective it will be. Under present arrangements it will still be perfectly possible (which it is not in Germany) for someone to go straight into employment at 16 and to receive no training at all.[33] And even if the Youth Training Scheme does well, there will remain major shortcomings at the level of technician training and school education.[34]

Age

There are two dimensions of supply which the individual is powerless to affect: age and sex. Over time, youth unemployment has risen hugely relative to adult unemployment. This is due partly to relative wages, partly to relative population movements, and partly to general economic conditions. For the period 1959–85, the following regression explained relative male youth unemployment quite well:[35]

$$\log \frac{u_Y}{u_A} = 2.31 + 3.4 \log \frac{W_Y}{W_A} + 0.42 \log \frac{POP_Y}{POP_A} - 0.20 \log v$$
$$\qquad\qquad (7.0) \qquad\qquad (0.9) \qquad\qquad\qquad (2.1)$$

s.e. $= 0.14$, D.W. $= 1.37$ (*t*-statistics in brackets)

where W_Y/W_A is relative hourly earnings, POP_Y/POP_A is 15–19-year-olds relative to 15–60-year-olds, and v is the vacancy rate.

Up to the mid-1970s, relative wages were a potent force in explaning the rise. No one fully understands why relative wages rose so much, but the best explanation seems to be the desire of collective bargainers to pay adult rates at ever earlier ages (Layard 1982). Since the late 1970s relative youth wages have if anything fallen, presumably in response to relative unemployment. But at the same time the economic situation has worsened and relative population movements have been adverse to youth (up to now, but with an improvement hereafter). All in all, however, the performance of the British labour market in providing jobs for young people in recent years has been nothing but dismal.

Sex

When we come to sex differences in the workforce, we have to start with the huge increase in female participation. This is one of the most profound social changes of our time. After a small hiccough in the early 1980s, it seems to be proceeding unabated. The increase is entirely on the part of currently married women, the participation rate of other women having been more or less constant for the last 30 years. Most of the increase has been of part-time work.

What has caused the rush of women to the labour market? The natural first step is to look at wage levels. Women's hourly wages were very stable relative to men's up to the early 1970s (at nearly 65 per cent). The Equal Pay Act outlawed separate pay scales for men and women, and as a result women's earnings rose to around 75 per cent of men's, where they have stayed ever since. How much of this difference reflects continuing discrimination is a difficult issue. Zabalza and Arrufat (1983) argue that at least two-thirds of it reflects differences in work experience and other measurable variables; Stewart and Greenhalgh (1984) seem to indicate something more like a half.

But how far do wage movements explain the rise in women's labour supply? Up to the mid-1970s the real wages of men and women rose at roughly the same rate. Rises in men's wages tend to decrease women's labour supply (through negative income and substitution effects); rises in women's wages tend to increase it (through a large positive substitution effect, offset by a small income effect). The key issue is the relative size of these two effects. As Joshi *et al.* (1985, p. S149) show, elasticities estimated from cross-section data suggest that general wage changes cannot explain by any means all of the increase in women's participation in the early 1970s. They are however quite successful at explaining the rise in women's participation *since* the early 1970s. It is, however, remarkable that these changes have persisted so strongly in the face of the adverse economic situation.

This brings us to the question of women's employment. One would suppose on the demand side that the externally imposed rise in relative wages would have reduced relative employment. The reverse has happened. Even if we confine ourselves to the private sector, the ratio of female person-hours to male has risen since the early 1970s (see Joshi *et al.* 1985).

Two factors must account for this. The first is the shift in labour demand towards more female-intensive industries (especially services). This indeed accounts for a part of the increase. But a fixed weight demand index[36] accounts for only half of the rise in relative female employment since 1970.

What can account for the rest? Relative wage movements would have suggested a fall. Against this, the Sex Discrimination Act which also became operative in 1976 outlawed discrimination in employment on grounds of sex. This might have been interpreted to mean that employers should not reduce relative employment when relative wages were raised by the Equal Pay Act. But one would not have expected a rise in relative employment.

One explanation may be employment protection. This might lead firms to prefer part-time workers; but in fact, only those working less than 16 hours a week are exempt and two-thirds of part-time women work more than this. (Until 1975, all workers under 21 hours were exempt—or about two-thirds of part-time women workers.)

Given the buoyant employment position of women, one naturally asks whether there might not have been a growing mismatch in terms of sex between the pattern of jobs on offer and the pattern of labour supplied. To answer this, we first need evidence on the relative unemployment rates of men and women. Using survey-based estimates, we find that in the early 1970s female unemployment was about 50 per cent higher than male, becoming similar in the late 1970s and about 20 per cent lower than male in the 1980s (see Table 5.3). This suggests that mismatch may have been lower in the late 1970s. However, to obtain a more exact measure, we need to estimate the share of vacancies that was 'female-oriented'. To do this, we take the vacancies in each two-digit industry and divide them between men and women in proportion to employment in that industry. We then construct the index $U_f/U - V_f/V$ and find some evidence that this was positive in the 1970s and negative in the 1980s (see Table 5.3). However, the mismatch now in favour of women is not much greater than the mismatch in favour of men earlier.

Conclusion

In sum, the behaviour of relative wages does not do much to even out the relative imbalances in the labour market generated by shocks to demand (as between industries, regions, or skills) or to supply (as with changes in the number of young people). There is however *some* flexibility in relative wages by skill, but this is not enough to prevent a large relative oversupply of the less-skilled.

Table 5.3
Mismatch in job opportunities by sex

	Unemployment rates			Index $\dfrac{U_f}{U} - \dfrac{V_f}{V}$
	Male	Female	Female − male	
	(1)	(2)	(3)	(4)
1971	3.4	5.1	1.7	−1.0
1972	4.6	7.9	3.3	6.2
1973	3.4	5.5	2.1	9.7
1974	4.0	4.9	0.9	2.7
1975	4.9	5.0	0.1	−3.4
1976	6.5	8.5	2.0	6.9
1977	6.4	8.5	2.1	8.0
1978	6.8	8.6	1.8	−6.4
1979	6.9	7.4	0.5	1.7
1980	6.6	6.9	0.3	−1.4
1981	10.8	10.1	−0.7	−6.1
1982	12.7	10.0	−2.7	−7.4
1983	12.2	9.4	−2.8	−9.8
1984	12.8	11.4	−1.4	−6.4

5. Productivity

Having considered the extent to which potential labour resources are utilized, we now turn to the productivity of those resources that are actually used. In Figure 5.21 we see the path of output per head in both the whole economy and the manufacturing sector. The main features of both these series are summarized in Table 5.4. Until 1973 there is a period of relatively rapid growth, but this is followed by a dramatic slowdown. During the recession from 1979–81 this slowdown is even more marked, but from 1981 onwards

Table 5.4
Productivity growth rates
(% per year)

	1960–73	1973–9	1979–80	1980–4
Output per head				
Whole economy	2.5	0.9	−2.6	2.8
Manufacturing	3.5	0.9	−3.9	5.4
Output per person-hour				
Manufacturing	3.9	1.1	−1.2	5.0

there is a sharp improvement. These features are common to both series, but we shall now focus on manufacturing, since it is only here that we have enough information to enable us to analyse these changes.

The first point to note is that these shifts in productivity growth are not due to fluctuations in measured hours worked. As we can see from the third row of Table 5.4, the movements in the growth rate of output per person-hour are much the same, so we must clearly look elsewhere for an explanation. Let us first focus on the slowdown after the first oil shock. Much has been written about this phenomenon, which was common to almost all OECD countries (see, for example, Matthews 1982; Lindbeck 1983; Giersch and Wolter 1983; Denison 1983). As we can see from Figure 5.22, there was a significant reduction in the growth of the recorded gross capital stock, both for the whole economy and in manufacturing. This is clearly a contributing factor, but equally clearly it is not the whole story,[37] since the growth rate of total factor productivity (TFP) also falls sharply after 1973. In Table 5.5 we present the capital stock and TFP growth rates for manufacturing, which have a similar structure aside from 1979–80.[38] The latter series is taken from Mendis and Muellbauer (1984), which is the most careful analysis of British manufacturing productivity in the postwar period currently available. This study is based on an estimated production function which not only takes account of factor utilization but also corrects for various biases in the recorded output

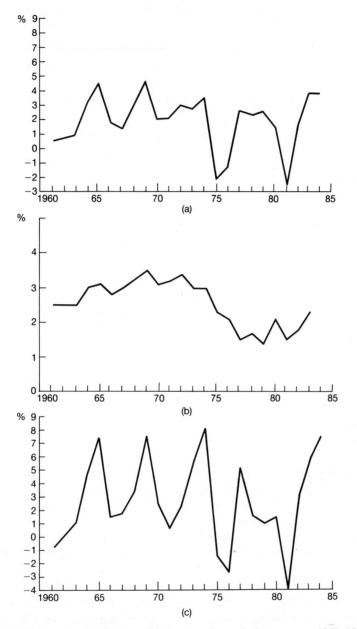

Fig. 5.21 (a) Growth of real value added per worker: whole economy, 1961–1984. (b) Growth of total factor productivity: whole economy, 1961–1983. (c) Growth of real value added per worker: manufacturing, 1961–1984.

Note: (b) is centred 5-year average.

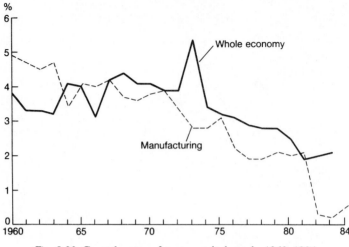

Fig. 5.22 Growth rates of gross capital stock, 1960–1984.

Table 5.5

Growth rates of capital stock and total factor productivity in UK: manufacturing
(percentages)

	1960–73	1973–9	1979–80	1980–3
Capital stock	4.0	2.3	2.0	1.0
Total factor productivity	2.5	0.8	−2.3	2.5

measure,[39] although these do not include quality changes. So the changes in total factor productivity growth can be put down to some combinations of 'technical progress' (e.g., changes in technology or working practices), trending measurement error in the quality or quantity of output, or the inputs and changes in holiday time. The latter can be disposed of quite rapidly; for, although there has been a considerable increase in paid holidays over the relevant period, this would account for a growth slowdown of only 0.1 percentage points, according to Mendis and Muellbauer.

In their view, the key to the slow-down in measured TFP lies in the measurement of the gross capital stock. Two points are worth noting here. The strong correlation between capital stock growth and TFP growth which is clear from Table 5.5 (see also Layard and Nickell 1986a, Figure 5) suggests that technical progress is embodied in new capital goods, and therefore that the slow-down in capital accumulation has a larger effect than might appear from a standard production function estimate.[40] The second and perhaps more important point is that the measured gross capital stock is based on the assumption of fixed service lives for different types of capital assets. In fact, however, scrapping of capital goods is hardly likely to be independent of economic circumstances. In particular, when demand is severely depressed, or when fuel and raw materials prices rise strongly in relative terms (as in 1973), then scrapping is likely to accelerate. In consequence, the measured capital stock series would overestimate the true series. There is some evidence in favour of this view. For example, Kilpatrick and Naisbitt (1986) present some evidence to the effect that energy-intensive industries experience a greater than average slow-down in measured TFP after 1973. More direct evidence is provided by Wadhwani and Wall (1986), who have corrected the CSO manufacturing capital stock series using firm data on a large sample of quoted companies in the manufacturing sector. Over the period 1972–4 they calculate that the CSO underestimated capital stock growth by 1.63 per cent over the two years and during 1974–80 overestimated capital stock growth by a cumulated 2.86 per cent. So the slow-down in capital stock growth after the first oil shock is indeed significantly more marked than would be implied by the published data.

Turning now to the more recent past, there was a dramatic fall in the rate of growth of output per person-hour in 1979–80, but since 1981 it has been rising rapidly, as Table 5.4 indicates. The initial decline is partly a cyclical phenomenon, but it does correspond to a similar decline in measured TFP, which is corrected for factor utilization. The key factor here is probably the extensive unrecorded scrapping of capital equipment which took place during this period. Thus, Wadhwani and Wall (1986) estimate that between 1979 and 1982 the manufacturing capital stock fell by 1.76 per cent, whereas the published data show a rise of 2.14 per cent over the same period.

Since 1981, output per person-hour has been rising at 5 per cent per annum. TFP growth appears to be back at its pre-1973 level of 2.5 per cent per annum according to Mendis and Muellbauer, and this is clearly part of the story. However, given that the capital stock growth remains below its pre-1973 level, there must be other factors involved, particularly with regard to the utilization of labour. Information on this is provided by the Percentage Utilization of Labour (PUL) series collected by Smith-Gavine and Bennett (1985). This series is based on a representative panel of some 131,500 operatives in manufacturing and directly measures their hourly work effort using standard work-study techniques. The series is pictured in Figure 5.23 and indicates that there has been a considerable rise in work effort over the period from the end of 1980. Indeed, hourly work effort is now around 5 per cent higher than its average in the period 1973–9 and around 7 per cent higher than its trough in the winter of 1980–1. The other relevant factor here is the fact that the capital equipment that was scrapped at the beginning of the 1980s would have been the least efficient, and this would have produced a significant one-off boost to productivity growth.

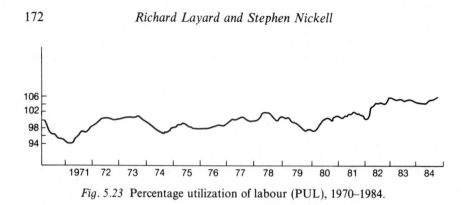

Fig. 5.23 Percentage utilization of labour (PUL), 1970–1984.

Conclusion

In summary, therefore, the recent high level of productivity growth reflects three factors: first, the reversion of total factor productivity growth to its pre-1973 level; second, a considerable growth of hourly work effort; and third, an initial boost owing to the extensive scrapping of outdated equipment. The sustainability of these factors is problematic. The continuing low growth of the measured capital stock is a danger for the first of them, and the recent flattening of the work effort (PUL) series indicates problems for the second. The third cannot be sustained by definition.

Notes

1. Non-employed job-seekers registered at employment exchanges.
2. OECD *Employment Outlook*. September 1985. The figures are standardized OECD figures for unemployed as proportion of labour force (including self-employed), and read UK 13.1, France 7.7, Germany 7.6, Italy 6.6, and USA 7.2. They relate to 1984.
3. Any tendency to use elements of historic capital cost in the price-setting process will, of course, tend to exacerbate the squeeze on profit.
4. We have found that total factor productivity has no effect in our equations. This is quite explainable (Layard and Nickell 1986a).
5. It is worth pointing out that the model (5.1), (5.2) is not (econometrically) identified as it stands, although it could be in dynamic form. However, one would not estimate it in this form but would clearly estimate the structural price equation containing the level of output market activity, along with some form of dynamic labour demand function (see Layard and Nickell 1986a). Identification would then be less problematic.
6. One of the elements of wage pressure—real import prices—is not strictly exogenous since it depends on the real exchange rate. So the NAIRU described here is conditional on this variable. In the very long run we might expect the real exchange rate to adjust to maintain trade balance, and a very long-run NAIRU would allow for this. In practice, this would not make a very huge difference (Layard and Nickell 1986a).
7. The price equation (5.1′) is a re-estimated version of that in Layard and Nickell

(1986a), and is derived by eliminating the demand variable σ from the employment equation of the form in their Table 4 and the first price equation in their Table 5. Small terms in $\Delta^3 u$, Δl, and Δk are omitted. All the relevant details may be found in Nickell (1987). Equation (5.1') corresponds to equation 24) in that paper. The wage equation is equation (5.7) below, with (5.7') being used to substitute for R. Small terms in $\Delta^3 u$ and its lags have been omitted. (5.1') and (5.7') were estimated jointly. The data are annual (1956–83) aggregates for Britain.

8. It is worth noting that, in order to generate stable inflation in the face of a reduction in wage pressure, real demand must rise. If the rise in demand is brought about, at least in part, by tax cuts, it is easy enough to achieve a zero fall in consumption wages. This point comes over clearly in the simulation in the Treasury Paper on Wages and Employment, 1985.

9. For a formal treatment of the models of wage determination being discussed here see Johnson and Layard (1986) and Nickell and Andrews (1983).

10. A simple model that captures these points is as follows. Suppose each worker in the ith firm yields net output $e\{W_i/W(1-u)\}$ where $W(1-u)$ is his expected earnings outside. The firm will choose the wage so that

$$e'\left\{\frac{W_i}{W(1-u)}\right\} \frac{1}{W(1-u)} - 1 = 0$$

with $e'' < 0$. The equilibrium wage is got by setting $W_i = W$.

11. In an extreme situation they could actually lose their jobs and be replaced by unemployed workers—as in Rupert Murdoch's fortress at Wapping.

12. The kind of model implied here is captured by the notion that the ith union chooses W_i to maximize expected rents $N_i\{u(W_i) - u(W)(1-U)\}$ subject to a perceived demand curve $N_i = f(W_i, I_{i,-1})$ where $I_{i,-1}$ is last year's inflow into unemployment from the firm. Taking the first-order condition and *then* setting $W_i = W$ and $I_{i,-1} = I_{-1}$ gives a national wage equation $W = g(U, I_{-1})$.

13. If so, there would still be a long-run natural rate of unemployment. For even if the wage equation was flat, the price equation has a slope. But the implied natural rate would be very sensitive to wage pressure (z).

14. Our wage equation confirms that the labour force (L) affects employment through its effect on wage behaviour. We find that the log of the unemployment rate $(1 - N/L)$ is the best explanatory variable. If $\log N$ is entered in addition, it is insignificant. To see whether the labour force was generally significant in wage equations, David Grubb has estimated the following equations for 19 OECD countries on annual data 1952–82 (the coefficients and t-statistics are unweighted averages):

$$\dot{w} - \dot{w}_{-1} = 1.7 + 0.69(\dot{p} - \dot{w})_{-1} - 0.33(w - p)_{-1} - 1.91l + 2.00n - 0.17h + 0.26T$$
$$\quad (3.0) \qquad\qquad (1.5) \qquad\qquad\qquad (1.6) \quad (2.3) \quad (0.2) \quad (0.3)$$

where h is log hours per worker and T is time.

15. This is based on equation (3) of Table 1 in Nickell (1986). In estimating that equation (which is based on annual data), it was impossible to detect an effect of the $\Delta^2 p$ term. However, from the quarterly wage equation in Layard and Nickell (1986), we know that such an effect exists (albeit rather a small one, compared with that in the price equation), and we have used the estimate from that equation to obtain the coefficient on an equivalent annualized variable. The coefficients in the Nickell (1986) equation are consistently estimated despite the presence of an

omitted variable $(p-p^e)$ since the latter is orthogonal to the instruments used in estimation.

16. They found that the doubling in the proportions of long-term unemployed since 1979 would predict about a 20 per cent rise in the level of unemployment at given vacancies. We shall show below that in fact changes in duration explain rather more than this. There are two reasons why the proportions fall with duration. One is the way in which duration affects workers' morale and employers' perceptions (i.e., the duration-dependence of the chances of outflow for a given individual). The other is a selectivity effect—that the more motivated and desirable workers find jobs quicker, so that the proportion finding jobs is lower at long durations. To the extent that we are using the duration structure to explain the falling average outflow probability, we are assuming a constant level of true state-dependence and a constant distribution of characteristics among those becoming unemployed.

17. If the proportions p_t leaving unemployment after duration t fall by a common multiple (λ) at all durations, the overall proportions leaving unemployment fall by more than λ. This applies in the steady state, and follows from the shift in the duration structure towards long durations. It can be illustrated easily in the case where the proportion leaving is λp up to duration T and $\lambda p'$ $(<\lambda p)$ thereafter. Suppose an inflow of unity. The stock of unemployed is then

$$\frac{1}{\lambda p}(1-e^{-\lambda pT})+\frac{e^{-\lambda pT}}{\lambda p'}=\frac{1}{\lambda}\left\{\frac{1}{p}+e^{-\lambda pT}\left(\frac{1}{p'}-\frac{1}{p}\right)\right\} \qquad \left(\text{with } \frac{1}{p'}>\frac{1}{p}\right).$$

when λ falls, this rises by a multiple exceeding $1/\lambda$. It follows that the average proportion leaving has fallen more than in proportion to λ. Figure 5.13 shows how the fall in the average proportion leaving can be decomposed into (1) the direct effect of changes in the ps and (2) the effect of changes in the duration structure (largely owing in turn to changes in the ps). Comparing the beginning and end-year, we can write the change in the average proportion leaving as

$$p_1 f_1 - p_0 f_0 = p_1(f_1-f_0)+f_0(p_1-p_0)$$

where p is the vector of ps and f the vector of proportions (f_t) with duration t. Looking at the right-hand side, the fall in the dotted line measures $p_1(f_1-f_0)$, which is approximately half the total change.

18. This requires U_i/V_i to be the same everywhere. Two alternatives are less relevant:

    (a) the ratio U_i/N_i, but this does not take into account that the unemployed get employed by finding vacancies;
    (b) the ratio $(U_i+N_i)/V_i$, but this does not take into account the fact that almost half of all vacancies are filled by the unemployed. Thus the fraction of unemployed who are looking for work exceeds the fraction of the employed looking for work by roughly the ratio N_i/U_i. If one knew exactly what fraction of employed workers were looking (λ_i), a good index might be $(U_i+\lambda_i N_i)/V_i$.

19. This is taken from Jackman and Roper (1987). For an alternative index see Nickell (1979).

20. The remarks are approximate and are based on the following line of thought. Suppose two regions, with region 1 the high-unemployment region: then, first,

$$mm=\frac{U_1}{U}-\frac{V_1}{V}.$$

If U_1/U falls, *mm* falls unless there are offsetting falls in V_1/V, which is unlikely.

Second,

$$SU = U_1 - \frac{V_1}{V} U.$$

So

$$\frac{dSU}{dU} = \frac{dU_1}{dU} - \frac{V_1}{V}$$

assuming V_1/V unaltered. This is positive if

$$\frac{dU_1}{L_1} > \frac{dU}{L} \frac{V_1/L_1}{V/L}.$$

Since $V_1/L_1 < V/L$ (since 1 is the high-unemployment region), $dU_1/dL_1 > dU/L$ is sufficient for $dSU/dU > 0$.

21. If one wished to argue that regional imbalance had worsened, one would need to argue that the share of *involuntary* unemployment in the North had risen. If we assume that voluntary unemployment is the same in all regions, this would require a huge growth in voluntary unemployment. An example is given in the table, where the total columns are actual and the other columns are hypothetical. Alternatively, we could assume more voluntary unemployment in the North (and smaller growth in voluntary unemployment in each region). But this seems implausible.

	South-East			North		
	Voluntary	Involuntary	Total	Voluntary	Involuntary	Total
1979	1	2	3	1	6	7
1985	7	3	10	7	11	18

22. That is, $\frac{1}{2}\sum|\Delta e_i|$ where e_i is the employment share. This shows the extent to which unemployment is moving from one sector to another.
23. See Layard and Nickell (1986a, Table 11), which also provides the source for similar remarks below about other z variables.
24. For a discussion of the benefit system see Layard (1986). See also Atkinson and Micklewright (1985).
25. The elasticities with respect to incomes in work were 0.96 and 0.87, respectively. This implies that, as incomes rise at a given replacement ratio, job-finding increases and thus unemployment falls. In time-series this proposition seems implausible.
26. For a fuller discussion of the shift in the u/v curve see Pissarides (1986).
27. Note that there are other effects on output through effects on productivity. Average effects on output via strikes cannot be large since in an average year only $\frac{1}{4}$ per cent of man-days are lost that way.
28. The holiday argument is as follows. A worker will choose to be unemployed if, in the week in question, $u^i(W_c, H) < u^i(B_i, 0)$. The search argument adds in to the right-hand side an extra term reflecting the present value of the expected gain in future utility from searching rather than accepting a job at W_c.
29. Even in 1978, the duration of vacancies was as follows: skilled manual 6.2 weeks,

semi-skilled and personal service 2.6 weeks, unskilled 1.5 weeks (Jackman *et al.* 1984). Vacancy rates were similar in all occupations.

30. The limits were 1977–8, 10 per cent; and 1978–9, 5 per cent.
31. Pissarides and McMaster (1984a). In 18 sectors real wages were regressed on log national vacancies and on log sector-specific vacancies, with six and five signs wrong respectively and the sum of the two effects always positive. But real wages were significantly affected by national vacancies in eight sectors and by sector-specific vacancies in three sectors only.
32. If wages are log normal, the mean exceeds the median and the median voters will gain from equalization (Ashenfelter and Layard 1983).
33. In January 1985, 28 per cent of 16-year-olds were in the Youth Training Scheme and 13 per cent in employment.
34. School education is dealt with in the fuller version of this paper (Layard and Nickell 1986b).
35. For a fuller discussion (up to 1979) see Layard (1982). See also Wells (1983) and Joshi *et al.* (1985).
36. The index is

$$I_t = \sum_i \left(\frac{F_i}{M_i}\right)_{70} \frac{M_{it}}{M_t}$$

where F is female person-hours, and M is male person-hours.
37. Indeed, Mendis and Muellbauer (1984) calculate that the direct effect of the slow-down in capital accumulation explains less than one-quarter of the decline in productivity growth.
38. There is considerable evidence that the official statistics for capital stock growth in 1979–80 are highly misleading in the sense of being subject to a strong upward bias. This is discussed later.
39. The biases corrected for include the following. (a) Gross output bias, which arises because the Central Statistical Office approximates changes in value added by using gross output changes with value added weights. So if raw materials become more expensive, value added tends to increase faster than gross output because of substitution away from raw materials, inducing a downward bias in published data. (b) Domestic price index bias: about two-thirds of manufactured output is based on current price data deflated by wholesale price indices for *home* sales. So if the ratio of foreign to domestic wholesale prices rises, the measured price increase based on home sales is too low and thus the measured volume increase is too high. (c) List price bias: although the price indices used are supposed to measure transaction prices, they are, at least in part, based on list prices. A reduction in competitive pressure is likely to reduce discounts (on the list price), and so the measured price rise understates the true price increase leading to an overstatement of the volume increase. (d) Finally, there are price controls. These tend to be widely evaded by spurious quality improvements or relabelling, and thus official price indices tend to rise more slowly than true indices when price controls are in operation with the opposite effect on output. This bias, of course, moves into reverse when controls are removed, and Darby (1984) makes much of this argument in his analysis of the US productivity slowdown.
40. Attempts at estimating putty–clay production functions do not, however, provide any evidence either way on this issue (see Malcolmson and Prior 1979, and Mizon and Nickell 1983).

References

Ashenfelter, O. and Layard, R. (1983), 'Incomes Policy and Wage Differentials'. *Economica*, 50, 127–45.

Atkinson, A. B. and Micklewright, J. (1985), *Unemployment Benefits and Unemployment Duration*. London: London School of Economics, Suntory–Toyota International Centre for Economics and Related Disciplines.

Bain, G. S. (ed.) (1983), *Industrial Relations in Britain*. Oxford: Basil Blackwell.

Batstone, E. (1984), *Working Order*. Oxford: Basil Blackwell.

Bean, C., Layard, R., and Nickell, S. (1986), 'The Rise in Unemployment: A Multi-Country Study'. *Economica*, 53, S1–S23.

Bennett, A. J. and Smith-Gavine, S. A. N. (1985), *The Index of Percentage Utilisation of Labour: Bulletin to Co-operating Firms*, no. 40. Leicester: Leicester Polytechnic, School of Economics and Accounting.

Blanchard, O. and Summers, L. H. (1986), 'Hysteresis and the European Unemployment Problem'. Massachusetts Institute of Technology, mimeo.

Bruno, M. and Sachs, J. (1985), *Economics of Worldwide Stagflation*. Cambridge, Mass.: Harvard University Press.

Budd, A., Levine, R., and Smith, P. (1986), 'Unemployment, Vacancies and the Long-Term Unemployed', London Business School, Centre for Economic Forecasting Discussion Paper no. 154.

Darby, M. (1984), 'The US Productivity Slowdown: A Case of Statistical Myopia'. *American Economic Review*, 73, 301–22.

Denison, E. F. (1983), 'The Interruption of Productivity Growth in the United States'. *Economic Journal*, 93, 56–77.

Giersch, H. and Wolter, F. (1983), 'Towards an Explanation of the Productivity Slowdown: An Acceleration–Deceleration Hypothesis'. *Economic Journal*, 93, 35–55.

Hall, R. E. (1975), 'The Rigidity of Wages and Persistence of Unemployment'. *Brookings Papers on Economic Activity*, 2, 301–50.

Hughes, G. and McCormick, B. (1981), 'Do Council Housing Policies Reduce Migration Between Regions? *Economic Journal*, 91, 919–37.

Jackman, R., Layard, R., and Pissarides, C. (1984), 'On Vacancies'. London School of Economics Centre for Labour Economics, Discussion Paper no. 165 (Revised).

Jackman, R. and Roper, S. (1987), 'Structural Unemployment', special issue on Wage Determination and Labour Market Flexibility. *Oxford Bulletin of Economics and Statistics*, forthcoming.

Jackman, R. and Williams, C. (1985), 'Job Applications by Unemployed Men'. London School of Economics Centre for Labour Economics, Working Paper no. 792.

Johnson, G. and Layard, R. (1986), 'The Natural Rate of Unemployment: Explanation and Policy'. In O. Ashenfelter and R. Layard (eds.), *Handbook of Labor Economics*. Amsterdam: North-Holland.

Joshi, H. E., Layard, R., and Owen, S. J. (1985), 'Why are More Women Working in Britain?' *Journal of Labor Economics*, 3(1), S147–S176.

Kilpatrick, A. and Naisbitt, B. (1986), 'Energy Intensity, Industrial Structure and the Productivity Slowdown'. National Economic Development Office, mimeo.

Layard, R. (1982), 'Youth Unemployment in Britain and the US Compared'. In R. Freeman and D. Wise (eds.), *The Youth Labor Market Problem*. Chicago: University of Chicago Press.

—— (1985), 'How to Reduce Unemployment by Changing National Insurance and Providing a Job-Guarantee'. London School of Economics Centre for Labour Economics, Discussion Paper no. 218.

—— (1986), *How to Beat Unemployment*. Oxford: University Press.

——, Metcalf, D., and Nickell, S. (1978), 'The Effects of Collective Bargaining on Relative Wages'. *British Journal of Industrial Relations*, 16, 287–302.

—— and Nickell, S. (1986a), 'Unemployment in Britain'. *Economica*, special issue on unemployment.

—— (1986b), 'The Performance of the British Labour Market'. London School of Economics Centre for Labour Economics, Discussion Paper no. 249.

Lewis, H. G. (1963), *Unionism and Relative Wages in the US*, Chicago: University of Chicago Press.

Lindbeck, A. (1983), 'The Recent Slowdown of Productivity Growth'. *Economic Journal*. 93, 14–34.

—— and Snower, D. (1984), 'Involuntary Unemployment as an Insider–Outsider Dilemma'. Institute for International Economic Studies, University of Stockholm, Seminar Paper no. 282.

Malcolmson, J. and Prior, M. (1979), 'The Estimation of a Vintage Model of Production for UK Manufacturing'. *Review of Economic Studies*, 46, 719–36.

Matthews, R. C. O. (ed.) (1982), *Slower Growth in the Western World*. London: Heinemann.

Mendis, L. and Muellbauer, J. (1984), 'British Manufacturing Productivity 1955–1983: Measurement Problems, Oil Shocks, and Thatcher Effects'. Oxford, Nuffield College, mimeo.

Micklewright, J. (1983), 'Male Unemployment and the Family Expenditure Survey 1972–1980'. *Oxford Bulletin of Economics and Statistics*, 46(1), 31–53.

Minford, P. (1985), *Unemployment: Cause and Cure* (2nd edn). Oxford: Basil Blackwell.

Mizon, G. and Nickell, S. (1983), 'Vintage Production Models of UK Manufacturing Industry'. *Scandinavian Journal of Economics*, 85, 295–310.

Narendranathan, W., Nickell, S., and Stern, J. (1985), 'Unemployment Benefits Revisited'. *Economic Journal*, 95, 307–29.

Newell, A. (1984), 'Annual Indices of the Changes in the Structure of Employment by Industry and Region'. London School of Economics Centre for Labour Economics, Working Paper no. 617.

Nickell, S. J. (1979), 'Unemployment and the Structure of Labour Costs'. *Journal of Monetary Economics*, Supplement: Carnegie-Rochester Public Policy Conference, no. 11.

—— (1982), 'The Determinants of Equilibrium Unemployment in Britain'. *Economic Journal*, 92, 555–75.

—— (1987), 'Why is Wage Inflation in Britain so High?' *Oxford Bulletin of Economics and Statistics*, 49(1), 103–29.

—— and Andrews, M. (1983), 'Trade Unions, Real Wages, and Employment in Britain 1951–79', *Oxford Economic Papers*, 35, Supplement.

Nissim, J. (1984), The Price Responsiveness of the Demand for Labour by Skill: British Mechanical Engineering: 1963–78'. *Economic Journal*, 94, 000–00.

Oswald, A. (1984), 'Efficient Contracts are on the Labour Demand Curve: Theory and Facts'. Industrial Relations Section, Princeton University, Working Paper no. 178 (July).

—— and Turnbull, P. (1985), 'Pay and Employment Determination in Britain: What are Labour Contracts Really Like?' *Oxford Review of Economic Policy*, 1, 80–97.

Pissarides, C. (1978), 'The Role of Relative Wages and Excess Demand in the Sectoral Flow of Labour'. *Review of Economic Studies*, 45, 453–67.

—— (1986), 'Unemployment Flows in Britain: Facts, Theory, and Policy'. *Economic Policy*, 1(3), 499–540.

—— and McMaster, I. (1984a), 'Sector-specific and Economy-wide Influences on Industrial Wages in Britain'. London School of Economics Centre for Labour Economics, Working Paper no. 571 (2nd Revision).

—— (1984b), 'Regional Migration, Wages, and Unemployment: Empirical Evidence and Implications for Policy'. London School of Economics Centre for Labour Economics, Discussion Paper no. 204.

Prais, S. J. (1981), 'Vocational Qualifications of the Labour Force in Britain and Germany'. *National Institute Economic Review*, no. 98, 000–00.

Smith-Gavine, S. A. N. and Bennett, A. J. (1985), 'Index of Percentage Utilisation of Labour', *Bulletin to Co-operating Firms*, no. 49.

Stewart, M. B. (1983), 'Relative Earnings and Individual Union Membership in the UK'. *Economica*, 50, 111–25.

—— (1985), 'Collective Bargaining Arrangements, Closed Shop and Relative Pay'. University of Warwick, mimeo.

—— and Greenhalgh, C. A. (1984), 'Work History Patterns Patterns and the Occupational Attainment of Women'. *Economic Journal*, 94, 493–519.

Wadhwani, S. (1985), 'Wage Inflation in the UK', *Economica*, 52, 195–208.

—— and Wall, M. (1986), 'The UK Capital Stock: New Estimates of Premature Scrapping'. *Oxford Review of Economic Policy*, 2(3), 44–55.

Wells, W. (1983), 'The Relative Pay and Employment of Young People'. Department of Employment Research Paper no. 42.

Zabalza, A. and Arrufat, J. (1983), 'Wage Differentials Between Married Men and Women in Great Britain: The Depreciation Effect of Non-Partivipation'. London School of Economics Centre for Labour Economics, Discussion Paper no. 151.

CHAPTER 6

Policy for Industry

John Kay and David Thompson

London Business School and Institute for Fiscal Studies

1. Introduction

This paper assesses the role of industrial policy, in principle and in practice, in a competitive economy. In this environment the obvious role of government is to correct market failure, to create competition where competition does not exist, and to regulate it where it does not work.

Intervention to tackle market failure, however, may be confronted by regulatory failure. The principal merits of a market-based approach to resource allocation are those of efficiency in the use of information, and incentive compatibility. Information is used efficiently because it is sufficient that individual agents—firms or consumers—know the prices that prevail in the market and their own costs or preferences. Firms do not need to know the cost structures or production processes of other firms, or the preferences of actual or potential consumers. Nor is it necessary for the government to obtain this information. Incentive compatibility implies a structure that is robust to selfish or opportunistic behaviour by individuals. Firms are efficient not because they are persuaded of the social benefits of efficiency, but because it is in their own interests to be efficient.

Any regulatory intervention is subject to these problems of information and incentives, and it is this that leads to the possibility of regulatory failure. The regulator may not have sufficient information to define his objectives for the regulated, and the regulated may not have incentives to provide it. Nor will the regulated firm necessarily wish to achieve what the regulator prescribes. It is apparent that the problems of information and incentives are closely linked. If the regulator held all necessary information he would not need to be concerned about the motives of those he was regulating; and if he was confident about their motives, his requirements for information would be correspondingly reduced.

The policies we shall describe in this paper began their recent evolution in the late 1940s, when competition policy was introduced and important sectors of British industry were nationalized. We can characterize the approach adopted then as one of concern for market failure without realization of the likelihood of regulatory failure. The newly formed public corporations were

The authors are grateful for comments and suggestions made by participants at the Conference and by Jim Fairburn, Dennys Gribbin, Dieter Helm, and David Starkie. Particular thanks are due to John Vickers who acted as discussant to an earlier draft of this paper. The authors are grateful for financial support from the Economic and Social Research Council; the usual disclaimer applies.

given a rather general objective of pursuing the 'public interest', with little more specific guidance. It was assumed that they would be able to establish what that public interest was, and would wish to promote it.

But the possibility of regulatory failure became increasingly apparent, and promoted changes in the style of intervention. It is only a mild exaggeration to suggest that the pendulum has now swung fully in the opposite direction, and that current policy is motivated primarily by concern for regulatory failure even at the expense of ignoring market failure. This has led to anxiety to restrict the scope of the Monopolies and Mergers Commission (as it now is) and other agencies of competition policy and, more radically, to the privatization of the nationalized industries. The deficiencies of government regulatory policy are perceived as so great that it is considered better to leave the activities of the formerly nationalized industries to market forces.

It will become apparent that we do not believe that either market failure or regulatory failure can be neglected. Market failure is as endemic in market economies as regulatory failure is in centrally planned ones. But policy for one should recognize the probability of the other. This suggests a regulatory structure that seeks to use market forces, and to make them work more effectively, rather than to supplant them.

In the concluding sections of this paper we consider what such a policy might involve. Sections 2 and 3 review the nature of market failure and regulatory failure. Sections 4 and 5 examine how policy has evolved in practice in the light of this analysis, leading from nationalization to privatization; while Section 6 reviews competition policy. Section 7 suggests the appropriate shape of future policy.

2. Market Failure

Under familiar assumptions, competitive markets yield efficient outcomes. Allocative efficiency is secured because competition leads to relative prices which reflect costs of production. Productive efficiency is achieved because firms that fail to achieve best-practice input–output combinations earn inferior profits and face the threat of bankruptcy or take-over. Thus competitive, privately owned firms will secure efficiency provided the other conditions of the fundamental theorems of welfare economics are fulfilled. Market failures occur when these assumptions are violated. Competitive solutions may not exist, or they may exist and not be achieved, or they may be achieved but not produce socially desirable outcomes.

Many industries can be regarded as uncontestable natural monopolies in which competitive solutions do not exist. This is most obviously the case in utilities that involve distribution networks (for example, gas or electricity distribution). In each of these, the costs of providing two competing networks would probably not be a great deal less than twice what it would cost to provide a single network. These are not only natural monopolies but also sustainable monopolies (see Sharkey (1982)). Not only is it inefficient for competition to emerge, but also it is improbable that it will in fact emerge.

In other areas competition may be possible but may not be achieved. In general, profit-maximizing companies will seek to reduce the product market competition they face. The most obvious routes to achieving this—mergers with important competitors or operating price cartels in co-operation with them—are now effectively precluded. While policy prevents visible horizontal restrictions on competition, others remain. Public policy towards vertical restraints is a controversial issue. Businesses frequently seek to impose restrictions of various kinds on their suppliers or their customers, such as resale price maintenance, exclusive dealing arrangements, territorial franchising, tie-in-sales, or aggregated rebates. Traditionally, both economists and policy-makers have viewed these practices with hostility. More recently, however, an influential school of thought has sought to deny that any market failure is to be found in these cases (see Hay 1985), and in the United States, particularly, many vertical restraints are now regarded as benign.

We suspect, however, that many vertical restraints reflect one of two common sources of market failure: asymmetries in information, or the pursuit of entry-deterring strategies. Over-charging for spare parts or after-sales services is a frequent subject of anti-trust investigation. While this is treated as abuse of a monopoly position in the post-sale market, it may more often reflect manufacturer exploitation of consumer ignorance of the full cost of purchase. This difference in the information available to buyers and sellers is a common reason why markets may require regulatory intervention—as with financial services, for example.

Firms may also engage in practices to restrict entry or encourage exit by their competitors. Predation is one weapon they may employ. Others may include tie-in sales, or geographical or other territorial restrictions. The difficulty for policy is to distinguish cases where these practices are used to inhibit competitive entry from those that reflect a manufacturer's genuine concern for the association of his own reputation with the ways in which his products are sold.

Policies whose objective is to deter the market entry of new competitors may not involve explicit restrictions or collusive activity, however. Recent theoretical developments in the analysis of competition in oligopolistic markets (see Vickers 1985 for a discussion) suggest that, under plausible assumptions, outcomes similar or identical to those that would result from co-operative collusion may be arrived at as a result of independent action. Furthermore, entry may be deterred by characteristics of the incumbent (in particular, the strength of bankruptcy constraint that it faces) and by actions (such as investment in capacity) whose anti-competitive content is likely to be extremely difficult to define. All of these considerations make the achievement of competitive outcomes a complex policy task.

Furthermore, where product markets are not competitive, profit maximization may no longer promote the achievement of productive efficiency. In oligopolistic markets, profit-maximizing strategies may involve deterring new entrants to the market by undertaking expenditures (e.g., in R&D or capacity) that would not otherwise be worthwhile.

In other areas, competition is both possible and may be achieved, but is perceived as having adverse results. Nationalized industry policy has usually reserved a role for 'wider economic and social objectives' (a blanket term covering a range of non-specified factors). In principle, the presence of externalities or policies that aim to discriminate in favour of particular consumer groups (e.g., the old) does not present a direct obstacle to the operation of competitive markets. A suitably designed tax/subsidy policy could be envisaged to 'internalize' external benefits and costs or achieve the desired re-distributional goal. And in practice, some limited policy initiatives have been taken along these lines (e.g., old age pensioners' travel concessions, which provide for subsidized travel on competing public transport services). However, in most cases where 'social factors' are sometimes supposed to preclude the operation of competitive markets, the obstacle is in reality either the existence of natural monopoly (e.g. rural rail services) or a perception that particular re-distributional policies are achieved more efficiently when implemented directly through pricing policy as opposed to implementation through taxes/subsidies (e.g., OAP's fuel bills).

Other areas of perceived market failure have led governments to seek to intervene in the private sector. The economics of expenditure on research, development, and innovation has received substantial elaboration in both the theoretical and empirical literature, identifying the problem of appropriability (see for example Dasgupta and Stiglitz 1980, and Spence 1984). Essentially, the incentive to undertake R&D depends on the returns earned by the investing firm. But optimal utilization of the results of research effort implies their dissemination at marginal cost, and because this will often be low (by comparison with the original research expenditure), the incentive to invest will be correspondingly reduced. In these circumstances there may be under-investment in research and development and inefficient duplication of research efforts across a number of firms. Patents are the classic policy instrument used to internalize research benefits, but only at the expense of the short-term under-utilization of research findings. In these circumstances, subsidization of research activity may show a positive cost–benefit return. (see Spence 1984 for a theoretical analysis, and Shonfield 1981 for a review of empirical findings.) It is not, however, necessarily the case that in an unregulated market there will be under-investment in research activity. In an oligopolistic market, investment in research may be carried out to signal to rivals a commitment to producing high levels of output with the intention that rivals may in consequence reduce their own planned levels of output (see Brander and Spencer 1983). In these circumstances the outcome may be over-investment in research activity. (See Vickers 1985 for an elaboration of the conditions under which over-investment and under-investment are likely to arise.)

The promotion of domestic producers, or their support in the face of capital market pressures indicating withdrawal, appears as a motivating factor in many industrial rescues. It is a familiar result that, in an open economy, subsidizing the domestic production of goods with a highly elastic import supply leads to a net economic loss; higher-cost domestically produced goods are substituted for imports at the margin. If, however, the import supply is not highly elastic, then subsidization of domestic production may confer benefits to the country concerned through an alteration in the terms of trade: the literature on optimal tariff levels elaborates the trade-off between the costs associated with higher-cost domestic production and the benefits associated with more favourable terms of trade.

Where the international market in the particular product is oligopolistic, then subsidization of domestic production may yield additional benefits by providing a first-mover advantage to the domestic producer (see Yarrow 1985); whether this is the case clearly depends, in particular, on the responses made by other firms and governments. In these circumstances government support for domestic producers may enable profitable entry into oligopolistic markets to take place where, without such support, entry could be successfully deterred by incumbents (see Dixit and Kyle 1985).

Concern to reduce the transitional costs associated with changing market and industrial structures also appears as a common interventionist rationale. Rigidities in the labour market (either between geographic areas or between skills) may lead to a divergence between the private and social opportunity costs associated with continued production. This divergence will (or should) decline over time because transitional costs are, by definition, transitory. Inappropriately specified support packages may, however, convey adverse incentives (in terms of geographic or skill relocation) whose effect may cancel out the static net benefits generated by the support.

Market failure may be characteristic not just of product markets but also of capital markets. We have already noted that take-over may be a method of restricting product market competition as well as a means of replacing inefficient management. Take-overs that reduce the achievement of competitive solutions may include not only the horizontal merger of important competitors but also the merger of vertically linked companies, each holding significant market power (requiring joint entry into the two markets by potential competitors), and conglomerate take-overs which allow the acquirer to exploit the scope for entry deterrence more effectively than the target company.

Shareholders may not be effective in enforcing the pursuit of profit or value-maximizing strategies upon management. This is particularly likely where companies are large (and the threat of take-over correspondingly lower) and where shareholdings are widely dispersed. Singh (1971) shows that size is more important than profitability in reducing the probability of acquisition. Free of pressure from shareholders, managers may pursue various alternative objectives, including growth maximization, sales maximization, output maximization, expense preference, or satisficing. A particular implication is that mergers may be implemented which serve these other objectives and whose impact upon efficiency, and profits, may be negative.

The taxonomy of market failures developed here is long but by no means exhaustive. It explains why governments have repeatedly involved themselves in the operation of markets, by nationalization, by industrial policy, and by competition policy. The range, and complexity, of possible sources of market failure also explain why intervention has often been piecemeal and pragmatic. This in turn has exacerbated the problems that these interventions face, problems to which we now turn.

3. Regulatory Failure

Where markets do not work effectively, governments may seek to impose regulatory solutions. The advantages of competitive markets are to be found in their use of information and incentives; the difficulties that regulation faces lie in these same areas. Private firms and their managers will not necessarily see the pursuit of the public interest as their primary concern or, indeed, be well placed to determine what that public interest is. It is, however, these managers who have access to the best information about costs, demand, and production possibilities, and day-to-day responsibility for a range of decisions that no government or regulatory authority can hope to supervise in any detail.

Where markets fail, two solutions appear possible. One is to persuade managers to seek welfare-maximizing policies, rather than profit maximization, and to give them advice on what the public interest is. The other is to confront them with a structure of incentives and constraints which will ensure that public and private interests coincide. The first suggests nationalization as an appropriate remedy for market failure; the second, regulation of private industry. The first makes severe demands of human nature; the second makes severe demands on the ingenuity of regulatory design and the information necessary to operate it. We consider each group of problems in turn.

The solution proposed to the supposed failure of markets to operate efficiently in the sectors where public corporations were created (primarily fuel, transport, and communications) was to substitute for private sector profit-orientated firms public corporations which, it was assumed, would seek to maximize welfare directly. As Herbert Morrison, the main architect of this approach, put it, 'The public corporation must not be a capitalist business . . . It must have a different atmosphere at its board table from that of a shareholders' meeting; the board and its officers must regard themselves as the high custodians of the public interest' (Morrison 1933). Welfare economists had already outlined the type of policies that such an organization should follow (in particular see Lange 1936, Lerner 1944, and Hotelling 1938). This demonstrated that a public corporation could mimic the welfare efficiency of a perfectly competitive market by implementating appropriately specified pricing and investment policies. More materially, where market failure was significant it could be shown that a public corporation could implement pricing and investment policies that were superior, in terms of economic efficiency, to the outcome that would result from an unregulated private market.

The critical question was whether, in practice, the corporations would choose to pursue the vaguely defined concept of 'public interest'. The Morrisonian framework provided few direct incentives to implement the policies for efficient pricing and investment suggested by the economic literature or to achieve productive efficiency (see Little 1952). It was assumed that the public spirit of managers freed from the constraints of self-interested shareholders would be sufficient. The development of the economic theory of property rights (see Furubotn and Pejovich 1972 for a survey) suggested that managers in public corporations would instead respond to the particular personal incentives they faced. If this were true, it would imply that corporations may pursue objectives very different to welfare maximization and the 'public interest'. For example, they may seek to maximize output (see Rees 1984 for an exposition), the size of their capital asset base, or what has been described by Hicks as 'the best of all monopoly profits'—that is, a quiet life. Whitbread suggested as early as 1971 that the British Airports Authority's objective was output maximization, a possibility subsequently examined by Starkie and Thompson (1985).

If public sector managers cannot be relied on to pursue the public interest, then government control of nationalized industries involves determining and implementing incentives that constrain their behaviour towards welfare-maximizing policies. Policy thus becomes very similar to that of public regulation of private firms, and indeed, this convergence has been apparent in the evolution of policy.

The problem can be characterized in a 'principal–agent' framework, in which the 'principal' (the regulatory authority or government department) relies on an agent (the corporation) to achieve its objectives in circumstances where the objectives of principal and agent diverge and in which the two parties' access to information is asymmetrical. (See Crew and Kleindorfer 1979 for an elaboration in relation to regulatory issues.)

This 'principal–agent' problem raises its own difficulties. Public corporations are in many cases statutory or natural monopolies with a corresponding dominance in information and technical expertise. The regulator must rely on the corporation for the detailed implementation of policy, and the difference in objectives may lead to inefficiencies and to a failure to achieve agreed objectives, which the regulator is unable to prevent because of inferior information.

Rate-of-return regulation of private corporations, as practised in the United States, offers little incentive to cost reduction, and positive inducements to over-capitalization (the Averch–Johnson effect). Again, regulators lack information on what would constitute an efficient level of costs. Other structures create their own distortions: the German insurance industry is limited to prescribed returns on premium income, and this leads directly to excessive marketing expenditure (Finsinger, Hammond, and Tapp 1985). Rate-of-return regulation also affects price-setting behaviour (Sherman and Visscher 1982); it encourages the use of multi-part tariffs, price discrimination, and, in some circumstances, the setting of prices below marginal costs for those activities that are comparatively capital-intensive.

The 'principal–agent' characterization supposes that the public interest objectives of the regulator are clear. In reality the government faces the same incentive problem itself: intervention may be motivated by day-to-day political pressures rather than by any clear public interest concerns. Discretionary interventions by ministers may obscure corporation objectives and blur responsibility for particular decisions and outcomes between management and government.

In the United States, the utilities are distanced from government intervention by the establishment of separate regulatory commissions. Here almost the opposite weakness has been identified, characterized as 'regulatory capture' (see Demsetz 1968 and Bailey 1973). It is argued that regulatory authorities, originally established to protect the interests of consumers against the potential market power exercisable by an industry, may come to form a symbiotic relationship with the regulated enterprise in which they effectively promote the interests of the industry (or its more dominant firms) as well as, or instead of, the interests of the industry's customers. This is a particular danger where the regulatory body is reliant on the regulated enterprise for the information and analysis that it requires to discharge its functions. The US airline industry, prior to deregulation, provides an example: the Civil Aeronautics Board, established largely to protect passenger safety, effectively became the co-ordinator of a cartel on behalf of the major carriers (Douglas and Miller 1974). It has been suggested (Starkie and Thompson 1986) that the UK Civil Aviation Authority is proposing policies on the access to scarce airport facilities which better serve the interests of the major incumbent airlines than the promotion of competition.

4. Nationalization

Nationalization in Britain was a response to market failure. The performance of certain industries of central economic importance was perceived inadequate by yardsticks of social efficiency. The answer was to substitute managers with different objectives—'high custodians of the public interest', in the striking phrase of Herbert Morrison's cited above.

The development of nationalized industry policy can be characterized as a progressive recognition that the original Morrisonian concept is flawed, and a progressive shift towards more formal 'regulation' of the public corporations. The evolution of policy can be seen through three successive White Papers in 1961, 1967, and 1978. The 1961 paper reflected a belief that in the 1950s nationalized industries had suffered from inadequate definition of objectives and weaknesses in financial control. The government therefore introduced financial targets, specified mainly as a rate of return on assets. The most elaborate framework was that of the next White Paper, in 1967: prices were to be set on the basis of long-run marginal costs, and cross-subsidization was to be eliminated. Investment was to be evaluated against a test discount rate. Social responsibilities were to be supported and accounted for separately. Financial targets were to be retained to encourage efficiency (how this might work was left unexplained), and the conjunction of a pricing rule, an investment criterion, and a financial target appears to over-determine the system. The 1978 White Paper retained the basic framework while making it less specific: prices were to take account of costs, rather than being based on long-run marginal costs: the investment programme as a whole (rather than individual projects) was to achieve a required rate of return.

The most detailed critique of the control framework for nationalized industries came from the National Economic Development Office NEDO) in 1976. NEDO was particularly critical of the extent of government intervention outside the scope of the formal objectives established in the White Papers. The most visible example was the requirement in the early 1970s for corporations to hold down price increases as part of the government's counter-inflation strategy. Separate legislation—the Statutory Corporations (Financial Provisions) Act 1974—was introduced to pay subsidies to the corporations. This clearly broke any link between prices and long-run marginal costs. More seriously, NEDO concluded that *ad hoc* interventions had substantially undermined the separation of responsibilities between government and the corporations. In practice, 'the resulting confusions lead to a situation in which Boards are not effectively required to account for their performance in a systematic or objective manner, whether it be to Parliament, to Ministers, to other legitimate interest groups or to the "wider public".' NEDO indentified two separate but interrelated problems. The first concerned the timing of decision-taking; here the concern was with short-term intervention which changed previously agreed plans and strategies. The second related to the level of decision-taking: the problem here was that intervention related not just to corporations' financial performance and overall strategy but also, in some cases, to quite detailed operating decisions (e.g., in relation to cutting bus services or closing railway lines).

In NEDO's assessment, government had responded to the deficiencies resulting from the absence of a proper framework of objectives and control by increasing the frequency of specific intervention on particular subjects. This response undermined managerial responsibility further and led to a further deterioration in performance. NEDO recommended the creation of an additional body (the Policy Council) intermediate between government and the corporations to insulate the latter from *ad hoc* intervention. Although this proposal was rejected, and only limited changes were made to the institutional framework in the 1978 White Paper, intervention has been less obviously apparent in the subsequent periods.

The additional mechanism of external financing limits does, however, provide government with further means for intervention in corporations' pricing and investment policies. It is frequently maintained that industries' capital programmes are subject to short-term restrictions, and it has recently been argued that the external financing limit (EFL) has been used to raise electricity prices above marginal costs (see Yarrow 1985). Whether such implicit taxation is appropriate is not the issue; it illustrates that intervention is not precluded by the existing framework, and the fact that it is less obviously apparent may simply reflect the current government's aim of avoiding intervention, rather than any change in the underlying framework.

These weaknesses have been reflected in the performance of the industries. NEDO undertook assessments of their productive efficiency: subsequent work by Pryke (1981), Molyneux and Thompson (1987) and reports by the Monopolies and Mergers Commission (MMC) have dealt with similar issues. Evaluation of the productive efficiency of a public corporation where no similar activities are performed in the UK by other firms is by no means straightforward. NEDO concluded that financial targets had been an ineffective check on productive efficiency and that few attempts had been made to find some relevant indicator. Pryke (1981) observes a wide range of performance, with large unit cost reductions where technology had changed or input prices have fallen (airlines, telecoms, gas) but indifferent results elsewhere.

Efficiency audits from the MMC have also produced varying reports. In some cases the pursuit of efficiency is commended: 'we were impressed by the professional commitment of those whom we met and their desire to provide a good and cost-effective service' (MMC: Anglia and North West Water Authorities, 1982). More typically, there is a mixture of favourable and unfavourable conclusions. In some of these cases the result is probably little different to that which would be found from a similar audit of a private company in a more competitive environment. Finally, the performance of a number of industries is strongly criticized (for example, London Transport, the Post Office, Civil Aviation Authority). Although it would be difficult, from this evidence, to diagnose nationalized industry productive efficiency as a primary industrial problem, there is some scope for improvement in performance.

The attempts of nationalized industries to achieve allocative efficiency—to set a pricing structure that reflects relative costs and an investment strategy that responds to consumer needs as measured in the market—have been particularly open to criticism. NEDO established that few corporations had implemented marginal cost pricing, and that it had generally been argued that most investment was 'essential' for the maintenance of a network or system (as in telecoms or gas distribution) whose size and nature was statutorily determined. Departments had ususally acquiesced in this. It may therefore be concluded that the attempt to impose rules derived from welfare economics had little effect on anything that the nationalized industries had actually done.

Little seems to have changed subsequently. Pryke concluded in his study that prices in many sectors were below long-run marginal costs and that 'extensive cross-subsidization is to be found at those public corporations that produce a range of goods and services'. The MMC's more recent efficiency audits point to the same conclusion. In a number of industries no attempt had been made to match the structure of prices to relative costs, and in some cases the corporation did not even measure the marginal costs of supplying different markets (see for example, Post Office and Buses). A failure to implement efficient pricing policies is also identified in studies of British Gas (see Hammond, Helm, and Thompson 1985 for a survey) British Airways (see Ashworth and Forsyth 1984), the British Airports Authority (see Starkie and Thompson 1985), and British Telecom (see Vickers and Yarrow 1985; DIW 1986).

NEDO found that little progress had been made, at the time of its study, to account for and evaluate non-commercial objectives separately. The most visible initiative was the intention, implemented in the 1968 Transport Act, to subsidize explicitly loss-making, but socially desirable, railway lines. By the time it was abandoned in 1974, this system had become largely equivalent to the deficit financing of the pre-existing rail network.

The MMC studies show that, more typically, corporations have interpreted their statutory duties to mean that certain markets should be served at prices and/or levels of service quality that result in a financial loss (rural bus services, for example). The corporations' market power is used to cross-subsidize this provision by raising prices above the efficient level in other markets. Typically, the benefits of pursuing such policies are not systematically evaluated by the corporations or government—nor, in some cases, are the costs (see MMC on Buses and Post Office, for example). In practice, it seems likely in many cases that a pattern of cross-subsidization has arisen largely in consequence of changes in demand patterns or relative costs to which the corporation has failed to respond quickly. Thus, the falling relative cost of trunk telecoms services has resulted in the cross-subsidization of local calls. It is extremely unlikely that such policies will be welfare-maximizing. More probably, they are likely to be significantly inefficient (see for example Beesley, Gist, and Glaister 1983 on London Transport), not least because they allow corporations the scope to escape the costs associated with responding to changing markets and technologies.

In summary, it seems clear not only that the Morrisonian concept has been abandoned, but also that the policies that have replaced the Morrisonian concept have, at least in relation to the achievement of allocative efficiency, also failed. The two important characteristics of the framework established by 1950 were the independence of the public corporations from day-to-day political intervention, and the assumption that a suitably constituted corporation would, left largely to its own devices, pursue the public interest. Experience in the early part of the postwar period showed that neither of these objectives was being successfully fulfilled. As a result, policy in successive White Papers has shifted towards the establishment of a regulatory framework whose purpose is to constrain the public corporations towards the achievement of economically efficient policies. With this recognized, however, the rationale of public ownership itself comes into question.

5. Privatization

Introduction

Disillusion with the performance of the public corporations has led to the most fundamental reform of policy since they were established. After its election in 1979, but most especially since 1984, the Conservative government has been following a policy of privatization in which ownership is transferred back to the private sector. We distinguish sharply between privatization, in this sense, and deregulation—the removal of statutory restraints on competition—which we discuss in Section 6.

Proceeds from asset sales have risen from a total of £377 million in 1979/80 to £2.6 billion in 1985–6. Initially, however, privatization concentrated on public sector assets (leases on motorway service areas, shares in BP) rather than enterprises, and the firms that were moved into the private sector were generally small and operated in markets where other, private sector, firms held stronger market positions. The sale of 51 per cent of the shares in British Telecom in November 1984 (for £3.9 billion, with payments staged over three years) marked the first large public corporation to be transferred to the private sector followed by British Gas (1986) and British Airways (1987).

The Conservative government now proposes to sell several further large corporations which hold dominant positions in the markets they serve—in particular the British Airports Authority, and, at some stage, the regional water authorities. Sale proceeds of £4.75 billion are anticipated in each year between 1986/7 and 1988/9.

It is apparent that the government sees the de-nationalization of public corporations as serving a multiplicity of objectives (and we have discussed elsewhere the trade-offs between these: Kay and Thompson 1986). The central concern, however, is to increase the efficiency of the public corporations (see in particular the policy statements by Moore 1983, 1985).

Privatization and Efficiency

Privatization does not necessarily lead to a change in the management structure of the companies being privatized. Indeed, it will often be the case that the same individuals as before will be in charge of the corporation after privatization policies are introduced. What does change as a result of privatization is the environment in which managers operate and the incentive system with which they are faced.

However, as we saw in Section 2, it is a combination of competition in both product and capital markets that promotes efficiency, and it is not clear that these observations have much relevance to the position of the newly privatized firms. The enterprises currently being de-nationalized are generally large, well established firms which will face little effective competition in their product markets. From the point of view of any company contemplating a take-over, these enterprises represent a very large expenditure. For example, the sale of the shareholding in British Telecom realized £3.9 billion, giving an implicit market valuation for BT at the time of sale of £7.8 billion. Although a number of large take-over bids have recently been launched on the UK stock market, enterprises such as British Telecom and British Gas are an order of magnitude larger. The effective threat of take-over to de-nationalized enterprises will be further circumscribed by statutory limitations on the maximum size of shareholdings and on holdings by overseas companies. It seems unlikely that an overseas buyer would be allowed to take control of enterprises such as British Telecom or British Gas, but an overseas company may be the most credible purchaser in many cases, because many of these enterprises hold a near monpoly (in the UK) of specialized management resources. The market for these firms may therefore be highly imperfect. The notion that the managers of British Telecom or British Gas will feel seriously threatened by the prospect of a hostile bid for their company stretches credulity, as does the prospect of their going bankrupt.

Our analysis of incentives shows that the promotion of efficiency (both allocative and productive) is substantially more complex than the simple substitution of private ownership for public ownership. This complexity is reflected in the findings of studies that have attempted to compare the performance of public and private enterprises. (See in particular articles by Pryke 1982, Millward 1982, Bocherding *et al.* 1982, Parker 1985, Yarrow 1986, and Domberger and Piggott 1986.)

We have suggested elsewhere, however (Kay and Thompson 1986), that two important themes can be established from this evidence. One is that competition tends to improve the performance of all firms, public or private. The second is that the industries in which public enterprises perform better than private enterprises—such as electricity supply in the United States and insurance in West Germany—are industries where competition in product markets is generally absent and where private enterprises are for this reason subject to regulation. We noted that the type of regulation that has been adopted has largely eliminated capital market incentives. Furthermore, regulation has frequently distorted the enterprises' own profit incentives, inducing the utilization of an inefficient combination of factor inputs, thus raising costs. Market failure is thus compounded by regulatory failure.

We would conclude from this that the introduction of competition is the most effective policy measure to improve the efficiency of the nationalized (and formerly nationalized) industries. De-nationalizing an enterprise into an uncompetitive environment in unlikely to be very beneficial. Inadequately executed, it could be positively harmful. De-nationalization will tend to improve performance only if supported by deregulation; if the two conflict, then deregulation is to be preferred.

6. Competition Policy

Competition policy in Britain began in 1948, at the same time as the principal public corporations described in Section 4 were established. Some market failures were to be dealt with by nationalization, others by ensuring that the private sector was to be more competitive. The Monopolies Commission was established and empowered to investigate industries where one firm, or group of firms acting in concert, controlled more than one-third (subsequently one-quarter) of the market. The policy was in due course extended to permit scrutiny of mergers and to inhibit the implementation of restrictive practices. The Office of Fair Trading, established in 1973, co-ordinates this activity. Further incentives to competition came from provisions of the Treaty of Rome, and from measures of deregulation—the removal of statutory restrictions on competition—which were introduced after 1980. We consider each of these areas of policy in turn.

Monopolies and Oligopolies

In the first 20 years of the life of the Monopolies Commission, the majority of references concerned industries in which a single firm was dominant. By 1970, most substantial markets of this kind had been the subject of at least one reference to the Commission. The development of competition policy in the 1970s was significantly influenced by macroeconomic preoccupations. A sense that oligopoly contributed to inflationary pressures by reducing an industry's incentive to resist cost increases had been one motive for a general reference to the Commission of the practice of parallel pricing. A series of oligopolistic industries—cables, petrol, bread—found themselves subject to particular references. The concept of the 'complex monopoly', by which the Commission could scrutinize a group of firms with market share in excess of 25 per cent, gave the Monopolies and Mergers Commission (MMC) wide-ranging jurisdiction. (See Sharpe 1985 for a critique of the 'complex monopoly' concept.)

But if its jurisdiction was, if anything, too wide, its powers were, if anything, too limited. The Commission's approach centred on 'things done', and hence on specific practices and their effects. We noted earlier that restrictions on competition in oligopolistic markets may be achieved without explicit collision, and also that entry may be deterred by behaviour whose anti-competitive content would be extremely difficult to determine. It is perhaps not surprising that the Commission often found little to complain of.

Nor is it clear, short of large-scale intervention to change the structure of oligopolistic markets, what remedies could have been proposed. These investigations often proved largely inconclusive and ineffective, although in a number of cases they uncovered unregistered agreements between the oligopolists that should have fallen to be investigated, and in all probability prohibited, by the Restrictive Practices Court. In other cases, practices that might deter entry were prohibited, although the Commission was not always successful in persuading the government to implement its recommendations. Where significant changes in market structure and/or performance have emerged following a Commission investigation, in many cases this can be attributed largely to changes in the characteristics of particular markets (the development of chemical fertilizers in place of organic ones, for example) rather than to the Commission's activities. However, their role in removing restrictions on entry has often had a beneficial impact (see Shaw and Simpson 1985).

The 1980 Competition Act introduced a new procedure for the investigation of 'anti-competitive practices'. The procedure begins with the Office of Fair Trading (OFT) establishing whether an anti-competitive practice exists. If it persuades itself that the practice is indeed anti-competitive, and fails to persuade the firm concerned to abandon it, the matter can be referred to the MMC for further scrutiny and a public interest evaluation.

Although there is merit in the ability of this procedure to focus on specific activities, the legislation is unhelpful in offering no definition of an anti-competitive practice, and the OFT has been little more successful in establishing one. Almost all business behaviour is, in some sense, anti-competitive. Any contract restricts the freedom of parties to it to compete. A supplier who, under pressure, concedes favourable terms to one of his customers is engaged in conduct that is at once competitive—in the ordinary sense of the word—and anti-competitive, because it favours one customer against his rivals. The first case to go through the full two stages of the procedure was Raleigh Bicycles, who had insisted on restricting supplies of their bicycles to specialist retailers. The two reports veer between the untenable view that any restriction on supply is *per se* anti-competitive, and the equally impossible position that it is only unreasonable restrictions on supply that are anti-competitive—which would collapse the two tests and two stages of the procedure into one (Kay and Sharpe 1982). The practical effect of the system has so far been disappointingly limited.

Mergers

In 1965 the responsibilities of the Monopolies Commission were extended to allow it to scrutinize proposed mergers and to recommend prohibition. The Director General of Fair Trading can recommend to the Secretary of State for Trade and Industry that a merger be referred to what is now the Monopolies and Mergers Commission. This power is in practice exercised through a non-statutory mergers panel of civil servants and representatives of the OFT. The Commission is required to judge whether or not the proposed merger is against the public interest. Policy is thus based on the presumption that mergers are generally beneficial (or at least neutral) in effect—in other words, that capital markets function broadly efficiently.

In practice, government policy in the 1960s was concerned to promote merger, not to restrain it. Industrial restructuring was a popular objective, and a government agency—the Industrial Reorganization Corporation—was a principal instrument. The result was certainly the largest merger wave since the 1920s, and possibly the most rapid series of amalgamations in British economic history (Hannah and Kay 1977).

A sceptical reaction to this phase in the early 1970s was shared by businessmen and by those who influenced competition policy. The MMC found little advantage, but also little detriment to the public interest, in the last and largest of the projected mergers of the 1960s—that of Unilever and Allied Breweries—but by the time it had reported, the two firms concerned had lost interest in combining. In the 1970s few large mergers were proposed—fewer still were horizontal mergers—and those that came before the Commission were generally coolly, if not necessarily unfavourably, received. In a number of cases, such as the merger between British Match and Wilkinson Sword, the reversal of the burden of proof canvassed in the 1978 Green Paper, which would have required the firms concerned to show that their proposals were of positive benefit to the public interest rather than merely not against it, would probably have led to an opposite outcome.

As Fairburn (1985) has shown, by the early 1980s it had become clear that large horizontal mergers were very likely to be rejected. But by this time many of the merger cases referred to the Commission raised no competition issues of significance at all. Some references—as in Amalgamated Industrials and, most conspicuously, the long-running battle between Lonrho and House of Fraser—appeared principally to reflect suspicion and distaste of particular industrial entrepreneurs and their ambitions. In others—such as the propsed acquisition of Davy Corporation by Enserch—the MMC was effectively invited to serve as a foreign investment review body. When both Standard

Chartered and Hong Kong and Shanghai Banks bid for the Royal Bank of Scotland, the likely competitive effects of the merger would have been positive since both prospective acquirors were seeking a base from which to make an aggressive entry into the UK retail banking market. The mergers were rejected because of fears for the future conduct of monetary policy and on account of the 'Scottish card'—fears that Scotland would suffer if control of a major financial institution were transferred from Edinburgh to London, or to Hong Kong.

These cases illustrate the increasing politicization of merger references. Lobbying for or against a reference became a major weapon in contested bids. When Sotheby's feared rape by an unwelcome American suitor, they pressed for and secured a reference to the Commission which delayed matters until a more acceptable marriage partner was found. The MMC concluded, shortly and correctly, that no public interest issues had been at stake. The Scottish card was played again by Anderson Strathclyde, resisting a bid from Charter Consolidated. The MMC opposed the acquisition, principally on the basis of doubts about the acquiror's management capabilities, although the Chairman of the Commission publicly dissented from his colleagues' conclusion. At this point the Minister intervened, and overturned the MMC recommendation.

The controversy that this aroused, aggravated by the irrelevant fact that the Trade Secretary had a modest shareholding in Charter Consolidated, led to a new policy statement that henceforth merger references would be based predominantly on competition grounds. But there are wider issues involved in the grandiose expansion plans of ambitious managers. From 1984 to 1986, a booming stock market led to a surge in merger activity rivalling that of the 1960s, with large conglomerate firms such as BTR and Hanson Trust as leading players. Pressure to secure or avoid reference again became central. But with competition issues now emphasized, threatened targets such as Imperial and Distillers succeeded in escaping reference of their favoured partnerships to the Commission by hasty reconstruction of their activities.

Anti-competitive arrangements between firms may stop short of full merger. Minority share acquisition is an increasingly important form of arrangement between companies which falls outside the scope of existing competition policy arrangements (although, if on a scale sufficient to constitute effective control, it could be the subject of a merger reference). The purchase of such a stake may often be a prelude to a full bid, but in fact the majority of such holdings appear to be maintained for a substantial period of time. The probable functions of such holdings would seem to be to support tacit agreements between potential competitors, or between customers and suppliers, and as such would seem to raise issues requiring the specific attention they would receive were the agreements explicit rather than tacit (see Meadowcroft and Thompson 1987).

Restrictive Practices

Since 1956, industries pursuing restrictive agreements had been obliged to put them on a public register, and these might be referred to the Restrictive Practices Court (RPC), where the industry concerned would be required to demonstrate that the agreement in question served the public interest as defined by a number of 'gateways'. The Court would then have to satisfy itself that if the agreement passed through the gateways it was, on balance, justified (the tail-piece provision). In practice, the Court had shown itself unsympathetic to such defences in a number of early cases (Stevens and Yamey 1965), and this had led to the abandonment of most controversial agreements. Resale Price Maintenance was subjected to similar scrutiny after the 1964 Resale Prices Act, with similar outcome. Thus, by the time the OFT was established in 1973, the Restrictive Preactices Court had become decidedly the less active of the two principal arms of British competition policy; its work, as defined by the initial legislation governing it, had largely been completed (see Swann *et al.* 1974 for an assessment).

This does not imply that all restrictions on competition had disappeared. The requirement for registration is a product of the form, rather than the effects, of an agreement; and considerable legal ingenuity has been expended on recasting agreements in the form of bilateral contracts which escape the provisions of the legislation (see Sharpe 1985 for an elaboration of this point). In 1976 the coverage of the legislation was extended to services. Few cases have come to court, and in the most substantial one that did—the agreements of the Association of British Travel Agents—the restrictions were mainly upheld as either providing consumer protection or acting in support of other restrictions that had that effect. But the existence of the legislation has significantly influenced behaviour, most notably in financial services. The Stock Exchange agreed to abandon its principal restrictions (leading to the 'big bang') in return for a period of grace and exemption from the general provisions of restrictive trade practices (RTP) legislation.

EEC Competition Policy

Since British entry into the EEC, the competition policy of the European Community has also been relevant to the operation of British business. The principal relevant legislation is found in Articles 85 and 86 of the Treaty of Rome. Article 85 prevents restrictions on trade between member states, and Article 86 prohibits abuse of a dominant position in any market within the community.

In some cases the European dimension has acted as a supplement to domestic policies. For example, the high level of car prices in the UK (see Ashworth, Kay, and Sharpe 1982), although essentially a domestic issue, has not been the subject of investigation by British competition policy institutions, perhaps as a result of political pressure from UK motor manufacturers. The Commission has, however, secured some lowering of prices by making a reduction in differentials within the Community a condition of exemption of the industry's selective distribution agreement from the provisions of Article 85 and has supported this by challenging attempts to restrict parallel imports in the European Court. More generally, however, the concern of EEC competition policy has been with restrictions that affect trade between member states. One example is the Commission's action to prevent price discrimination by Distillers' segmentation of the Community market in Scotch whisky.

The Commission of the European Communities is the principal agency for the enforcement of the provisions of Articles 85 and 86. The Commission may act on its own initiative or in response to complaints. It is, however, open to firms or industrialists who believe themselves damaged by violations to seek redress themselves in the European Court. This possibility of private enforcement is not normally available in domestic competition policy, which relies on initiative from the government or OFT (although much of this activity is complaint-led).

Such opportunities may currently exist, however, in relation to restrictive practices where it is widely believed that a customer harmed by an unregistered practice could recover damages from the parties to the illegal agreement. Although no cases have reached court, settlements have been reached—most prominently between the cable manufacturers and the Post Office—where unregistered cartels have been uncovered. Such provisions do, however, fall a long way short of those of the United States, which would provide for exemplary treble damages and possible criminal liability on the part of both the company concerned and its managers.

Deregulation

Deregulation, the removal of statutory restrictions on market entry, has been implemented in a number of sectors. The most significant case is telecommunications, where another supplier of telecoms services, Mercury, has been permitted to enter the market and British Telecom's statutory monopoly in the supply of equipment (such as exchanges or telephones) has been eliminated. And there is now more freedom for competing companies to provide Value Added Network Services (VANS).

In the case of express coaching, restrictions on entry on to particular routes have been completely removed and anyone who meets the various safety criteria can now start up a coach service. Liberalization of bus transport generally has followed. Electricity supply was deregulated in the 1983 Energy Act, which removed the public sector's statutory monopoly in the generation of electricity 'as a main business' and enabled private producers to supply customers by making use of the publicly owned distribution network at pre-specified charges. Private producers can also sell their output to the public distribution network, and again there are pre-specified charges (which, in principle, are to be based on the public sector's avoidable costs) at which the public authorities are required to purchase power offered by private producers. A similar liberalization of the gas industry was implemented in the Oil and Gas Act 1982, which allows private gas producers to rent the use of the (then) publicly owned distribution network to supply gas to large industrial customers.

The tendering of publicly financed services has been introduced for various local authority services (e.g. refuse collection) and health authority services (e.g. hospital cleaning). While there have been a number of well publicized examples of tendering (well publicized either because of the savings in costs that were claimed, or because of alleged failings in service quality), it has so far been implemented on only a comparatively small scale. For example, in the health service in 1984/5 private contractors supplied 11 per cent of laundry services, 2 per cent of cleaning and $\frac{1}{2}$ per cent of catering. The volume of services put out to tender is, however, four or five times this level. In the case of local authorities, 2 per cent of refuse collection services were supplied by private contractors and twice that level were put out to tender (see Domberger, Meadowcroft, and Thompson 1986).

Overall, competition policy has had marked effects in some areas—such as the virtual disappearance of cartels and resale price maintenance, and the prohibition of large horizontal mergers. The impact of deregulation policies has been mixed with significant changes in market performance in some cases (e.g. express coaches) and little change in others (e.g. gas supply). In other areas, competition policy has had very little impact, in particular, on the comfortable oligopolistic stuctures that characterize many important sections of British industry. We now consider how a policy for competition might be developed.

7. The Evolution of Policy

We have argued that government attempts to deal with market failure have generally been plagued by regulatory failure. The initial appeal to managers of nationalized industries to pursue the public good was not successful in defining managerial objectives, and it is clear that corporations have often followed other aims. Indeed, the government itself has often had confused and conflicting goals. Even when government has had a clear conception of the public interest and the implications of this for nationalized industry performance—as at the time of publication of successive White Papers—differences in objectives, incentives, and information have rendered the recommendations put forward largely ineffective. Particularly important is the nationalized industries' substantive monopoly of relevant information and expertise. For these reasons, the institutional framework within which the regulation of public corporations has been established has meant that this regulation has been particularly likely to fail.

This analysis, however, leads to the conclusion that privatization of existing monopoly corporations as a remedy for these difficulties is also likely to fail. The view that ownership is the key issue is not supported. Not only does it appear that ownership changes have little impact on performance outside a competitive market, but the underlying problems are associated with ownership only weakly. Those industries that have been nationalized are generally characterized by market failure, and attempts to deal with these failures by nationalization have been confronted by regulatory failure. Privatization may reduce the degree of concern for market failure questions on the part of government or industry managers. It will also give different form to the institutions of regulation. The regulatory agency is, on the one hand, less susceptible to the vicissitudes of day-to-day political pressures and, on the other, more vulnerable to the risk of regulatory capture. But privatization does not change these issues in any fundamental way. The fundamental problem of regulation—which does not work well in markets that do not work well—remains.

The thrust of policy, then, should be towards the promotion of competitive solutions. We begin by examining methods of promoting competition within the private sector and then go on to examine how competition can be made more effective within the traditional public sector.

Competition within the Private Sector

Three distinctive characteristics of UK competition policy require review. One is the absence of rules of behaviour. In the United States certain courses of conduct are clearly proscribed by legislation or statutory interpretation, and this is, to a lesser extent, true in the EEC also: UK policy requires an individual determination of the public interest in any, and every, case. Second, and associated with this, is the freedom to examine factors remote from competition. Although it is failure in competition that gives the British anti-trust agency—MMC, RPC, or OFT—its jurisdiction, once such a failure has been established it is permitted—indeed, obliged—to examine a wider range of issues. These include not only the efficiency of the investigated company's operations but all aspects of its activities—ownership, location, employment policies—which might bear on the public interest. Finally, British policy relies almost entirely on the activity of public agencies, while private enforcement is a major arm of US anti-trust policy and a significant element in the EEC.

The economic rationale behind the differences between Britain and the United States can readily be decribed in terms of the theory and history outlined in earlier sections of this paper. The ideology that framed US policy saw the absence of competition as the primary source of market failure. The task of policy was therefore to impose competition. Other possible kinds of market failure were substantially ignored. Where competition was clearly impossible, as in the natural monopolies, regulation was required. In Britain, however, monopoly was only one possible source of market failure, and action to remedy it had to be balanced against other perceived benefits.

Discontent with the evolution of policy in both countries has resulted from weaknesses of the regulatory process and has led to convergence of both practice and problems. In the United States, the judicial promotion of competition in principle precluded 'rule of reason' defences. Neither superior efficiency nor technological necessity could be cited in support of a monopoly position. In practice, cases against IBM and AT&T reached realistic settlement. Critics argued that a variety of apparently anti-competitive practices—particularly vertical restraints—did not represent a restriction in competition at all. And regulatory institutions were criticized for capture or for inflexibility. In the UK, the vagueness of the public interest criterion led to wide-ranging enquiry and difficulty in establishing consistency or precedent. Market failures not directly associated with the absence of competition came to concern the competition policy authorities. In both countries, there is pressure to define more precisely the scope of anti-trust policy.

There are some practices—such as predation or price cartels—which serve no purpose other than the destruction of competition, and for these it is apparent that outright prohibition is an appropriate response. Effective deterrence of these activities requires also that there should be a penalty for undertaking them—or at least, a penalty more effective than the present UK sanction of being asked to stop. Existing UK policy means that anti-competitive activity will nearly always be worthwhile, even if it is eventually discovered and prohibited. The imposition of fines would make policy more effective. In other cases, anti-competitive effects may need to be balanced against other possible market failures, but in the case of (for example) large horizontal mergers, the probability of sufficient balancing factors may be remote. Thus, there is scope for more systematic prohibition and guidelines in competition policy, but also a role for pragmatic intervention.

Where other kinds of market failure resemble weaknesses of competition in their nature or effect, it may be appropriate that these should remain within the scope of competition policy. Information deficiencies are examples of this; even if the market failure at the root of the spare parts cases is not fundamentally an issue of competition, the agencies of competition policy may nevertheless be appropriate vehicles for the application of policy. In other areas, such as foreign investment review, genuine issues of public policy arise; but it is not clear that the MMC is a body well equipped to pronounce, or that policy intervention in these issues should be restricted only to cases that appear to involve an issue of competition.

One approach to regulatory failure is to introduce competition among regulators. This points up a role for private enforcement; it has proved an important route to more effective policy in the United States, and there are advantages to be gained from its selective application in the UK.

Competition within the Traditional Public Sector

We have stressed that it is competition, rather than the transfer of ownership, that promises the most marked improvement in the performance of the public sector. There is considerable scope for introducing greater competition, by removing statutory restrictions, by reducing incumbent advantages, and by appropriate restructuring of the industries concerned.

It is supposed that much of the public sector is to be characterized by natural monopoly. However, the scope of natural monopoly is often less than existing market structures would suggest. For example, the government has accepted, in recent legislation, the case for operating London's airports under single ownership, although the economies of scale or scope that are achieved appear negligible (see Starkie and Thompson 1985). In other industries, natural monopoly is characteristic of only of a part of the activity of the industry. For example, in the UK there appears limited scope for competing distribution networks for electricity, telecoms (local services), or gas. However, the existence of the natural monopoly often provides the basis of control over other parts of the industry where no natural monopoly exists. For example, it is evident that the provision of rail track is a natural monopoly; but the provision of rail services on that track is not. The normal method of running railways, however, is for the owner of the track to run the trains. It is sometimes suggested that separation of the ownership of 'track' and 'trains' would enable a market in the supply of train services to develop. (See Starkie 1984 for a recent exposition.) In assessing the merits of this proposal, it would be necessary to offset the benefits of competitive provision of train services from the additional costs imposed by a more complicated, and somewhat more artificial, scheme of organization. Often, however, vertical integration goes far beyond the point at which it reduces costs. There is no real advantage, for example, in having the telephone instrument provided by the same firm that has the natural monopoly of the local telephone network. In electricity, where there has never been any assumption that appliances would be supplied by the distributors of electricity, most appliances are sold by independent retailers.

Thus, the first principle for promoting competition in these industries is to separate the ownership of natural monopoly activities from that of potentially competitive activities. Without such separation, it is unlikely that there will be any practical safeguard against unfair competition by the monopolist in the competitive market. This is illustrated by the failure of measures to deregulate gas supply (the Oil and Gas Act 1982) and electricity supply (the Energy Act 1983). In both cases private producers are allowed to rent the use of the public sector's distribution network to supply to customers. In the case of gas (see

Hammond, Helm, and Thompson 1985), British Gas's policy of setting prices significantly below the marginal cost of newly developed gas supplies, a policy made feasible by its contractual rights to lower-cost gas sources, means that profitable market entry is infeasible. In the case of electricity (see Hammond, Helm, and Thompson 1986), provision was made in the Energy Act to limit the incumbent's scope for deterring competitive entry. The Act required the public sector to purchase power supplied by private enterprises at prices based on its own avoidable costs. The flaw in the Act was to leave the interpretation and fixing of these prices to the incumbent. We have already noted the difficulties in measuring the marginal costs of electricity supply, and in the event the Energy Act tariffs have been set by the incumbent at levels that have not generally been attractive to entrants, and without the provisions for long-term contracts for supply that are often required to finance investment in electricity generation. This conclusion is reinforced by the comparative success of a similar deregulation in the United States, where the terms of entry are regulated not by incumbents but by independent commissions (see Henney and Thompson 1986).

Changes in technology imply that traditional natural monopolies are opened to competition, or that previously competitive industries become natural monopolies. The natural monopoly of broadcasting, for example, took over what had been competitive areas of provision of information and entertainment, and justified new forms of regulation. But in time, advancing technology has itself broken down this natural monopoly, and innovation seems more often to increase possible competition than to reduce it. Technological developments in telecoms have led to the perceived natural monopoly in trunk transmissions being questioned (see for example Beesley 1981, Beesley and Gist 1984, Vickers and Yarrow 1985), and in recent years competing suppliers of trunk services have emerged in the United States and latterly in the UK.

Where competition is not a feasible option—and in the UK the distribution networks in sectors such as gas appear genuine (and sustainable) natural monopolies—then unrestricted profit-maximizing private ownership will be inefficient in allocative terms, and some regulation is required. The weaknesses identified with regulation of these industries in private ownership overseas (discussed in Section 3) have led to a search for more effective measures to regulate newly de-nationalized enterprises in the UK. The main features of the new regulatory regimes have their origins in a report by Professor Stephen Littlechild (1983) on the comparative merits of alternative schemes to regulate a de-nationalized British Telecom. Littlechild's preferred solution was to place a regulatory control on increases in BT's prices. The scheme that has been adopted, the '*RPI* minus X' formula, permits BT to increase the prices of a bundle of its services by an amount that is X per cent below the increase in the retail price index. Littlechild concluded that the direct regulation of prices rather than profits would minimize the incentive to the choice of inefficient (over-capitalized) production techniques that is inherent in rate-of-return regulation. Furthermore, Littlechild believed that the simplicity of the proposed scheme, and the absence of significant scope for discretion by the regulatory authorities, reduced the dangers of regulatory capture.

Any verdict on the effectiveness of this type of regulation must await some experience of its performance in practice. However, several possible weaknesses have been identified. Vickers and Yarrow (1985) argue that the level of price control set for BT is not a particularly rigorous constraint, and that separate protection against anti-competitive pricing will also be necessary. Both of these considerations indicate that a simple price formula holds disadvantages as well as advantages. The re-specification of the price control in 1989 raises a separate issue. If the re-specification is based largely upon BT's actual cost performance, then in practice the result will be similar to rate-of-return regulation with its associated disadvantages. Further, if re-specification of the formula requires extensive negotiation with BT, then the dangers of reegulatory capture re-emerge. Vickers and Yarrow conclude that the problems of rate-of-return regulation may be hard to avoid in a regulated private monopoly.

We suggested earlier that the fundamental problem common to the control of nationalized industries in the UK, and to the regulation of private utilities in the United States, is the significant asymmetry in information and technical expertise that arises between a single monopoly enterprise and a regulatory authority. This suggests both that the $RPI-X$ framework may be ineffective and that the solution to more effective regulation in sectors where competition is not feasible is the creation of competing sources of information. One route to achieving this is to separate the ownership of geographically distinct natural monopolies of the type that occur in the distribution of electricity, gas, water, and telecoms. A second, perhaps complementary, approach would involve introducing competitive franchises for the operation of natural monopoly activities. (See Domberger 1986 for a discussion.)

Where there is no natural monopoly but there is statutory restriction on competition, the remedy appears obvious: remove the statute. But experience in a variety of industries has demonstrated that market structures developed behind the protection of statutory restriction cannot be changed so easily. Deregulation in express coaching (see Davis 1984, Jaffer and Thompson 1986), telecoms apparatus (see Gist and Meadowcroft 1986), and airlines (see McGowan and Trengove 1986) all show a similar pattern. In each case, market structure has not changed significantly and incumbents have continued to dominate the liberalized markets.

Incumbents have benefited from three advantages, each of which has implications for a policy of promoting competition. First, each incumbent has an established market reputation. This means that costs are higher for a new entrant than for the incumbent because of marketing outlays. A market position that is built upon many years of statutory monopoly (British Telecom is the best-known supplier of phones because for many years it was the only supplier of phones) provides a particularly striking example of cost asymmetry. Furthermore, where the product's perceived quality is enhanced by the continued presence in the market of the supplier (for example, many durable products require continuing specialist maintenance), the fact that consumers will generally perceive the incumbent to have a higher commitment to the market than a new entrant will provide a second source of competitive advantage. Both points suggest a strong case for sub-dividing incumbent enterprises prior to deregulation unless there are strong arguments in favour of forgone economies of scale or scope, or unless the particular reputation effects confer significant benefits to consumers (in which event regulation of product quality may be the most appropriate policy).

Second, each of the incumbents is particularly well placed to compete in newly liberalized markets. Oligopoly theory emphasizes the importance of the bankruptcy constraint and of the incumbent firm's objectives (see Vickers 1985). Where the incumbent's bankruptcy constraint is weak, this signals to potential entrants that they are unlikely to win a price- (or non-price) competitive war, while a sales- (or output-)maximizing incumbent is more likely to respond to entry with retaliation than is a profit-maximizer. Each deregulated incumbent is backed by the financial strength gained from operating in many other markets where its market power is strong. Effective competition requires the elimination of the asymmetry in bankruptcy constraint between incumbent and entrant, suggesting that the ownership of monopoly and competitive activities should be divided. Where the incumbent is in public ownership, financial regulation should seek to inhibit the pursuit of non-profit-maximizing objectives at the expense of entrants.

Third, incumbents are well placed financially and technically to adopt entry-deterring strategies, and have an incentive to demonstrate the possible high cost of entry (the chain store paradox: see Vickers 1985). Our earlier conclusions on the weaknesses of present UK policy in relation to anti-competitive practices thus apply *a fortiori* to newly deregulated markets. There are some indications that specific regulatory agencies (such as OFTEL) are proving more effective than existing institutions, although it must be doubtful whether they can be wholly successful in the absence of powers to obtain damages or impose equivalent sanctions.

8. Conclusions

The current debate on industrial policy can perhaps be characterized by two extreme views. The first emphasizes the significance of market failure and points to the scope for optimally directed intervention to correct for such failures and improve economic performance. The second is generally sceptical as to the quantitative importance of market failure and emphasizes the effect that intervention may have in reducing competition (in both product and capital markets), distorting incentives, and thereby reducing economic efficiency. It is an over-simplification, although not much of an over-simplification, to say that policy in the period up to 1970 was informed by the first of these views and policy since 1980 by the second.

We do not share either of these views. We believe, however, that it is possible to reach firmer conclusions than a mere balancing of the two hypotheses. First, we believe there is clear evidence that the operation of competition, in both product and capital markets, can be effective in improving the efficiency of enterprises. Product market competition appears effective regardless of ownership, although the benefits may be greater under private ownership. The effect of liberalization initiatives where competition was previously restricted by statutory monopoly is particularly marked in those industries where it has occurred.

Second, although competition generally enhances efficiency, there are important areas of economic activity where markets will not work well. This is particularly true of the sectors in which nationalized and formerly nationalized industries operate. The problems that nationalization was intended to remedy may remain even if we are no longer persuaded that the existing structure of public corporations is an effective way of dealing with them. There are other areas of the private sector—characterized, for example, by asymmetries of information or reliance on R&D expenditures—where unmoderated market forces may not produce efficient outcomes. There is a variety of trading relationships which may be adopted by participants to internalize these failures. Prohibitions *per se* may therefore be detrimental to economic efficiency, although the assessment of all cases on their merits may simply mean an absence of coherent or effective policy, and often has meant that.

Third, the framework for the regulation of monopolies—public or private—has not succeeded in providing an effective substitute for the disciplines and incentive structures of private markets. By the late 1960s it had become clear that public corporations would not adopt welfare-maximizing policies (whatever these might be) in the absence of a framework that constrained them to act in this way. Nor has such a framework been constructed since. Regulatory intervention has repeatedly been criticized for its inconsistent nature, and its undermining of managerial responsibility. There is no reason to suppose that these problems have now been solved. Where privatization involves a new regulatory framework—as in telecommunications—there may be a possibility that performance in non-competitive areas will be improved by it, although that has yet to be demonstrated. Where, as in gas, it involves only the creation of a new regulatory institution, expectations must be very low. The weakness of the privatization programme, then, is that it is not rooted in an analysis of why nationalization has failed, as distinct from the assertion that it *has* failed. The view that, since nationalized industries are unsuccessful, private ownership must be better is a slogan rather than a coherent industrial policy.

The policy that our analysis suggests relies on market forces, but this is very far from a regime of *laissez-faire*. On the contrary, making market forces work requires a range of specific interventions: to maintain competition within the private sector, to remedy specific instances of market failure, and to create—perhaps artificially—opportunities for competition where regulation would otherwise be demanded. The first of these types of intervention—the support of private sector competition—is evidently the task of competition policy; the second is the task of a (more or less extensive) industrial policy; the third requires a more sophisticated approach to restructuring nationalized industries than the present privatization drive. The common theme of all these policies is an intention to work with market forces rather than to supplant them.

References

Ashworth, M. H. and Forsyth, P. J. (1984), *Civil Aviation and the Privatisation of British Airways*, IFS Report Series 12. London: Institute for Fiscal Studies.

Ashworth, M. H., Kay, J. A., and Sharpe, T. (1982), *Differentials between Car Prices in the United Kingdom and Belgium*, IFS Report Series 2. London: Institute for Fiscal Studies.

Averch, H. and Johnson, L. (1962), 'Behaviour of the Firm under Regulatory Constraint', *American Economic Review*, 52, 1052–69.

Bailey, E. E. (1973), *Economic Theory of Regulatory Constraint*. Lexington, Mass.: D. C. Heath & Co.

Beesley, M. E. (1981), *Liberalization of the Use of the British Telecommunications Network*. London: HMSO.

——, and Gist, P. (1984), 'Strategic Planning in the Nationalised Industries: The Role of Market Forces'. In John Grieve Smith (ed.), *Strategic Planning in the Nationalised Industries*. London: Macmillan.

——, Gist, P., and Glaister, S. (1983), 'Cost–benefit Analysis: London's Transport Policies'. In *Progress in Planning*, vol 19, part III. Oxford: Pergamon Press.

Bocherding, T. E., Pommerehne, W. W. and Schneider, F. (1982), 'Comparing the Efficiency of Private and Public Production: The Evidence from Five Countries'. *Zeitschrift für Nationalokonomie*, supplement 2, 127–56.

Brander, J. and Spencer, B. (1983), 'Strategic Commitment with R&D the Symmetric Case'. *Bell Journal of Economics*, 14, 225–35.

Crew, M. A. and Kleindorfer, P. R. (1979), *Public Utility Economics*. London: Macmillan.

Dasgupta, P. and Stiglitz, J. (1980), 'Industrial Structure and the Nature of Innovative Activity', *Economic Journal*, 90, 266–93.

Davis, E. H. (1984), 'Express Coaching since 1980: Liberalization in Practice', *Fiscal Studies*, 5(1), 76–86.

Demsetz, H. (1968), 'Why Regulate Utilities?' *Journal of Law and Economics*, 11, 55–66.

Deutsches Institut für Wirtschaftforschung (DIW) (1986), *Economic Evaluation of the Impact of Telecommunications Investment in the Communities*. Berlin: DIW.

Dixit, A. K. and Kyle, A. S. (1985), 'The Use of Protection and Subsidies for Entry Promotion and Deterrence'. *American Economic Review*, 75, 139–52.

Domberger, S. (1986), 'Economic Regulation through Franchise Contracts'. In J. A. Kay, C. P. Mayer, and D. J. Thompson (eds.), *Privatisation and Regulation: The UK Experience*. Oxford: University Press.

Domberger, S., Meadowcroft, S. A. and Thompson, D. J. (1986), 'Refuse Services—Has Tendering Worked?' *Fiscal Studies*, 7(4), 69–87.

Domberger, S. and Pigott, J. (1986), 'Privatisation Policies and Public Enterprise—A Survey'. *Economic Record*, 62, 145–62.

Douglas, G. W. and Miller, J. C. (1974), *Economic Regulation of Domestic Air Transport*. Washington DC: Brookings Institution.

Fairburn, J. (1985), 'British Merger Policy', *Fiscal Studies*, 6(1), 70–81.

Finsinger, J., Hammond, E. M., and Tapp, J. (1985), *Insurance: Competition or Regulation? A Comparative Study of the Insurance Market in the United Kingdom and the Federal Republic of Germany*, IFS Report Series 19. London: Institute for Fiscal Studies.

Furubotn, E. G. and Pejovich, S. (1972), 'Property Rights and Economic Theory: A Survey of Recent Literature'. *Journal of Economic Literature*, 6, 1137–62.

Gist, P. and Meadowcroft, S. A. (1986), 'Regulating for Competition: The Newly Liberalised Market for Branch Exchanges'. *Fiscal Studies*, 7(3), 41–66.

Hammond, E. M., Helm, D. R., and Thompson, D. J. (1985), 'British Gas: Options for Privatisation'. *Fiscal Studies*, 6(4), 1–20.

—— (1986), 'Has the Energy Act Failed?' *Fiscal Studies*, 7, 11–33.

Hannah, L. and Kay, J. A. (1977), *Concentration in Modern Industry*. London: Macmillan.

Hay, G. A. (1985), 'Vertical Restraints', *Fiscal Studies*, 6(3), 37–50.

Henney, A. and Thompson D. J. (1986), 'Deregulating Electricity Supply in the US and UK'. Memorandum to Energy Select Committee in 'Combined Heat and Power: Lead City Schemes' H.C. 488.

H. M. Treasury (1961), *Financial and Economic Obligations of the Nationalised Industries*, Cmnd 1337. London: HMSO.

—— (1967), *Nationalised Industries: A Review of Economic and Financial Objectives*, Cmnd 3437. London: HMSO.

—— (1978), *The Nationalised Industries*, Cmnd 7131. London: HMSO.

Hotelling, H. (1938), 'The General Welfare in Relation to Problems of Taxation and of Railway and Utility Rates', *Econometrica*, 6(3), 242–69.

Jaffer, S. M. and Thompson, D. J. (1986), 'De-regulating Express Coaches: A Re-assessment'. *Fiscal Studies* 7(4), 45–68.

Kay, J. A. and Sharpe, T. (1982), 'The Anti-competitive Practice'. *Fiscal Studies*, 3, 191–8.

Kay, J. A., and Thompson, D. J. (1986), 'Privatisation: A Policy in Search of a Rationale'. *Economic Journal*, 96, 18–32.

Lange, O. (1936), 'On the Economic Theory of Socialism'. *Review of Economic Studies*, IV, Part I, 53–71, Part II, 123–42.

Lerner, A. P. (1944), *Economics of Control*. London: Macmillan.

Little, I. M. D. (1950), *A Critique of Welfare Economics*. Oxford: Clarendon Press.

Littlechild, S. C. (1983), *Regulation of British Telecommunications' Profitability*. London: Department of Industry.

McGowan, F. and Trengove, C. (1986), 'European Aviation—A Common Market', IFS Report Series 23. London: Institute for Fiscal Studies.

Meadowcroft, S. A. and Thompson, D. J. (1987), 'Partial Integration: A loophole in Competition Law?' *Fiscal Studies*, 8(1), 24–47.

Millward, R. (1982), 'The Comparative Performance of Public and Private Enterprice', in Lord Roll (ed.), *The Mixed Economy*. London: Macmillan.

Molyneux, R. and Thompson, D. J. (1987), 'Nationalised Industry Performance: Still Third Rate?' *Fiscal Studies*, 8(1), 48–82.

Monopolies and Mergers Commission (1982a), *Buses*, HC 442. London: HMSO.

—— (1984a), *London Transport Executive*, Cmnd 9133. London: HMSO.

—— (1983), *Civil Aviation Authority*, Cmnd 9068. London: HMSO.

—— (1982b), *Anglian Water Authority*, Cmnd 8726. London: HMSO.

—— (1984b), *The Post Office Letter Post Service*, Cmnd 9332. London: HMSO.

Moore, J. (1983), 'Why Privatise?' Speech given to the annual conference of City of London stockbrokers Fielding, Newson Smith at Plaisterer's Hall, London Wall, 1 November. HM Treasury Press Release 190/83.

—— (1985), 'The Success of Privatisation'. Speech made when opening Hoare Govett Ltd's new City dealing rooms on 17 July, HM Treasury Press Release 107/85.

Morrison, H. (1933), *Socialisation of Transport*. London: Constable.

National Economic Development Office (NEDO) (1976), *A Study of UK Nationalised Industries*. London: HMSO.

Parker, D. (1985), 'Is the Private Sector More Efficient?' *Public Administration Bulletin*, 48, 2–23.

Pryke, R. (1981), *The Nationalised Industries: Policies and Performance Since 1968*. Oxford: Martin Robertson.

—— (1982), 'The Comparative Performance of Public and Private Enterprise'. *Fiscal Studies*, 3(2), 68–81.

Rees, (1984), 'A Positive Theory of the Public Enterprise'. In M. Marchand, D. Pestieau, and H. Tulkens (eds.), *The Performance of Public Enterprises*. Amsterdam: North-Holland.

Sharkey, W. W. (1982), *The Theory of Natural Monopoly*. Cambridge: University Press.

Sharpe, T. (1985), 'British Competition Policy in Perspective'. *Oxford Review of Economic Policy*, 1(3), 80–94.

Shaw, R. and Simpson, P. (1985), 'The Monopolies Commission and the Process of Competition', *Fiscal Studies*, 6(1), 82–96.

Sherman, R. and Visscher, M. (1982), 'Rate of Return Regulation and Two-part Tariffs', *Quarterly Journal of Economics*, 97, 27–42.

Shonfield, A. (1981), 'Innovation: Does Government have a Role?' In C. Carter (ed.), *Industrial Policy and Innovation*. London: Heinemann.

Singh, A. (1971), *Takeovers*. Cambridge: University Press.

Spence, M. (1984), 'Cost Reduction, Competition, and Industry Performance'. *Econometrica*, 52, 101–21.

Starkie, D. N. M. (1984), 'BR: Privatization without Tears'. *Economic Affairs*, 5(1), 16–19.

—— and Thompson, D. J. (1985), *Privatising London's Airports*, IFS Report Series 16. London: Institute for Fiscal Studies.

—— (1986), 'Slot Trading—Opening up Access to Heathrow'. *Lloyds Aviation Economist*, 3(4), 18–19.

Stevens, R. B. and Yamey, B. S. (1965), *The Restrictive Practices court: A Study of the Judicial Process and Economic Policy*. London: Weldenfeld & Nicolson.

Swann, D. *et al.* (1974), *Competition in British Industry*. London: George Allen and Unwin.

Vickers, J. (1985), Strategic Competition Among the Few—Some Recent Developments in the Economics of Industry'. *Oxford Review of Economic Policy*, 1(3), 39–62.

—— and Yarrow, G. (1985), *Provatization and the Natural Monopolies*. London: Public Policy Centre.

Yarrow, G. (1985), 'Strategic Issues in Industrial Policy'. *Oxford Review of Economic Policy*, 1(3), 95–109.

—— (1986), 'Privatisation in Theory and Practice', *Economic Policy*, 2, 323–64.

CHAPTER 7

The Welfare State

Anthony Atkinson, John Hills, and Julian Le Grand

London School of Economics

1. Introduction

In the past 15 years, the welfare state has been under attack in at least two different respects. First, there have been the attacks on its *extent*. Successive governments have attempted to cut public spending on welfare, and under the Thatcher administration we have seen in addition the abolition of programmes, and the privatization of functions. Second, there have been attacks on its *effectiveness*. It has been argued that the welfare state programmes have failed to meet their objectives, that poverty has not been abolished, and that inequalities in various aspects of welfare remain undiminished. Others go further and suggest that the welfare state has been counterproductive. Like Charles Murray in *Losing Ground* (1984) in the United States, the critics argue that the state programmes have created adverse incentives and undermined individual responsibility.

These two attacks have fed on each other. The alleged ineffectiveness of present programmes has made it easy to argue that cuts in resources in the welfare state can be accommodated by increased efficiency. Many of those opposed to such cuts had previously been emphasizing the shortcomings of the present position in the effort to increase resources, and they found it difficult to reverse direction. The cuts themselves often served to highlight the problems with the state services and to reinforce the claims that they were ineffective.

In this chapter, we seek to document the experience of the British welfare state over the 1970s and the first part of the 1980s, and to examine the record with regard to its extent and effectiveness. As such, the chapter falls into three main sections. Section 2 provides a selective account of the policies pursued by the Conservative government of 1970–4, by the Labour government of 1974–9, and by the Conservative government from 1979 to the time of writing (1986). The account is selective in that we concentrate on polices in the fields of health care, housing, and social security. Section 3 is concerned with the effect of these policies on the *extent* of the welfare state, and with how far it has indeed been cut back. Has the frontier been shifted back to the extent suggested by the rhetoric of both opponents and proponents? Here we must

We are very grateful for computational help from Fiona Coulter, Maria Evandrou, and David Winter. Helpful comments on earlier drafts were received from Nick Bosanquet, Rudolph Klein, Richard Layard, Alan Maynard, James Mirrlees, Ray Robinson, Clive Smee, and Christine Whitehead.

take account of the external factors that have affected its role—most importantly, rising unemployment. Section 4 considers some of the arguments concerning *effectiveness*. There are two obvious difficulties here. The first is that outputs are notoriously more difficult to measure than inputs in this field. The second is that we must construct a counterfactual situation against which to measure the impact of the welfare state.

This plan is ambitious, and we should warn the reader that the chapter is both limited and preliminary. The most obvious limitation is that, even within the conventional definition of the welfare state in terms of public spending categories, we focus on three particular areas and exclude personal social services and education. Despite the obvious importance of these two areas, and the fact that there are crucial links between different types of spending, we felt that some restriction was necessary to keep the paper within manageable length. The analysis is described as 'preliminary' in the sense that it largely makes use of aggregate data on the extent and effectiveness of the welfare state. Thus, in Section 3 we consider information on total public spending and its movement in relation to overall demographic variables; in Section 4 the sources we use are, for example, measures of life expectancy, the total number of unfit homes, or the number of low-income families. From this kind of evidence it is difficult to obtain a fully satisfactory picture of the impact of policies at the level of individual families, and in particular of the relation between policies in different fields. As part of our future research programme, we plan to address this issue through analysing the evidence in the General Household Surveys, covering more than 10,000 households a year, from 1973 to 1982. These surveys provide a rich source of information, whose time-series aspect has not really been exploited to date.

2. Health, Housing, and Social Security Policy, 1970–1985

At the start of the 1970s, the welfare state retained the confidence of both major parties. The objective of the government could be described as that of maximizing some measure of the benefit derived from welfare spending subject to a limit on its total. To quote Mr Wilson, 'we shall . . . of course, continue to pursue our social objectives as fast as the growing stength of the economy will permit' (*Poverty*, Autumn 1967, p. 13). The record of the 1964–70 Labour government was criticized (see, for example, Townsend and Bosanquet 1972) for failing to redistribute resources, but the expansion of the social budget was seen as a vehicle for progress. The failure to eliminate poverty, poor housing and poor health was a result of inadequate resources and lack of social planning rather than of any shortcomings in the welfare state itself.

Conservative Government 1970–1974

The Conservative government that took office in 1970 under Mr Heath was not committed to a root-and-branch attack on the role of government provision in the welfare area. Indeed, rather the reverse: the manifesto on which the Conservatives won the election stated clearly that 'Our aim is to develop and improve Britain's social services to the full' (p. 19).

This was particularly evident in the case of health care, where there was little significant difference between the incoming government's commitment to the national health service (NHS) and that of the previous administration. The NHS budget actually grew at a faster annual rate in real terms over the period 1970–4 than in 1964–70 (Klein 1983, p. 67). There were no moves towards privatization, through contracting-out or stimulating the private sector. Although accurate estimates on private spending on health care are difficult to obtain (partly because of definitional problems, such as the status of private nursing homes), it is unlikely that the amount diverged much from the 3 per cent of total expenditure on health care estimated by the Royal Commission on the National Health Service for 1976 (1979, p. 289). Indeed, the only development that could be interpreted as increasing consumer power at the expense of that of the state was distinctly 'corporatist' in nature: the creation of Community Health Councils in 1974.

Instead, the policy emphasis in the health field throughout the period was a continuation of the previous decade's concern with what Klein (1983) has termed 'technocratic change'. There were three problem areas: the general need to ration an apparently infinitely expanding demand for medical care; the 'Cinderella' services (focusing on the elderly, the mentally ill, and the mentally handicapped); and an increasing awareness of the unequal provision of services between regions. The answer to all these problems was perceived as an *organizational* one, an approach that was explored in a number of remarkably similar government documents produced under both Labour and Conservative governments (Ministry of Health 1968; DHSS 1970, 1971, 1972) and that culminated in the major reorganization of the NHS in 1974. This reorganization was justified principally in terms of increasing managerial efficiency, a theme that will recur.

In the housing field, too, there was some continuity of policy. The late 1960s had seen the total number of new housing starts fall from its position as the centre of housing policy. Whereas the National Plan of 1965 (Department of Economic Affairs 1965) had set a target half a million houses to be built each year, and had emphasized the use of 'industrialized' and high-rise building for local authorities, the ending of special subsidies to blocks of more than five storeys, as well as the Ronan Point disaster in May 1968, had led to a fall in the proportion of new high-rise building to 8 per cent of tenders by 1970. By that time, the idea of system-building as a way of winning the numbers game had been abandoned. In its place came the beginnings of a number of policies that were to run through the subsequent 15 years. The 1968 White Paper, *Old Houses into New Homes*, marked the beginning of a trend towards renovation rather than clearance and redevelopment which continued throughout the period. A series of measures favouring owner-occupation—the abolition of 'Schedule A' taxation of owner-occupiers' imputed rents in 1963, the exemption of owner-occupied houses from the new Capital Gains Tax, the introduction of Option Mortgage Subsidy, and the protection of mortgage interest tax deductibility—were all in place when the Heath government took office in 1970.

That government's objectives for housing were described in its 1971 White Paper, *Fair Deal for Housing*. As well as the traditional, if undefined, aim of 'a decent home for every family at a price within their means', a formulation that remained part of most expressions of policy until 1979, the White Paper also gave the objectives of a 'fairer choice between owning a home and renting one' and 'fairness between one citizen and another in giving and receiving help towards housing costs'. What this meant as implemented by the Housing Finance Act was a compulsory increase in local authority rents towards 'fair rent' levels, to be phased over several years, combined with a mandatory national rent rebate scheme and equivalent rent allowances for private unfurnished tenants. The increased incomes for local authorities resulting from the higher rents were to be used first as part of the mechanism to redistribute subsidies from council tenants in general towards those eligible for means-tested assistance, and then, if surpluses emerged, to reduce rates and national Exchequer subsidies to housing. Although the aims of this strategy for current spending sound familiar 15 years later, the Heath government's attitude to capital spending was rather different. While capital spending on housing benefited from the general increases in public spending plans in 1972, it was specifically exempted from the subsequent round of cuts at the end of 1973. Meanwhile, restrictions on the ability of local authorities to sell their houses to sitting tenants were removed, but a positive Right to Buy became part of Conservative policy only in its manifesto for the 1974 general election.

In social security, also, there were no major policy departures. In 1971 the Conservatives introduced the new income-tested benefit, the Family Income Supplement (FIS). But they also initiated some new universal benefits, notably the constant attendance allowance for the disabled and the new pension for the over-80s, for those not previously qualifying. In the field of pensions more generally, an immediate casualty of the 1970 election was the Labour plan for national superannuation, which under the Social Security Act 1973 was replaced by provisions of a different kind, with a state reserve scheme for those not covered by occupational pensions. The Conservatives issued a Green Paper on a tax credit scheme, involving integration of benefits and the personal income tax, although no legislation was introduced before the election.

Perhaps the main departure in welfare state policy over this period was the introduction of greater means-testing, which followed from the view that public spending was insufficiently targeted. The Chancellor of the Exchequer, for instance, said in October 1970 that the government's aim was to 'confine the scope of free provision more closely to what is necessary on social grounds' (quoted in *Poverty*, no. 16/17, p. 5). Greater means-testing took a variety of forms. There were the introduction of FIS and of the national rent rebate scheme already mentioned. Prescription charges were raised in April 1971, but at the same time more people could claim a means-tested exemption. The same applied to school meals, and to dental and optical charges. Cheap welfare milk was abolished, but this was accompanied by a raising of the income levels below which families qualified for free welfare milk. The extended means-tested schemes were backed by a large-scale advertising campaign.

At the same time, the extent of the movement in the direction of greater means-testing should not be exaggerated. The model for the rent rebate scheme had already been provided by the rate rebate scheme established in 1966, so that for many tenants it was not a new development. The number of families eligible for FIS is unlikely to have exceeded a quarter of a million. Despite the increase in prescription charges, the revenue they raised as a percentage of total NHS income, which the previous Labour government had actually increased in its last years (from 2.3 per cent in 1967/8 to 3.5 per cent in 1969/70), remained virtually constant during the Conservative period.

Labour Government 1974–1979

The Labour government elected in February 1974, and re-elected in October of that year, was seen by many of its supporters as having the opportunity to make the radical changes that had eluded the 1964–70 administration. It is indeed often portrayed as having embarked on radical policies but as having been blown off course by the IMF in December 1976. This is an over-simplification, but it is true that the major changes took place in the early years of the administration. Some of these, such as the state earnings-related pension scheme, the decision to phase out private beds in NHS hospitals, or the taxing as an employee benefit at all levels of remuneration of medical insurance paid for by the employer, represent a definite reversal of policy, but others reflected the concerns of the previous government.

In the health field, this was the case with the reallocation of resources to the relatively deprived regions and to the Cinderella services. In 1976 the Resource Allocation Working Party (RAWP) reported (DHSS 1976). It recommended the adoption of a new formula for allocating NHS resources between the regions. The principal innovation was the inclusion of measures of need (chiefly, demographic factors and mortality rates) among the factors used to determine the allocation of funds. The effect of this was to divert resources that otherwise would have gone to regions that (relative to need) were well endowed (primarily, London and the other south-eastern regions) towards poorly endowed ones (most of the rest of the country). Despite obvious problems (such as the omission of morbidity as an indicator of need, the existence of extensive areas of deprivation even within the wealthier regions, and the neglect of inequalities other than geographical ones), the operation of RAWP during the period did manage a measure of redistribution between regions and has been judged a success by Bosanquet (1980).

The attempt to reallocate resources to the Cinderella services was less successful. Notwithstanding a major policy document promising better services for the mentally ill (DHSS 1975), spending on this group in real terms hardly rose at all, while expenditure per head on the elderly probably fell (Bosanquet 1980, p. 217). Perhaps part of the reason for these failures was the government's preoccupation with the third major issue of the period: the removal of private beds from NHS hospitals. Despite the bitterness of the struggle, the success of this too was very limited. By 1980, when the policy was reversed by the new Conservative government, the number of paybeds in England had been reduced by less than a third, while the average daily bed occupation by private patients in NHS hospitals had fallen by less than 12 per cent (Health Services Board 1980; Central Statistical Office 1986, p. 12).

One of the by-products of the compromise over pay-beds was the setting up of a Royal Commission to examine the overall state of the NHS. This reported in 1979, and provided, in the words of one commentator, 'an overwhelming—though not uncritical—endorsement of the NHS's achievements' (Klein 1983, p. 133). It was the last such endorsement the NHS would receive for some time. Another important enquiry initiated in this period was a response to one of the criticisms of RAWP; that it concentrated too heavily on regional differences, and did not address possibly more fundamental inequalities, particularly those associated with social class and income. In 1977 a DHSS Working Party was set up under the chairmanship of Sir Douglas Black to investigate these 'social' inequalities in health. However, the committee did not produce its report (Black 1980) until after the Conservative government had taken office, and its conclusions did not fit in with the philosophy of the new government. Only a few copies were made available, and for a few years the Report 'acquired something of the novelty of an underground *samizdat* publication from Eastern Europe' (Paterson 1981). However, it became more widely available with the eventual publication of a commercial edition (Townsend and Davidson 1982).

In the field of housing, the incoming Labour government dismantled the Housing Finance Act's compulsion on local authorities to move to fair rents and restored the 'no profit' rule for local authority Housing Revenue Accounts, but left the structure of rent rebates and allowances in place, and extended the rate rebate scheme. Council rents were initially frozen in nominal terms as part of the Social Contract and were subsequently increased by amounts that did not keep up with general inflation (see Table 7.4 below). On the capital side, expenditure continued to increase (and with it the number of new public sector housing starts) until 1976, when it became a major casualty of the cuts associated with the IMF. The scale of local authority new house-building has continued to decline ever since.

More fundamental changes to housing policy were referred to the Housing Finance Review, which eventually resulted in the *Housing Policy* Green Paper (DoE 1977). Although the review was initially announced as an attempt to settle the questions of equity between the tenures and to sort out the 'dog's breakfast' of housing finance, the Green Paper proposed no fundamental changes. Major changes in subsidy and tax arrangements were ruled out for fear of their effects on 'the household budgets of millions of families—which have been planned in good faith in the reasonable expectation that present arrangements would broadly continue' (p. iv). The aim of a 'decent house' at a price within the means of all families was restated, some minor concessions to new owner-occupiers were introduced, and the Housing Investment Programme (HIP) system, which continues to control local authority capital programmes, was proposed, as were the broad principles of the system of current subsidies to local authorities eventually implemented by the Conservative government's 1980 Housing Act.

In the area of social security, the policy of the Labour government may again be seen in part as the development of that of its predecessor. Further progress was made with benefits for the disabled: non-contributory invalidity pension was introduced in 1975, followed by mobility allowance and the invalid care allowance. The government introduced the first benefit explicitly intended for one-parent families; child interim benefit, now one-parent benefit. This followed the Finer Report, which had concluded that 'in terms of families with children . . . there can be no other group of this size who are as poor as fatherless families' (Finer 1974, p. 269). It may be noted that this benefit did not replace the additional tax allowance which had been introduced in 1969. The latter continues today at a cost of some £150 million (Treasury 1986, Table 2.24), compared with an expenditure of £138 million on one-parent benefit (Treasury 1986, Tables 3.15 and 3.18.42).

Differences in policy did of course exist. The Labour government was not attracted by the tax credit idea. However, it took over one element: the conversion of income tax allowances for children into a single tax-free cash benefit. Child benefit replaced both the tax allowances and family allowances, previously paid for the second and subsequent children, with effect from April 1977. The episode was however fraught with controversy and enlivened by leaks from Cabinet Minutes (Field 1982), and the political pressure necessary to bring about even this limited reform was seen as a measure of the difficulty in extending state support.

The field of pensions was also controversial, but by compromising in key respects the government reached some form of accommodation with the pension industry; and the Conservatives acquiesced (at least until 1985—see below) in the operation of the 1975 Social Security Act, which brought in the new state earnings-related pension scheme (SERPS). The scheme provided no benefit to existing pensioners, but Labour made a substantial increase in current pensions and introduced a 'ratchet', according to which pensions were indexed in line with whichever rose faster, prices or earnings. It also rejuvenated the Supplementary Benefits Commission, with David Donnison as chairman, who in turn initiated a review of the operation of this major income-tested scheme, the findings of which led to changes by the 1979 Conservative government.

Conservative Government 1979–1986

The Thatcher government is widely thought to represent a distinct break in welfare state policy, but its radical nature should not be exaggerated. The government has not, for example, made any serious attempt to dismantle the National Health Service. Indeed, ostensibly at least, it never intended to do so. The 1979 Conservative Manifesto stated: 'we do not intend to reduce resources going to the National Health Service'; the 1983 manifesto was not quite so explicit in terms of overall resources, but made a number of specific spending commitments (notably, to hospital building and maintenance, to the Cinderella services, and to the underprovided regions). Neither made any reference to large-scale privatization of the service, although the 1983 manifesto did 'welcome the growth in private health insurance in recent years' (p. 28).

The policy interventions in the health field by the Conservative government are in part a continuation of earlier concerns. For example, there have been two major organizational changes, both in the name of efficiency. The 1982 reorganization removed one tier of administration; the changes following the Griffiths Report (National Health Service Management Inquiry 1983) increased the role of professional management. Prescription and other charges within the NHS have been raised, but this was the policy of the earlier Heath administration; and, although the increase is very considerable (with a rise in prescription charges of nearly 1000 per cent from 1979 to 1986), since about three-quarters of all prescriptions are actually exempt from charges, this has not meant any substantial increase in the proportion of NHS funding coming from charges: from 4.4 per cent in 1979/80 to 4.8 per cent in 1985/6 (Central Statistical Office 1986, p. 132).

What, then, are the differences under the Thatcher government? First, there have been measures to stimulate the private sector: through abolition of the Health Services Board that had regulated its activities, through changes in consultants' contracts that increased the opportunities for private practice, and through the restoration of exemption of employer-provided medical insurance from tax for employees below a certain level of remuneration. In the early years the effect was spectacular, with a 26 per cent increase in the number of subscribers to private medical insurance in 1980, followed by a 13 per cent increase in 1981. The rate of increase has now fallen sharply; by 1984 it was a mere 3 per cent (Central Statistical Office 1986, p. 127). Also, the entry of commercial, and chiefly American, firms into the market for providing hospital care has had the paradoxical effect of driving *up* the costs of private care, prompting the memorable complaint by the Chief Executive of BUPA that 'private medicine is threatened by commercialism' (*Daily Telegraph*, 8 January 1986). However, despite the reversal of the pay-beds policy, the average daily bed occupation by private patients in NHS hospitals continued to fall, to 1300 by 1983. Overall, the private sector remains small, with only 10 per cent of all beds in health care institutions, 2 per cent of outpatient attendances and 5 per cent of inpatient stays being private in 1982/3 (Central Statistical Office 1986, p. 126).

Second, there has been the 'contracting-out' of NHS ancillary services, such as catering and cleaning. In numerical terms, this has to be counted something of a success, with (as of September 1985) 365 tendering exercises having been undertaken by health authorities. However, the actual amount of 'privatization' is less impressive; of that 365, nearly 70 per cent were awarded to in-house organizations. Nor are the savings remarkable, amounting to just £29 million over the whole period up until September 1985 (DHSS press release, 11 December 1985). Thus, privatization in the forms either of stimulating the private sector or of contracting-out has not amounted to a great deal in numerical terms, and it seems reasonable to assert that, overall, there was a strong element of continuity in health policy, a conclusion also reached by Klein (1985).

By way of contrast, in housing there have indeed been major changes.The housing programme has been the worst casualty of attempts to cut public spending, falling (on current White Paper definitions) from nearly 6 per cent of the public expenditure planning total in 1979/80 to 2 per cent in 1985/6. The new building programme has been severely hit, with new public sector housing starts down to 43,000 in 1984, compared with a peak of 180,000 in 1976. The dominant policy has been the promotion of owner-occupation, and the share of the national housing stock owned by local authorities has begun to fall for the first time. Council tenants have been given a statutory 'Right to Buy', and, although the scale of sales has meant a very large flow of net capital receipts to the local authorities, restrictions on the use of these receipts have meant that much of this has accumulated rather than being applied to new capital spending.

At the same time, there are clear links with the policies of earlier governments. As far as current subsidies to local authorities are concerned, the policies are very similar to those of the Heath government, but using methods that have proved much more effective. It has not been compulsory to raise rents, a strategy that had led to direct confrontation with recalcitrant councils such as Clay Cross following the Housing Finance Act. Instead, the subsidy system and Rate Support Grant system have been used to make it very expensive not to do so through increases in the 'local contributions' that local authorities are deemed to make to their Housing Revenue Account (HRA) from either rents or rates. The 'no profit' rule has been abolished again, but this time the HRA surpluses are applied directly to reducing rates (although in 1981/2 the 'deemed' surpluses on the HRA resulting from raising rents in accordance with the government's wishes did result in lower Rate Support Grant).

In the same way, the reform of income-related assistance with housing costs to produce 'housing benefit' may be seen as following on from the proposals for a unified housing benefit advocated by the Labour chairman of the Supplementary Benefits Commission. This largely administrative change involved transferring responsibility for rebating the rents of supplementary benefit recipients (who receive benefit equalling their rents) from the DHSS to local authorities. While this created a great deal of administrative chaos, it made little change to the basic structure of income-related assistance established by the Housing Finance Act of 1972, apart from shifting benefits towards pensioners at the expense of other claimants and making the rules less generous in certain respects.

In the field of social security, discussion of the Conservative government's policies has tended to be dominated by the reviews launched by Mr Fowler in 1984 which led to major legislation in 1986. The preceding years had seen significant changes, but these had, at least in part, followed from the concerns of the previous governments. The problems with the administration of a complex benefits system, particularly the income-tested supplementary benefit, led to a re-casting of that system in the Social Security Act 1980, and to reviews of other elements by Lord Rayner. The policy was however distinctive in that it reduced the value or scope of universal benefits and, to a limited degree, embarked on privatization. The 1980 Act did away with the earnings/prices ratchet which had favoured pensioners, and abolished the statutory indexation of short-term benefits. The earnings-related supplement for the unemployed, sick, and widows was abolished. Unemployment and supplementary benefit for the unemployed became subject to income tax. Under the statutory sick pay provisions, employers became liable to pay sickness benefit for an initial period off work.

The twin themes of a greater reliance on income-testing and a reduction in state provision are developed in a much more major fashion in the 1986 legislation. Although the government has drawn back from the total abolition of the state earnings-related pension scheme (having aroused the opposition of the CBI, the National Association of Pension Funds, and several major life assurance companies—as well as the expected lobbies), it has substantially scaled down the benefits, for example changing the formula from 25 per cent of the best 20 years of earnings to 20 per cent of the lifetime average, and halving the pension inherited by the spouse. This will be accompanied by measures designed to increase the number who opt out of the state scheme, introducing a new option of personal pensions, and offering rebates on national insurance contributions. The effects on state spending are however quite delayed: even by the year 2003, the reduction is estimated to be only some £100 million.

On the income-testing side, supplementary benefit is again to be re-fashioned, and rechristened 'income support'. The criteria for eligibility will be simplified. The payment of single sums to cover exceptional needs will be stopped, to be replaced by a mixture of loans and grants from a Social Fund. The universal maternity and death grants are to be abolished. A new family credit scheme, to replace FIS, will extend income-tested support for families with children higher up the income range. The main part of these changes is due to be introduced in April 1988.

The Conservatives under Mrs Thatcher have made little progress in the direction of a unified tax and benefit system. After having taken major steps towards legislation in 1972/3 and announced their intention to go further in the 1979 manifesto, it is noteworthy that the reviews of social security took place independently of the Green Paper on the reform of personal taxation (Chancellor of the Exchequer 1986) and that this latter document discusses proposals for integration under the heading of 'The Tax System in the *Longer Term*' (italics added).

Conclusions

In his book *The Jekyll and Hyde Years*, Michael Stewart argued that:

both Labour and Conservative parties, while in opposition, have succumbed to the temptation to condemn a large proportion of the government's policies and have promised to reverse many of these policies when they themselves took office. The result has been a fatal lack of continuity. Incoming governments have spent their first year or two abolishing or drastically modifying the measures [of their predecessors]. After a year or two they have come to closer terms with reality. [Stewart 1977, p. 240]

In the case of welfare state spending in the period with which we are concerned, this has been true of some aspects of policy, but does not seem to have been universally the case.

Family Income Supplement and housing rebates are examples of policies, both introduced by the Conservatives in the 1970s, that were continued by the subsequent Labour government. In turn, the 1979 Conservative manifesto 'welcomed the new child benefit'. Disability benefits have been improved slowly, and much remains to be done, but they have not been a political football. This term may be more apposite in the case of earnings-related pensions, where two successive Acts were torn up by incoming governments, but the 1975 Act was deliberately designed as a compromise and was accepted as such by the Conservative opposition spokesmen. Contrary to the Jekyll-and-Hyde thesis, it was only *after* some five years of Conservative government that the abolition of SERPS became a serious proposal.

In the field of housing, there have been sharp differences in policy with regard to the local authority sector, including rent levels and council house sales, but the promotion of owner-occupation has been a consistent objective of all governments. The 1973 White Paper, *Widening the Choice: The Next Steps in Housing*, spoke of the need to 'reinforce the momentum towards home ownership', and the 1977 Green Paper described owning one's own home as 'a basic and natural desire' for most people. With the exception of the discouragement of council house sales in 1974, measures to assist owner-occupation introduced by one administration have not been reversed by the next. There has similarly been continuity in the trend away from the promotion of new house-building towards repair and renovation of the existing stock, although its pace has varied.

The position is even clearer in the case of health care, where perhaps the most striking feature of health policy over the period has been its continuity. There were ideological skirmishes on the periphery (over pay-beds, tax concessions to private medicine, and contracting-out), but the main concerns of all the governments involved were broadly the same: managerial reorgainzation, regional and other inequalities, and the Cinderella services.

However, it would be wrong to conclude from this that the social security system, the NHS, or, still less, housing are in the same state in 1986 as in 1970. There has undoubtedly been a loss of confidence in the effectiveness of the welfare state and in its ability to cope with changing circumstances. The administrative problems of social security, particularly with regard to means-tested benefits, intensified by changes in policy such as the new housing benefit scheme, have imposed serious costs on recipients and staff and have weakened public support. Even without this, the system would have been hard put to deal with the strain of greatly increased unemployment; and if governments can plead 'not guilty', at least until recently, to the charge of making sudden changes in policy, this leaves them open to indictment on grounds of failing to adjust to changing circumstances. It is indeed striking that the White Paper of December 1985 (DHSS 1985) contains no more than five lines on benefits for the unemployed. The problems of disrepair and homelessness demonstrate that all is not well with housing policy. On the health side, although overall public support for the principles behind public provision of health care remains high (see Bosanquet's contribution to Jowell and Airey 1984), there has been a noticeable loss in confidence in the ability of curative medicine in general, and of the NHS in particular, to meet the nation's health needs. There is a widespread perception, among both practitioners and the general public, that the NHS is in crisis, that it is being denied resources, and that it is being turned into a residual service. More generally, there seems to be an overall belief that the NHS has in some sense failed; that neither the average level nor the inequalities in health and health care has improved significantly, and that they may even have got worse.

But is this loss of confidence soundly based? Have there been significant reductions in the extent or effectiveness of the welfare state? In the remaining sections of this chapter we examine some of the evidence.

3. The Extent of Welfare State Spending

We examine here the trends in welfare expenditures over the period 1973/4–1983/4, thus covering the Labour government and the first Thatcher administration. What we are measuring, albeit imperfectly, is the inputs into welfare 'production'; the next section is concerned with the 'outputs'. At the same time, we recognize that public spending is only one of the inputs relevant to welfare policy. The objectives of securing adequate income support, or health status, may be attained by private spending, and that private spending may be support by the state in forms other than direct public spending. Thus, for instance, transfer of sick pay to employers under the Statutory Sick Pay Scheme caused state payments to fall, but there was a rise in employer sick pay, for which employers were reimbursed via a reduction in their national insurance contributions.

This example illustrates the difficulties in interpreting the statistical evidence; more fundamentally, it draws attention to the need to consider the 'parallel' welfare provisions in the form of occupational schemes and tax expenditures, or what Titmuss (1958) called 'occupational welfare' and 'fiscal welfare'. It is clear that the present government wishes to see a shift in the balance between these forms of provision. The proposals on earnings-related pensions, for instance, aim to reduce state spending, to increase occupational spending, and—implicitly—to increase the cost of tax expenditures for pension scheme contributions.

We begin with the public spending figures. Because of category changes over time, differences between Blue Book and Public Expenditure White Paper definitions, and problems concerning the appropriate deflator, it is far from easy to obtain consistent time-series for public expenditure on the welfare state in real terms over the whole of our period (see Robinson 1986 for a detailed discussion of the difficulties). However, Winter (forthcoming) has constructed a series for various welfare programmes covering the period 1973/4–1983/4 and these are provided in Table 7.1. Although we confine our subsequent discussion to health, housing, and social security, for comparative purposes we have included expenditures on personal social services and education in the lower part of the table. The figures for social security spending are classified by 'functional' categories (although it is recognized that this may be done in a variety of ways), so as to aid further analysis of the sources of change over the period.

Overall, the figures show that the changes in real public spending have not been uniform across time, or across spending categories, and we examine below the individual categories. We conclude the section with a brief discussion of the overall distributional impact of these changes.

Social Security

With the first social security category—child-related spending—we immediately encounter problems of classification. The abolition of child tax allowances in the mid-1970s and their incorporation in child benefit gives a distorted picture if we take only the public spending figure. In Table 7.2 we have given estimates of a number of items under the heading of 'parallel' welfare provisions, including tax expenditure figures taken from the official

Table 7.1
Direct public expenditure on the welfare state, Great Britain, 1973/4–1983/4
(£ billion, 1980 prices)

Programme	1973/4	1974/5	1975/6	1976/7	1977/8	1978/9	1979/80	1980/1	1981/2	1982/3	1983/4
Social security											
Child-related[a]	0.93	0.79	1.00	0.88	1.24	2.34	3.19	2.92	3.02	3.05	3.20
Age-related[b]	7.58	8.28	8.97	8.96	9.15	9.57	9.88	10.37	10.75	11.13	11.51
Income-related[c]	2.44	2.26	2.60	2.29	2.49	2.43	2.32	2.66	3.68	4.03	5.18
Unemployment[d]	0.47	0.49	0.85	0.90	0.89	0.82	0.74	1.24	1.49	1.22	1.19
Other[e]	2.85	2.98	3.60	3.69	3.87	4.09	3.96	3.77	3.87	3.88	3.87
Total	14.27	14.80	17.02	16.72	17.64	19.25	20.09	20.96	22.81	23.32	24.95
NHS[f]											
Hospital and community health services	6.72	7.31	8.03	7.81	7.79	7.90	8.08	8.51	8.56	8.56	8.30
Family practitioner services	1.55	1.79	2.01	1.96	2.14	2.25	2.27	2.31	2.37	2.57	2.53
Other NHS	0.62	0.64	0.68	0.81	0.61	0.58	0.59	0.65	0.70	0.74	0.74
Total	8.88	9.74	10.72	10.57	10.54	10.73	10.93	11.46	11.63	11.86	11.56
Housing											
Current[g]	1.25	1.87	2.01	2.29	2.08	2.23	2.56	2.53	1.76	1.27	1.07
Capital[h]	3.68	5.40	4.40	4.90	3.92	3.37	3.63	2.78	1.75	1.60	2.05
Income-related[i]	1.58	1.23	1.17	1.18	1.18	1.16	1.08	1.16	1.65	1.97	1.96
Total	6.50	8.50	7.58	8.37	7.18	6.76	7.27	6.46	5.16	4.85	5.08

Personal Social Services[j]	1.50	1.72	1.90	1.95	1.92	1.96	2.09	2.26	2.29	2.34	2.44
Education[k]											
Nursery	0.04	0.05	0.07	0.07	0.05	0.06	0.06	0.06	0.06	0.05	0.06
Primary	3.11	3.26	3.02	3.03	2.89	3.17	2.88	2.91	2.78	2.73	2.70
Secondary	3.80	4.07	3.78	3.85	3.82	3.84	3.75	3.83	3.76	3.77	3.77
University and advanced and further	2.68	2.85	2.69	2.90	2.81	3.10	2.91	2.99	2.90	2.93	3.02
Other	2.95	2.77	2.72	2.68	2.56	2.04	2.75	2.62	2.50	2.55	2.60
Total	12.58	13.00	12.28	12.53	12.13	12.21	12.35	12.41	12.00	12.03	12.15

[a] Child benefit and one-parent benefit; deflated by retail prices index (RPI).
[b] National insurance and non-contributory pension; deflated by price index for two-person pensioner household.
[c] Supplementary pensions and allowances and FIS; deflated by RPI.
[d] Deflated by RPI.
[e] Deflated by RPI.
[f] Deflated by implicit NHS deflator in the National Income and Expenditure Accounts.
[g] Deflated by RPI.
[h] Deflated by GDP price deflator.
[i] Deflated by RPI.
[j] Deflated by GDP price deflator.
[k] Education statistics are for the UK, deflated by implicit education deflator in the National Income and Expenditure Accounts.

Source: Winter (forthcoming); see also Atkinson, Hills, and Le Grand (1986, Table 1).

Table 7.2

'Parallel' welfare expenditures, United Kingdom, 1973/4–1983/4
(£ billion, 1980 prices)

	1973/4	1974/5	1975/6	1976/7	1977/8	1978/9	1979/80	1980/1	1981/2	1982/3	1983/4
Tax expenditures[a]											
Child tax allowance	2.48	2.63	2.35	2.47	1.36	0.67	0.01	0.01	0.01	0	0
Single-parent allowance	0.05	0.03	0.06	0.06	0.08	0.09	0.08	0.08	0.10	0.11	0.12
Age allowance	0.09	0.09	0.40	0.46	0.36	0.33	0.32	0.36	0.34	0.37	0.38
Other special allowances[b]	0.09	0.09	0.07	0.05	0.05	0.04	0.03	0.02	0.03	0.03	0.04
Exemption of social security benefits	1.03	0.88	0.92	0.81	0.85	0.92	0.77	0.80	0.92	0.65	0.38
Occupational expenditures											
Occupational pensions	3.46	3.30	3.16	3.51	3.23	3.69	3.90	4.21	4.89	5.13	5.56

[a]The age allowance and occupational pensions deflated by the index for two-person pensioner household. Remaining expenditures deflated by the retail price index. Mortgage interest relief is shown in Figure 7.1.

[b]Widow's bereavement allowance, blind person's allowance, dependent relative allowance, housekeeper allowance, and allowance for son's or daughter's services.

Sources: Public Expenditure White Papers, Cmnd 9143-II, Table 4.10, and Cmnd 8789-II, Table 4.7; *Inland Revenue Statistics, 1982*, Table 1.5, 1981, Table 1.5, 1980, Table 1.12, 1979, Table 1.10, 1978, Table 1.5; and Willis and Hardwick (1978, Table 8.2). Some figures have been interpolated. Occupational pensions are calendar-year figures from Government Actuary (1978, Table 5.1; 1981, Table 4.1), interpolated and extrapolated using the Blue Book series for pensions and other benefits paid.

series published by the Inland Revenue. These figures, like those for public spending, are 'first-round' costs, not taking account of any behavioural changes that may accompany removal of the provision.

The concept of 'tax expenditures' is difficult, and one cannot simply take these figures at face value. The problems may be illustrated by the treatment of the taxation of benefits. The table includes the Inland Revenue estimate of the amount of income tax lost through the tax-free status of certain national insurance and other benefits, but the Inland Revenue figures do not make allowance for the fact that child benefit is tax-free. In order to put the figures on a consistent basis, we adopt the convention of measuring the net transfer to families in terms of tax-free income. In the specific case of child-related benefits, we take the value of the child tax relief (and single-parent allowance) as shown in Table 7.2, add this to the value of child benefits and family allowances, and subtract an estimate of the tax paid on family allowances prior to April 1977. (This is an approximate figure, based on information from the Inland Revenue Surveys of Personal Income.) In the case of age-related benefits, which are essentially the retirement pension (supplementary pensions being included under 'income-related'), we add the value of the age allowance and again subtract an estimate of the tax paid on retirement pensions. Third, we take the total of income-related and unemployment benefits and subtract the tax that became payable by the unemployed after July 1982 (which shows up in the reduction in the last two years in the item 'Exemption of social security benefits' in Table 7.2). In each case, we are taking as the counterfactual position one in which there is neither direct public expenditure nor tax allowances relating to the client group concerned.

The resulting estimates of the net transfer are shown in Table 7.3 in the form of indices for 1978/9 (end of the Labour government) and 1983/4 (end of first Thatcher government). It is of interest to compare the trends revealed in these figures with changes in the needs for the programmes concerned. The concept of need in relation to the welfare state is a problematic one, partly because of difficulties of definition, but also because in several areas (such as unemployment benefits, income-related benefits, and health care) it may be argued that needs are at least partly endogenous. We shall resolve the definitional issues by examining changes in the potential 'clients' for some of the relevant programmes, accepting that in certain cases these will not be independent of changes in the programmes themselves.

Consider, first, *age-related* expenditures. Here the potential clients are the 'elderly': males aged 65 and over, and females aged 60 and over. The total of all age-related expenditures, including the age allowance, shows an increase in real terms of 25 per cent over the period of the Labour government, while the number of elderly increased by only 4 per cent (Le Grand and Winter 1987). The equivalent figures for the Conservative period are almost identical. This rather surprising finding for the later period may be checked against an alternative set of figures for the period 1978/9–1983/4: those published in the

Table 7.3
Changes in real spending, 1973/4–1983/4

	Index of real spending (1973/4 = 100)		
	1973/4	1978/9	1983/4
Social security (UK)[a]			
Child-related	100.0	97.2	105.2
Age-related	100.0	125.1	152.9
Income-related and unemployment	100.0	112.3	210.6
Health (Great Britain)			
Hospital and community health services	100.0	117.6	123.5
Family practioner services	100.0	145.2	163.2
Total NHS	100.0	120.8	130.2

[a]The social security spending figures from Table 7.1 have been increased to allow for Northern Ireland.

Sources: Tables 7.1 and 7.2, and approximate calculations of taxes paid on benefits.

Public Expenditure White Papers for the total benefit spending (Great Britain) by broad groups of beneficiary (Treasury 1984, Table 2.12.3; 1985, Table 3.12.5). These are less satisfactory in that they do not include the tax aspects just discussed; they do, however, incorporate supplementary pensions and housing benefit, including rate rebates. They show that total real spending on the elderly as measured in this way increased by 25.1 per cent between 1978/9 and 1983/4.

How did this increase come about? We can divide the expenditure shown in the Public Expenditure White Papers into 'insurance' and 'income-related'. The former category, which includes the national insurance pensions, the non-contributory pension, and the Christmas bonus, has increased in real terms by 18.6 per cent, or somewhat less than the average (Treasury 1984, Table 2.12; 1985, Table 3.12). In turn, this increase may be seen as generated by an increase in number of recipients, estimated at 7.6 per cent over the period (Treasury 1984, Table 2.12.2; 1985, Table 3.12.4), and by an increase in the real value of basic pension of 7.9 per cent (increase November 1978–November 1983, deflated by the two-person pensioner price index). It is apparent that these two factors together account for the greater part of the overall increase. In particular, over this period the SERPS pensions contributed only 0.5 per cent to the overall real improvement.

One of the principal aims of SERPS is to reduce the dependence of the elderly on income-tested benefits. Its limited contribution over this period can have allowed little change in this respect. On the other hand, there was a large growth in occupational pensions, where Table 7.2 shows a 60 per cent increase in real spending, and official figures report a 35 per cent increase in the number of occupational pensions in payment (*Employment Gazette*, December 1985). Despite this, the income-tested support to the elderly increased, according to the Public Expenditure White Paper figures, over 70 per cent in real terms, which is a much faster rate than the total. As a result, particularly on account of the introduction of housing benefit, income-related transfers increased from 12.0 per cent of the total to 16.6 per cent.

The number of potential clients for *child-related* expenditures is a little more difficult to determine, since the eligibility rules for the various programmes in that category differ. If we take the number of children under 16, then this fell substantially in both periods, suggesting that there was a real improvement per head over these periods. This conclusion has to qualified in so far as there may be differences between one-parent and other families. The year 1976 saw the introduction of a new benefit for this group, and there has been a growth in the number of one-parent families.

The large increase in expenditure on *income-related* benefits, and particularly those to the unemployed, cannot be considered independently of the change in the number of claimants. In order to explore this over the period 1978/9–1983/4, we take the Public Expenditure White Paper figures for benefits to the unemployed, including national insurance benefit, supplementary allowances, and housing benefit, and make an approximate adjustment for the taxation of benefits. This shows a 110.6 per cent increase in real spending over the Conservative period, which is less than the increase in the number of claimants of 138.4 per cent (*Social Security Statistics 1982*, Table 1.32; *1984*, Table 1.32). This real decline in benefit per claimant was not due to the movement of the basic benefit rate, which increased by some 3 per cent in real terms, but reflected the abolition of the earnings-related supplement, the taxation of benefits, and the fact that a much larger proportion of the unemployed do not receive the *insurance* benefit and are dependent on supplementary benefit. The percentage with national insurance benefits declined from 41 to 31 per cent; and spending on income-related benefits grew at a much faster rate. The reason for this is to be found in the fact that the income maintenance system for the unemployed is little different today from that introduced in 1934. There are two tiers, with eligibility for the upper (insurance) tier being both conditional on past employment record and limited in duration. The proposal of Beveridge for unlimited duration of insurance benefit was not accepted. (See Atkinson and Micklewright 1986 for further discussion.)

Thus, income-testing has come to play a much larger role under the Conservative government—in part because of conscious policy decisions, in part on account of long-standing problems with the income maintenance system.

Health

The changes in the levels of real spending on health care over the two periods
1973/4–1978/9 and 1978/9–1983/4 are shown in the lower part of Table 7.3.
For both hospital and family practitioner services, there was a real increase in
both periods. Overall, real spending on the NHS increased by 20 per cent
under Labour, and more modestly (by 8 per cent) under the first Thatcher
government.

   This finding of rising real spending on health care is clearly at variance with
the widespread perception noted above that the National Health Service is in
serious decline. This is not a new phenomenon. Klein (1983) noted earlier
discrepancies between the rhetoric of crisis and increasing real resources; he
ascribed it to a number of factors, including the demands of technological
developments and international comparisons with the health systems of
wealthier countries. Undoubtedly, these same factors are currently at work,
creating a faster growth in expectations than in resources. A government
minister has indeed suggested that additional spending of 0.5 per cent year is
necessary on account of medical advance (letter from B. Hayhoe to the
Chairman of the Institute of Health Services Management, 28 January 1986).
Another possible explanation, discussed by Robinson (1986), concerns
changes in the *composition* of spending. There has certainly been differential
growth between different parts of the service. Table 7.3 shows a 5 per cent rise
for hospital and community health services from 1978/9 to 1983/4, compared
with a rise of more than 12 per cent for family practioner services. The success
of the reallocations to the deprived regions and the Cinderella services has also
created tensions; in each case, the losers are acute hospitals in the South-East,
institutions with powerful friends and loud voices.

   Is it, however, possible that the real spending has been mis-measured? The
recent report of the Social Services Committee (House of Commons 1986) has
drawn attention to the problems that arise in attempting accurately to assess
real expenditure in the area, and to the very different figures that can be given.
Our figures follow the Select Committee in applying a specific NHS deflator,
intended to take account of factors such as the Clegg pay settlement in 1980
and thus avoiding the misleading impression that would be created if one
applied the retail price index or the GDP deflator (as has been done in
government statements). At the same time, our figures are not identical to
those of the Select Committee: for example, they cover Great Britain as a
whole, rather than being limited simply to England, as in the case of those
given by the Select Committee (a fact that is not easily ascertained from their
tables). But, while the year-to-year movement differs, the overall picture is
similar, with for example both sets of figures indicating a 5 per cent real rise in
hospital and community health services between 1978/9 and 1983/4. Our
series does not cover more recent years, but it may be noted that the Select
Committee figures show little rise since then. Moreover, evidence from other

sources suggests that the increases in expenditures do reflect real increase in input volumes. For instance, in the period 1979–83, there was a 7 per cent increase in the number of (whole-time equivalent) directly employed NHS staff in England (Treasury 1986, p. 220; see, also, Robinson 1986, pp. 12–13), including an 8 per cent increase in medical staff and an 11 per cent increase in nursing staff (not all of which was necessary to counteract the reduction in the working week).

How does this modest rise in real spending compare with indicators of demand? It is difficult to specify the potential clients for health expenditures, since demand for health services is clearly interrelated with the patterns of use. However, the DHSS constructs an indicator of changes in the 'demographic demand' for hospital and community health services, based on the utilization of these services by different age-groups and changes in the age distribution. This increased by 1.4 per cent during the Labour period and by 3.4 per cent in the Conservative one (calculated from estimates provided in *Hansard*, 20 March 1984). On this basis, there was only a very small increase in expenditure per unit of 'need' in the Conservative period, compared with a much larger increase under Labour.

This evidence suggests that the continuity of policy concerns in the health field should not be equated with continuity of levels of spending.

Housing

The figures conventionally presented as representing public expenditure on housing are in many respects unsatisfactory. The current Public Expenditure White Paper formulation presents numbers that give total spending on housing as including, among other items: current subsidies to Housing Revenue Accounts (the difference between current spending on housing by local authorities and their rental and other income), grants to the private sector for improvement and insulation; capital expenditure by local authorities financed by loans from central government and elsewhere; and the total of net loans and grants paid to housing associations for capital development. Even in conventional accounting terms, this total has limited meaning. Furthermore, comparison between years is made difficult by the changes in definition as to what constitutes the housing programme in each successive White Paper. In particular, the treatment of income-related subsidies has been inconsistent and the geographical scope of the totals has varied.

Correcting for these problems, Table 7.1 and Figure 7.1 present consistent series for public expenditure on housing in Great Britain. The table gives estimates of the volume of spending, using specific deflators in line with the other entries. Income-related subsidies are shown as the total value of rent rebates and allowances plus a sum equal to the estimated rents of Supplementary Benefit recipients. This gives a total equivalent to what is now counted as 'housing benefit' in the DHSS social security programme. Figure 7.1, which covers the longer period 1971/2 to 1984/5, is based on the same data as the figures presented in Table 7.1 but is in 'cost' terms; that is, the cash figures have been adjusted to 1984/5 prices by an index of general inflation (the GDP deflator at market prices).

Bearing in mind the significant limitations referred to above, we may see from Table 7.1 and Figure 7.1 a number of the results, intended and unintended, of the policies described earlier; but we also supplement the global picture by Table 7.4, which shows several key variables for the local authority sector in England and Wales. Overall, real spending rose until 1976/7 and has declined since then. However, the different components have not followed a uniform pattern. Despite the real rent increases achieved by the Housing Finance Act (see Table 7.4), general subsidies (current expenditure excluding income-related subsidies) rose between 1971/2 and 1973/4, reflecting increases in both management and maintenance expenditure by local authorities and debt charges. The decline in real rent levels under the Labour government combined with continued increases in spending levels, led to further increases in current general subsidies, which reached a peak in 1979/80. Although the nominal rent increases set by the incoming Conservative government were large, so, initially, was the rate of inflation. As can be seen from Table 7.4, it was in 1981/2 and 1982/3 that the increases in real rent levels occurred, taking them to 40 per cent above 1979/80 levels. Gross rental income (before deducting housing benefit) rose rapidly, and by 1983/4 the real level of general current subsidies was back down to its 1971/2 level. It is worth noting from Table 7.4 that the decline in current subsidies does not reflect a decline in gross current expenditure on management and maintenance, the real level of which rose steadily throughout the period, its 1983/4 level being 150 per cent higher than that of 1970/1 in real terms.

Movements in income-related subsidies are, as one would expect, something of a mirror image of those of the general subsidies. Supplementary benefit recipients receive benefit equal to their rents, and the structure of the rebate system means that others on housing benefit receive an increase in benefit equal to 60 per cent of any real increase in rents. In addition, the higher rent levels are, the more people are eligible for benefit. Table 7.4 shows that the Housing Finance Act resulted in a rise in the proportion of local authority tenants in England and Wales receiving means-tested assistance with their rents, from just under 30 per cent to just under 40 per cent. The proportion stabilized at this level until 1979/80, but since then rising unemployment and the increase in real rents have led to an increase to 60 per cent. This increase does not reflect any improvement in the inherent generosity of the benefit structure; the real value of the 'needs allowance' about which the scheme is structured has declined since 1974/5. The cost of income-related assistance increased by 50 per cent between 1971/2 and 1973/4 (see Figure 7.1) but then fell back again under Labour to its original level until 1980/1. The cost then

Table 7.4

Indicators of local authority housing income and expenditure and housing benefits, England & Wales, 1970/1–1983/4

	Indices 1970/1 = 100 (real terms)				% of tenants receiving housing benefits[c]	Index of real value of housing benefit needs allowance[d]
	Rents[a]	Spending on management & maintenance[b]	Gross rental income[b]	Total income and expenditure[b]		
1970/1	100	100	100	100	29	N/A
1971/2	102	104	99	100	30	N/A
1972/3	106	134	102	105	29	100
1973/4	121	142	119	120	38	113
1974/5	122	164	110	136	39	130
1975/6	105	171	101	133	40	122
1976/7	101	177	104	140	41	118
1977/8	100	185	106	138	42	115
1978/9	98	200	105	143	42	116
1979/80	97	211	100	149	41	114
1980/1	96	224	104	153	44	112
1981/2	127	227	135	151	52	108
1982/3	137	238	142	148	59	111
1983/4	137	255	137	142	59	111

[a] Adjusted by RPI.
[b] Adjusted by GDP deflator.
[c] No. of tenants receiving rent rebates or supplementary benefit, as % of local authority stock.
[d] Needs allowance for married couples adjusted using RPI.

Sources: Housing and Construction Statistics, 1969–79: Tables 96, 119, 120, and 121; 1974–84: Tables 9.3, 10.25, 11.1, 11.2, and 11.3.

rose rapidly in the next two years, directly reflecting the 40 per cent increase in real rent levels. Indeed, given the numbers of benefit recipients, very nearly half of the increased gross revenue resulting from the higher real rent levels will have been absorbed in benefits. Further increases in the cost of income-related expenditure have resulted from rising unemployment. Figure 7.1 shows that the combined total of general subsidies and income-related expenditure has remained little changed since 1976. It is worth noting that the increase in the cost of income-related expenditure pre-dated the switch to housing benefit in 1983/4: local authorities were told not just to take on the cases previously dealt with by the DHSS, but to cope with a total case-load 50 per cent greater than it had been two years earlier, most of the increase in which reflected higher rents.

On the capital side, the peak was reached in 1974/5. By 1979/80 net capital spending was already down to two-thirds of its peak level, and by 1984/5 it was only one-third of the peak. As with current expenditure, this does not simply reflect cuts in the level of gross expenditure, however. Table 7.5 shows the composition of the capital programme in England (which accounts for 80 per cent or more of the total for Great Britain). The major fall since 1976/7 has come in local authority new house-building, the major component of 'other gross capital' which has collapsed to less than a fifth of its starting level. The overall fall in gross spending has not been so rapid, however, as a result of the increase in spending on public sector improvement and renovation over the period as a whole, the increase in improvement grants since 1980/1, and the more moderate decline in net loans and grants to housing associations. A significant part of the decline in net capital spending has also come from the increase in net receipts (after deducting lending by local authorities to finance purchases) since Right to Buy sales started in earnest.

Finally, Figure 7.1 shows the almost continuous rise in the real value of mortgage interest relief (including Option Mortgage Subsidy). The extent to which mortgage interest relief represents the value of the effective subsidy given by the tax system is controversial; but, like the equally dubious measure of subsidies to council tenants given by HRA deficits, changes in it do give some indication of trends in the relative help given to the different tenures. Whereas in1971/2 the value of general current expenditure (mainly on HRA deficits) equalled that of mortgage interest relief, by 1984/5 mortgage interest relief was two and a half times as large, its cost approaching the combined cost of general current expenditure and income-related assistance with rent. It had risen from a level less than 20 per cent of public expenditure on housing to more than 50 per cent. This 150 per cent rise in the real value of the relief was much more rapid than the rise in the number of owner-occupier households or mortgagors (41 and 46 per cent, respectively). This underlines the importance of the 'parallel' welfare provisions.

The Distribution of Expenditure

The changes outlined above might have been expected to lead to significant

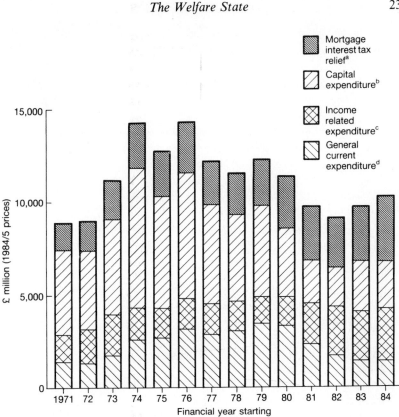

Fig. 7.1 Public expenditure on housing in Britain, 1971/2–1984/5.

Notes:
[a] Mortgage interest tax relief figures include Option Mortgage Subsidy and are on UK basis. Recent figures from Public Expenditure White Papers, earlier figures from *Housing Policy Review Technical Volumes.*
[b] Capital expenditure figures are net of receipts and are taken from successive *Public Expenditure White Papers,* supplemented by *Scottish Housing Statistics* and *Welsh Housing Statistics* to give a breakdown for Great Britain between current and capital expenditure.
[c] Equivalent of what is now counted as housing benefit, formerly rent rebates and allowances and the rents of supplementary benefit recipients. Costs of rent rebates and allowances before 1982/3 estimated on the basis of numbers of recipients from *Housing and Construction Statistics* and *Social Security Statistics* and average rents from *Housing and Construction Statistics* and *Scottish Housing Statistics.*
[d] General current expenditure consists mainly of deficits on local authority housing revenues accounts met by Rate Fund contributions and Exchequer subsidy. Figures from successive Public Expenditure White Papers supplemented by *Scottish Housing Statistics* and *Welsh Housing Statistics* to give a breakdown for Great Britain between current and capital expenditure

Sources: Winter (forthcoming); Atkinson, Hills, and Le Grand (1986, Fig. 1).

Table 7.5

Public capital expenditure on housing in England, 1976/7–1985/6
(£ billion, 1984/5 prices[a])

	Public sector improvement & renovation	Improvement grants etc.	Net loans and grants to housing associations	Other gross capital	Total gross capital	Net receipts	Total net capital
1976/7	0.8	0.1	1.0	4.4	6.3	0.6	5.7
1977/8	0.7	0.1	1.0	3.4	5.3	0.8	4.5
1978/9	0.9	0.2	0.9	2.8	4.8	0.9	3.9
1979/80	1.2	0.2	0.9	2.5	4.8	0.7	4.1
1980/1	1.0	0.2	0.8	1.8	3.7	0.7	3.0
1981/2	0.8	0.3	0.7	1.2	2.9	1.2	1.8
1982/3	1.1	0.5	0.9	1.0	3.5	1.9	1.6
1983/4	1.2	1.0	0.8	1.0	4.0	1.9	2.0
1984/5	1.1	0.8	0.7	0.9	3.5	1.5	2.0
1985/6	1.1	0.6	0.6	0.8	3.1	1.6	1.5

[a] Adjusted using GDP deflator.
[b] Estimated out-turn.

Sources: Public Expenditure White Papers. 1986, Cmnd 9702-II, Table 3.9; 1985, Cmnd 9428-II, Table 3.7; 1984, Cmnd 9143, Table 2.7; 1983, Cmnd 8789-II, Table 2.7; 1982, Cmnd 8494-II, Table 2.7.

changes in the distribution of government expenditure. Table 7.6 reproduces the analysis by the Central Statistical Office using Family Expenditure Survey data published annually in *Economic Trends*. This suggests that, although there have been significant changes in the pattern of beneficiaries from particular programmes, their overall impact has contributed to a remarkable stability in the distribution of final incomes after taxes and allocable items of government expenditure (at least, as far as the broad grouping of the income distribution shown is concerned).

However, considerable caution is required in interpreting the results of this kind of analysis (see Le Grand 1986 for a detailed discussion of some of the pitfalls). The distribution of original income (income before the payment of taxes or the receipt of benefits) is not independent of the distribution of those taxes and benefits. There are difficulties in making appropriate judgements about the incidence of different taxes and items of expenditure. In addition, although we have chosen the years and items presented to minimize the problems, there are changes in definition which mean that the figures for different years are not completely comparable. The most important of these are that the 1973 figures for original income include owner-occupier's imputed rents; that rent rebates and allowances (now 'standard housing benefit') are included under housing subsidies in 1973 but under 'other cash benefits' in 1979 and 1984; and that the 1973 housing subsidies also include rail subsidies (accounting for about 10 per cent of them), as it was not possible to separate them out in the form required. As a result of the 1982/3 reform to housing benefits, the 1984 figure for 'other cash benefits' no longer includes the payments made to cover the rates of supplementary benefit claimants; these are now reflected as greater progressivity in indirect taxes. The effects of the switch from child tax allowances to child benefit are also apparent in Table 7.6.

Over the period, *orginal* income has become notably more skewed, the share of the bottom 40 per cent halving from 12 to 6 per cent. At the same time, the distribution of *final* incomes has been much more stable. The share of the bottom quintile has in fact risen slightly, mainly at the expense of the one above it (for a more detailed examination of these trends, see O'Higgins 1986). The main reason for this has been the increase in the importance of cash benefits, rising from the equivalent of 12 per cent of final incomes to 22 per cent. This has resulted not just from the switch to child benefit, but also from the greatly increased volume of other cash benefits associated with rising unemployment. The age-related benefits (mainly the retirement pension) have become somewhat less progressive over the period, a phenomenon that reflects the gradual exit of part of the elderly population from the bottom quintiles as the incomes of the younger elderly improve. Conversely, the impact of child-related benefits has become less regressive as families with children have moved down the income distribution.

The health service figures are not allocated according to the actual use by

Anthony Atkinson et al.

Table 7.6
Distribution of incomes and benefits, UK, 1973–1984

	Share of quintile group by original income					Total as % of final income
	1st	2nd	3rd	4th	5th	
1984						
Original income	0	6	18	28	49	110
Age-related	41	38	12	5	4	10
Child-related	12	12	24	29	23	3
Other cash	46	27	13	9	6	9
All cash benefits	39	30	14	10	7	22
Gross income	7	10	17	25	42	132
Post-tax income	8	11	17	24	40	81
Health service	23	21	19	19	19	9
Housing subsidies	40	25	18	11	7	1
Final income	10	12	17	23	37	100
1979						
Original income	1	9	19	27	45	111
Age-related	51	32	7	5	5	9
Child-related	5	15	30	27	23	3
Other cash	44	28	11	9	8	5
All cash benefits	41	27	13	10	9	17
Gross income	6	11	18	25	40	128
Post-tax income	7	12	18	24	39	81
Health service	24	20	20	18	19	8
Housing subsidies	27	22	21	16	14	2
Final income	9	13	18	24	36	100
1973						
Original income	1	11	19	26	44	113
Age-related	53	26	9	6	5	8
Child-related	6	17	27	29	24	1
Other cash	44	25	14	9	7	3
All cash benefits	47	25	12	9	7	12
Gross income	6	12	18	24	40	125
Post-tax income	7	12	18	24	39	84
Health service	19	19	21	21	21	6
Housing subsidies	36	19	19	15	12	2
Final income	8	13	18	24	37	100

Sources: Economic Trends, January 1980, p 116, Table 3; December 1982, p 118, Table 4; December 1985, p 107, Table 3. The analysis relates to households (independent of size).

the different income groups; instead, each individual of the same age and sex is assumed to make the same use of the service. Hence any changes over time reflect only demographic changes in the groups concerned, rather than actual changes in the distribution of use. The fall shown in the progressivity of housing subsidies between 1973 and 1979 is simply a result of the reclassification of rebates as a cash benefit. The rise in the progressivity of general subsidies between 1979 and 1984 appears to be a result of the substantial cuts in the programme: only a minority of local authorities continue to receive subsidy, and these are concentrated in regions where tenants are poorer.

4. Effectiveness

The government White Papers on Public Expenditure contain statements of the 'aims and objectives' of each spending programme. For example, in the case of health spending we are told that 'the Government's primary objective for the NHS is to make the best use of the resources available to help the individual to stay healthy and to provide effective and appropriate treatment' (Treasury 1985, p. 157). One view of such statements is that they are likely to be acceptable to governments of different political persuasions and that the main difference between, say, a Labour government and a Conservative one would be in the different weights attached to the constraints. An alternative government might permit a higher level of spending and hence allow more generous financial help or faster progress towards narrowing health care disparities. On this basis, what we are concerned with is shifts along the trade-off frontier between the level of benefits and the level of taxation—of the kind considered in the theoretical literature on optimum taxation.

An alternative view of the White Paper statements is that they are anodyne to a degree that conceals the genuine doubts that have come to be held about the effectiveness of the welfare programmes in achieving their objectives. If one takes, for example, the objective of helping 'the individual to stay healthy', then there are two important stages in the argument. First, there is the provision of health care, where NHS spending is an important input, but only one of the inputs. Health care may also be provided by private purchase or by occupational health services; and one important difference between governments is in their views of the relative desirability and efficiency of private versus public provision. Second, there is the contribution of health care to health. Here there is room for disagreement about the effectiveness of particular treatments, there being some notorious cases where this seems dubious, and about the effectiveness of the allocation of health care in achieving equity objectives. There is, for example, the—controversial—conclusion of the Black working party (Black 1980) that inequality in health had actually widened during the period of the NHS. This conclusion was reached through comparing the mortality experience of the Registrar General's Social

Classes, a comparison that showed, for example, that the gap between the mortality rates (standardized for age differences) for Classes I (professionals) and V (unskilled manual workers) had increased between 1931 and 1971. It hardly needs to be pointed out that this, and other conclusions based on measures of health status, should take account of the many factors apart from health care which affect health.

This complex relationship between inputs and final goals raises a number of issues that have not been very fully examined. In the absence of research on crucial aspects, what follows is of necessity only a limited discussion.

Health

In the case of health care, the DHSS has produced a series of 'performance indicators', designed 'to help managers compare aspects of their services with other authorities' (Treasury 1986, p. 216). These in general refer to 'throughputs', and are therefore closer to measures of inputs rather than outputs. What would be the result if the government were to take measures of 'outputs'? There is a number of possible output measures, including mortality levels or rates, days off work and national insurance incapacity certificates, and self-reported morbidity based on household interviews, such as the General Household Survey. Of these, the most readily available at an aggregate level concerns mortality, and it is on this that we concentrate.

As illustrated in the Black Report, epidemiologists or medical sociologists conventionally use mortality data to construct and compare mortality rates for different groups in the population, such as social classes. This has a number of difficulties (detailed in Le Grand 1985, and Illsley and Le Grand 1987), especially when comparisons over time are concerned. In particular, the fact that the size of the classes (and sometimes the classification scheme itself) can change significantly over time implies that like is not being compared with like. An approach that does not suffer from this problem is to choose an indicator that can be attached to individuals rather than to groups, and then to examine trends in that indicator's mean and dispersion. Thus, for instance, economists exploring changes in income inequality over time have not compared, say, changes in the difference between the average income of Class I and Class V; rather, they have examined changes in a summary statistic, such as the variance or the Gini coefficient, based on differences between individual incomes throughout the population. This approach can be applied to mortality by using as an indicator an individual's length of life, that is, his or her age-at-death.

Some results employing this approach are provided in Table 7.7. This shows the mean, variance, and Gini coefficient for the distribution of age-at-death in England and Wales. The data are taken from the Registrar General's Statistical Reviews for the relevant years and from Office of Population Censuses and Surveys (1984). Estimates are provided for males, females, and

Table 7.7
Age-at-death, England and Wales, 1961–1983

	Males			Females			Aggregate		
	Mean	Variance	Gini	Mean	Variance	Gini	Mean	Variance	Gini
1961									
Actual	66.69	428.77	0.159	72.66	400.01	0.138	69.62	423.55	0.151
Standardized	69.11	354.96	0.137	76.19	323.19	0.116	72.83	353.36	0.130
Cohort	67.64	314.69	0.130	73.45	293.01	0.113	70.61	313.22	0.124
1971									
Actual	67.59	381.33	0.147	74.31	364.05	0.128	70.90	384.15	0.141
Standardized	69.49	331.18	0.132	76.25	314.17	0.115	72.86	336.47	0.127
Cohort	68.69	288.88	0.124	74.91	275.20	0.109	71.85	293.32	0.119
1983									
Actual	70.83	299.01	0.125	77.29	277.84	0.108	74.09	298.78	0.119
Standardized	70.40	296.40	0.125	76.84	280.19	0.109	73.62	298.31	0.120
Cohort	71.16	244.56	0.111	76.99	234.63	0.100	74.13	249.66	0.108

Source: Illsley and Le Grand (1987).

the total of males and females for 1961 as a point of comparison, for 1971 (at the beginning of our period) and for 1983, the latest year for which we have data. Three sets of estimates are provided: one based on actual deaths, one on 'standardized' deaths, and one on 'cohort' deaths. Standardized deaths are those that would have occurred at each age if the age distribution for each year had been the same; the procedure is designed to overcome the difficulty that observed changes in the distribution of age-at-death can be the product of changes in the age distribution. The cohort procedure is a method of generating a distribution of age-at-death that is based on conventional methods of calculating life expectancy; the details cannot be described here, but the basic procedure is to apply the mortality rates for a particular year to the birth cohort of that year. Two measures of dispersion are provided, the variance and the Gini coefficient. Each has different properties; of particular importance, given the change in the mean over the period, one (the variance) is translation-independent (that is, independent of translation by a constant) and the other is scale-independent (independent of multiplication by a constant). Further discussion of the methodology involved can be found in Le Grand and Rabin (1986) and Illsley and Le Grand (1987).

It is apparent from the table that two things have happened. There has been a steady rise in mean age-at-death over the period, and there has been a fall in its dispersion, as measured by either summary statistic. The latter is of particular interest since, as we have seen, it was one of the main contentions of the Black Report that, at least until 1971, inequalities in health as measured by differences in the (male) mortality experiences of the social classes were getting wider rather than narrower. The data that would permit comparisons between the social classes over our period have not been published in a form that makes such comparisons easy (OPCS 1986); however, it appears that the widening has continued (Marmot and McDowall 1986). But it is important to note that it is quite possible for there to be a fall in individualistic measures of inequality while there is an increase in the gaps between the social classes, if there are significant changes in the sizes of the latter over the period being compared. Certainly this seems to be what happened over the 1931–71 period (Le Grand and Rabin 1986), when there was a sharp fall in inequality in age-at-death for both males and females as measured by the Gini coefficent, while the gap in mortality rates between the classes widened.

The interpretation of this evidence poses several problems. First, they relate to *ex post* realizations, whereas our concern may be with the *ex ante* position. That is, the policy aim may be either that of equalizing the age of death for all or that of securing equal chances of attaining a given age at death, regardless of soical or economic position. Each is problematic as an objective. The first is obviously unrealistic, given that there will always be an irreducible minimum of stochastic variation in mortality. The second may allow 'too much' variation in actual mortality outcomes to be socially acceptable. In any case, the fall in inequality we observe could be due to a component common to all (thus contributing to *ex post* inequality) or to one specific to particular groups (thus contributing to both). From the data presented, we cannot determine which.

Secondly, since mortality is heavily affected by factors other than curative health policy, it is difficult directly to link any changes we may observe with changes in policy. Because of the absence of a proper counterfactual hypothesis as to what would have happened to mortality in the absence of the relevant policy (or under different policies), we cannot draw any unequivocal conclusions from this concerning the effectiveness or otherwise of health policy over the period. However, trends in mortality inequalities have been used in the past to criticize the performance of the Health Service (as in the introduction to Townsend and Davidson, 1982). Hence it is worth noting that this evidence suggests that there have been improvements in some key aspects of mortality outcomes, and therefore that criticism of the effectiveness of the welfare state based on the proposition that there has been a deterioration in these respects may be ill-founded.

Social Security

In the field of social security, there is nothing so stark as the mortality data; and the index we consider is the number of people living in families with incomes below the Supplementary Benefit (SB) level. This is perhaps more a performance indicator than a measure of output, since the level is of course set by the government itself. As is shown in column 1 of Table 7.8, the level rose by some 8 per cent in real terms between 1973 and 1983, with considerable year to year variation, and this needs to be borne in mind in interpreting the statistics for the proportion of the population below the SB level. (On the other hand, real personal disposable income rose by more than this percentage.)

The publication of these low-income statistics by the DHSS, which began in May 1974, was one of the most important developments in this field; and it is interesting that the series has been continued, albeit only every other year and with considerable lags, by the Conservative government. It should be noted that there have been changes in the methods employed (see the notes to the table); that the estimates are based on relatively small numbers and are subject to considerable sampling error; and that there is a number of features that complicate their interpretation—for example, the fact that, where the head of the family has been off work because of sickness or unemployment for less than three months, the assessment is based not on current income, but on the family's normal income when the head was in work. This is of especial significance when considering the impact of higher unemployment.

Table 7.8 shows the proportion of the population with incomes below the SB level and the much larger number within 40 per cent of this level (including those receiving SB) who are often described as being 'on the margin of poverty'. The estimates suggest that in the 1970s around 2 million people lived

Table 7.8

Persons in low-income families, Great Britain, 1973–1983

	Real level of SB (1973 = 100)	Below SB level		Below 140% SB level	
		('000)	(%)	('000)	(%)
1973	100	1,600	3.0	—	—
1974	103.1	1,410	2.7	—	—
1975	101.0	1,840	3.5	12,540	23.7
1976	101.9	2,280	4.3	14,870	28.1
1977	102.3	2,020	3.8	14,020	26.5
1977[a]		1,900	3.6	12,990	24.6
1979	103.0	2,130	4.0	11,580	22.0
1979[b]		2,090	4.0	11,570	22.0
1981	104.3	2,610	4.9	14,660	27.5
1983	107.8	2,780	5.2	16,380	30.5

[a]These figures and those for subsequent years are based on a comparison of incomes at the date of interview with the current SB scale; the estimates for earlier years adjust income to an end-of-year basis.
[b]These slightly revised figures are included to give a continuous series from the same publication covering the period of the first Thatcher government.

Sources: For 1973–9, see Atkinson (1983, p. 235); for 1979[b]–83, from DHSS *Low Income Families—1983*, published in July 1986. Real level of SB scale taken from *Social Security Statistics*, 1985, Table 46.10. The figures give the values of the single-householder ordinary-scale rate at the uprating date each year, adjusted by the RPI (excluding housing).

in families below the SB level, and that adding these to the number receiving SB and the number who are 'on the margin' gives a figure of nearly a quarter of the population in the latter half of the 1970s: 22 per cent in 1979. The figures for 1983, published in July 1986, reveal a substantial increase since 1979: if we take those below the SB level, then the number (2.8 million) is a third higher than in 1979. It seems highly unlikely that this rise could be attributed solely to the modest rise in the real SB scale. Similarly, there has been a noticeable increase since the late 1970s if we take the total number including SB recipients and those 'on the margin'. The official estimates show the percentage as rising from 22.0 per cent in 1979 to 30.5 per cent in 1983.

It is interesting to consider the breakdown of this substantial increase in the numbers living in low-income families. Table 7.9 shows the composition of the total low-income population, defined as those with incomes below 140 per cent of SB plus those receiving SB, and the incidence within each of the groups identified in the DHSS statistics. In terms of the incidence of low incomes,

Table 7.9
Incidence of low incomes[a] in Great Britain, 1979 and 1983

	1979		1983	
	% total population	Incidence of low incomes (%)	% total population	Incidence of low incomes (%)
Head over pension age	16.6	67.5	16.7	63.7
Head in full-time work or self-employed[b]	73.3	6.2	62.5	12.2
Head sick or disabled[c]	2.7	41.1	2.9	40.0
Head unemployed[c]	2.4	91.9	7.6	84.9
Other families[d]	5.1	58.7	10.3	44.3

[a]Low income is defined as income below 140% of supplementary benefit (SB) level or receipt of SB.
[b]Including those off work for less than 3 months.
[c]For 3 months or more.
[d]Including single parents, full-time students, those temporarily away from work for reasons other than sickness on part of no pay, persons looking after sick relatives and any others under pension age not working and not seeking work. There is a discontinuity for this category, and for the unemployed, because of the change in May 1983 in the benefit treatment of men aged 60–64.

Source: calculated from DHSS *Low Income Families—1983*, published in July 1986.

there has been a modest improvement for certain groups, including the unemployed, but a distinct worsening for families when the head is in full-time work (where the incidence has virtually doubled). The most important change, however, is in the composition, where there was a sharp fall in the number of families where the head is in full-time work, including self-employment (or where the head had been out of work for less than three months). The increase shows up among the unemployed and the 'other' group. Its significance may be seen from the fact that a 5.2 percentage-point shift from the working population to the unemployed, with the incidence in poverty held constant at the 1983 rates, would be associated with a 3.8 percentage-point rise in the overall incidence.

There seems little doubt that the recession has been associated with a rise in poverty, measured in this way. How far can the welfare state be criticized on this account? As with mortality, the rise may reflect factors other other than social policy. For example, there has been a shift in the earnings distribution, with the low paid falling behind. On the other hand, examination of the social security system suggests that it is inadequate to cope with rising unemployment and in particular with the lengthening duration of unemployment. As we have seen, income support for the unemployed has been reduced and we are now back with the same two-tier system introduced in 1934. Beveridge felt that reliance on means-tested benefits for the unemployed was 'wrong in principle', and the problem of incomplete take-up remains important 40 years later: the 1983 low-income figures show more than half a million people in families where the head had been unemployed for three months or more and which were below the SB level.

There is however another charge that can be levelled aginst the welfare state, which is that the welfare state itself is responsible at least in part for the rise in unemployment. This charge, which may be made more generally—for example, that the rise in the number of one-parent families is benefit-induced—is in effect the *Losing Ground* critique: 'we tried to provide more for the poor and produced more poor instead' (Murray 1984, p. 9).

If we take the effect of benefits on unemployment, this has been the subject of considerable controversy which has been reviewed in Atkinson and Micklewright (1986). A good example of the cross-section approach is the DHSS Cohort Study, a rich source of evidence about individual experience. This has been used to obtain estimates of the elasticity of unemployment duration with respect to benefits (Narendranathan *et al.* 1985), which are about a half to a third of the size found by earlier investigators for the early 1970s (e.g. Nickell 1979a, 1979b). The difference may reflect changing labour market conditions, but Atkinson and Micklewright (1986, Ch. 9) show that it is possible to generate a variety of results, and they suggest a lack of robustness in the findings.

In 1930, Beveridge wrote that 'the danger to be avoided lies less in the demoralising influence of a generous plan of assistance . . . upon the individual workman, than its effect on the minds of those in authority' (1930, pp. 408–9). There can be little doubt that the *belief* that benefits act as a disincentive has influenced public debate, as illustrated by the media coverage of 'scrounging'. (See, for example, the study by Golding and Middleton 1982.) The same is true of the 'poverty trap'. The quantitative significance of the poverty trap in terms of the number of families affected is small (see, for example Atkinson and Stern 1985; Dilnot and Stark 1986), but it has received a great deal of attention. The public choice analysis of why issues dominate political debate may be as important as studies of their actual economic impact.

Housing

Viewed in terms of the dominant aim of current housing policy, 'to encourage the widest opportunities for home ownership' (Treasury 1986), that policy has been remarkably effective. Figures from *Housing and Construction Statistics* for the relevant years on the ownership of dwellings show that exactly 50 per cent of the GB stock was owner-occupied at the end of 1970; by the end of 1984 this had risen to 61 per cent, the increase coming mainly at the expense of the private rented sector (the share of which fell from 20 to 11 per cent), but also, after 1978, the council sector (which fell from nearly 32 per cent in 1978 to under 28 per cent at the end of 1984). With 69 per cent of all households with a head aged between 30 and 44 in the owner-occupied sector in 1983 (*General Household Survey, 1983*), significantly more than in older cohorts, further increases can be expected in the future simply as a result of demographic factors.

Success in terms of the traditional aim of decent housing for all at a price they can afford is much harder to measure, not least because of the imprecision of the words 'decent' and 'afford'. According to government figures (as provided for the Housing Policy Review in the mid-1970s and more recently in *Social Trends*), there has been a gross surplus in the number of dwellings compared with households in Great Britain since the late 1950s, and this surplus doubled to about 1 million between 1970 and 1984. This surplus, however, masks the needs of concealed households and the problems of unfit and unavailable dwellings. When these are taken into account, there remains an overall deficit of nearly 1 million dwellings, according to the *Social Trends* estimates, even before allowing for the differences in the location of households and dwellings. The traditional measures of the size of unsatisfactory stock, and also measures to remedy it, have concentrated on the lack of basic amenities (hot and cold running water, inside WC, etc.) and statutory unfitness. As Table 7.10 shows, there was a continuation of the postwar progress in providing basic amenities between the 1971 and 1981 English House Condition Surveys, the number of dwellings without one or more of them falling from 2.8 to 0.9 million. At the same time, however, the reduction in the number of statutorily unfit dwellings has been much slower, from 1.2 to

Table 7.10

Unsatisfactory housing conditions in England, 1971–1981
(thousands of dwellings)

	1971	1976	1981
Lacking at least one amenity[a]	2815	1531	910
Lacking four or five amenities	1325	678	337
Unfit	1216	1162	1116
In serious disrepair[b]	864	859	1049
Unsatisfactory in some respect	3184	2223	2006
Unfit and in serious disrepair	538	464	475
Unfit, in serious disrepair, and lacking in least one amenity	453	308	263

[a]The amenities are: exclusive use of a WC inside the dwelling, a fixed bath or shower, a wash basin, a kitchen sink, and a hot and cold water system serving a bath, wash basin, and sink.
[b]Repairs needed costing over £7000 at 1981 prices.

Source: English House Condition Survey, 1981, Tables B, H, K, and N (DoE 1983).

1.1 million, and the number of dwellings in a state of serious disrepair (requiring repairs that would cost more than £7000 at 1981 prices) has *increased*, from 0.9 to 1.1 million.

The 1981 survey estimated that remedying every defect in the 24 per cent of the national housing stock that was unsatisfactory in some respect would cost about £30 billion (1983 prices), and that only 10–15 per cent of existing defects were remedied during 1981. The more recent Department of Environment (1985) inquiry suggests that remedying the problems of the local authority stock alone in 1985 would cost £19 billion—nearly £5000 per dwelling. The surveys also show that the problems of unfitness and disrepair are becoming more concentrated on particular social groups. While the proportion of households living in satisfactory dwellings which were without a member in paid employment rose from 23 to 29 per cent between 1976 and 1981, the proportion in dwellings that were fit but in serious disrepair rose from 20 to 35 per cent and the proportion in unfit dwellings from 30 to 47 per cent. The median household income of those in the satisfactory dwellings was more than twice that of those in the unfit dwellings.

The figures do give some indication that the problem of a shortage of enough 'decent' homes has changed over the period, from a lack of amenities to what appears to be a growing problem of disrepair. Whether it has become easier to 'afford' a decent home is less easy to judge from published aggregate statistics. Some indication of the tip of the iceberg of people being unable to afford decent housing is provided by the number of families accepted by local authorities as being homeless (although there are problems with even this, as acceptance policies vary over time). A relatively consistent series is available only since 1978, when the provisions of the Housing (Homeless Persons) Act took effect. The number accepted as homeless by English local authorities has risen year by year, from 53,000 in 1978 to 94,000 in 1985 (figures from *Social Trends* and DoE releases on homeless households). It appears to be becoming more difficult for local authorities in some parts of the country to deal with the problem. The Audit Commission (1986) found that in 1984/5, for every 100 relets available to London boroughs, 35 families were accepted as homeless, and in two boroughs the number exceeded 70. The number of otherwise homeless families placed by local authorities in bed and breakfast accommodation in London rose from 1330 in December 1980 to 4270 five years later (*Hansard*, 10 June 1986, cols. WA 127–8).

5. Concluding Comments

In this chapter we have argued that policy towards health and social security over this period exhibited much greater continuity than is commonly supposed, and that, while some elements of housing policy were reversed by incoming governments, others—notably, the encouragment of owner-occupation—were an abiding feature. There have been important shifts, such as a greater emphasis on income-tested benefits under the Conservative governments; and under the Thatcher government real levels of spending have risen less rapidly (health) or have fallen (current and capital spending on housing). None the less, the overall impression is more one of continuity than of rapid change in direction. Moreover, when there have been changes in policy (such as the greater emphasis on income-testing) these have emerged more as the result of small incremental movements, rather than the result of dramatic policy initiatives. Successive governments have been unwilling to consider radical departures, as evidenced by the timidity over child benefit, the dragging of heels over the integration of taxes and benefits, the limited progress with RAWP and the reallocation to the Cinderella services, and the failure to do anything significant towards reforming the structure of housing finance. The government has singularly failed to face the problems of providing adequate income support for the unemployed.

How can this behaviour be explained? Is it the product of administrative inertia or of deliberate decisions? Are the failures to make radical policy changes ones of omission or commission? To what extent do they reflect the influence of politicians, civil servants, the electorate, or specific pressure groups? Such questions take us beyond the scope of this chapter, but in our view this kind of 'public choice' research on the welfare state is going to be significant in the future. Understanding the way in which policies are made, including the electoral and political constraints, may be as important as understanding the effects of those policies.

References

Atkinson, A. B. (1983), *The Economics of Inequality* (2nd edn). Oxford: University Press.

—— (1985a), 'On the Measurement of Poverty'. London School of Economics: Taxation, Incentives and Distribution of Income Discussion Paper no. 90.

—— (1985b), 'Income Maintenance and Social Insurance: A Survey'. London School of Economics: Welfare State Programme Discussion Paper no. 5.

—— (1986), 'Social Insurance and Income Maintenance'. London School of Economics: Welfare State Programme Discussion Paper no. 11.

——, Hills, J., and Le Grand, J. (1986), 'The Welfare State in Britain 1970–1985: Extent and Effectiveness'. London School of Economics: Welfare State Programme Discussion Paper no. 9.

—— and Micklewright, J. (1986), *Unemployment Benefits and Unemployment Duration.* London: ST/ICERD.

—— and Stern, N. H. (1985), 'The Poverty Trap'. *Economic Review*, 2 (5), 30–4.

Audit Commission for Local Authorities in England and Wales (1986), *Managing the Crisis in Council Housing.* London: HMSO.

Beveridge, W. H. (1930), *Unemployment: A Problem for Industry.* London: Longman.

Black, D. (1980), *Inequalities in Health*, report of a research working group chaired by Sir Douglas Black. London: Department of Health and Social Security.

Bosanquet, N. (1980), 'Health'. In N. Bosanquet and P. Townsend, *Labour and Equality.* London: Heinemann.

Central Statistical Office (1986), *Social Trends No. 16.* London: HMSO.

Chancellor of the Exchequer (1986), *The Reform of Personal Taxation*, Cmnd 9756. London: HMSO.

Cooper, S. (1985), *Public Housing and Private Property 1970–1984.* Aldershot: Gower.

Department of Economic Affairs (1965), *The National Plan*, Cmnd 2764. London: HMSO.

Department of the Environment (DoE) (1971), *Fair Deal for Housing*, Cmnd 4728. London: HMSO.

—— (1973a), *Widening the Choice: The Next Steps in Housing*, Cmnd. 5280. London: HMSO.

—— (1973b), *Better Homes: the Next Priorities*, Cmnd 5339. London: HMSO.

—— (1977), *Housing Policy: A Consultative Document*, Cmnd 6851. London: HMSO.

—— (1983), *English House Condition Survey 1981 Parts 1 and 2.* London: HMSO.

—— (1985), *An Inquiry into the Condition of the Local Authority Housing Stock in England: 1985.* London: HMSO.

Department of Health and Social Security (DHSS) (1970), *Future Structure of the National Health Service.* London: HMSO.

—— (1971), *National Health Service Reorganisation: Consultation Document.* London: HMSO.

—— (1972), *National Health Service Reorganisation: England*, Cmnd 5055. London: HMSO.

—— (1975), *Better Services for the Mentally Ill*, Cmnd 6233. London: HMSO.

—— (1976), *Sharing Resources for Health in England*, report of the Resources Allocation Working Party. London: HMSO.

—— (1984), *Population, Pension Costs and Pensioners' Incomes.* London: HMSO.

—— (1985), *Reform of Social Security: Programme for Action*, Cmnd 9691. London: HMSO.

Dilnot, A. and Stark, G. (1986), 'The Poverty Trap, Tax Cuts and the Reform of Social Security', *Fiscal Studies*, 7 (1), 1–10.

Donnison, D. and Ungerson, C. (1982), *Housing Policy*. Harmondsworth: Penguin.

Dunleavy, P. (1981), *The Politics of Mass Housing in Britain 1945–1975*. Oxford: Clarendon Press.

Field, F. (1982), *Poverty and Politics*. London: Heinemann.

Finer, Morris (1974), *Report of the Committee on One-Parent Families*, Vol 1, Cmnd 5629. London: HMSO.

Golding, P. and Middleton, S. (1982), *Images of Welfare*. Oxford: Martin Robertson.

Government Actuary (1978), *Occupational Pension Schemes 1975*. London: HMSO.

—— (1981), *Occupational Pension Schemes 1979*. London: HMSO.

Health Services Board (1980), *Report, 1979*. London: HMSO.

House of Commons (1986), *Public Expenditure on the Social Services*, 387-I. London: HMSO.

Illsley, R. and Le Grand, J. (1987), 'The Measurement of Inequality in Health'. London School of Economics: Welfare State Programme Discussion Paper no. 16.

Inquiry into British Housing (1985), *Report*. London: National Federation of Housing Associations.

Jowell, R. and Airey, C. (1984), *British Social Attitudes, 1984 Report*. Aldershot: Gower.

Klein, R. (1983), *The Politics of the National Health Service*. Harlow: Longman.

—— (1985), 'Health Policy, 1979 to 1983: the Retreat from Ideology'. In P. Jackson (ed.), *Implementing Government Policy Initiatives: the Thatcher Administration 1979–1983*. Aldershot: Gower.

Le Grand, J. (1985), 'Inequalities in Health: the Human Capital Approach'. London School of Economics: Welfare State Programme, Discussion Paper no. 1.

—— (1986), 'On Researching the Distributional Consequences of Public Policies'. London School of Economics: Welfare State Programme Discussion Paper no. 6.

—— and Rabin, M. (1986), 'Trends in British Health Inequality, 1931–83' in A. Culyer and B. Jönsson (eds) *Public and Private Health Services*. Oxford: Basil Blackwell.

Le Grand, J. and Winter, D. (1987), 'The Middle Classes and the Welfare State', London School of Economics: Welfare State Programme, Discussion Paper no. 14.

Marmot, M. and McDowall, M. (1986), 'Mortality Decline and Widening Social Inequalities', *The Lancet*, 2 August.

Merrett, S. (1979), *State Housing in Britain*. London: Routledge & Kegan Paul.

Ministry of Health (1968), *The Administrative Structure of the Medical and Related Services in England and Wales*. London: HMSO.

Ministry of Housing and Local Government (1968), *Old Houses into New Homes*, Cmnd 3602. London: HMSO.

Murray, C. (1984), *Losing Ground*. New York: Basic Books.

Narendranathan, W, Nickell, S. J., and Stern, J. (1985), 'Unemployment Benefits Revisited', *Economic Journal*, 95, 307–29.

National Health Service Management Inquiry (1983), *Report* (the Griffiths Report). London: Department of Health and Social Security.

Nickell, S. J. (1979a), 'Estimating the Probability of Leaving Unemployment', *Econometrica*, 47, 1249–66.

—— (1979b), 'The Effects of Unemployment and Related Benefits on the Duration of Unemployment', *Economic Journal*, 89, 34–49.

O'Higgins, M. (1986), 'The Distribution and Redistribution of Income in the UK, 1971–1984'. Paper presented to Joint Studies in Public Policy Conference on New Directions in Public Spending, NIESR, London.

Office of Population Censuses and Surveys (OPCS) (1984), *Mortality Statistics Series DH* 1. *London: HMSO*.

—— (1986), *Occupational Mortality 1979–80, 1982–83*, Series DS no. 6. London: HMSO.

Paterson, K. (1981), 'The Black Report and Causality'. *The Lancet*, 6 June.

Office of Population Censuses and Surveys (OPCS) (1984), *Mortality Statistics Series DH* 1. *London: HMSO*.

—— (1986), *Occupational Mortality 1979–80, 1982–83*, Series DS no. 6. London: HMSO.

Paterson, K. (1981), 'The Black Report and Causality'. *The Lancet*, 6 June.

Robinson, R. (1986), 'Restructuring the Welfare State: An Analysis of Public Expenditure, 1979/80–1984/5'. *Journal of Social Policy*, 15, 1–21.

Royal Commission on the National Health Service (1979), *Report*, Cmnd 7615. London: HMSO.

Stewart, M. (1977), *The Jekyll and Hyde Years*. London: J. M. Dent.

Titmuss, R. (1958), *Essays on 'the Welfare State'*. London: Allen & Unwin.

Townsend, P. and Bosanquet, N. (1972) *Labour and Inequality*. London: Fabian Society.

Townsend, P. and Davidson, N. (1982), *Inequalities in Health: the Black Report*. Harmondsworth: Penguin.

Treasury, H. M. (1984), *The Government's Expenditure Plans, 1984–85 to 1986–87*, Vol. II, Cmnd 9143-II. London: HMSO.

—— (1985), *The Government's Expenditure Plans, 1985–86 to 1987–88*, Vol. II, Cmnd 9428-II. London: HMSO.

—— (1986), *The Government's Expenditure Plans, 1986–87 to 1988–89*, Vol. II, Cmnd 9702-II. London: HMSO.

Willis, J. R. M. and Hardwick, P. J. W. (1978), *Tax Expenditures in the United Kingdom*. London: Heinemann.

Winter, D. (forthcoming), 'Welfare State Expenditure, 1973/4–1983/4: A Data Mine'. London School of Economics: Welfare State Programme Research Note.

Comment on 'Monetary Policy'

Charles Goodhart

London School of Economics

In Chapter 1 above, Fischer has concentrated on the main macroeconomic policy issues facing the British monetary authorities (including the form of the Phillips curve relationship, the choice of intermediate target(s), the transmission mechanism of monetary effects, and the choice of methods of controlling the money stock), rather than delve into the minutiae of our institutional and operational details. He was surely well advised to stick to the high ground in this manner, since the British monetary authorities have succeeded in making the operational detail here peculiarly complex and opaque. I need mention only the statistical mistreatment of the Bank of England in our financial accounts, and the arcana of the relationships between the Bank and the discount houses. How many, for example, could explain the distinctions between 2.30 lending and 2.45 lending? I was, therefore, relieved that Fischer had refrained from much detailed probing of the arcana, with mercifully no reference to 'overfunding' and the 'bill mountain'.

I agree with the greater part of Fischer's commentary on these major issues, and there is virtually nothing in the first three sections with which I could find fault. I had more difficulty with Section 4, where Fischer assesses the British approach to monetary policy from a US viewpoint. While he is clearly correct in his comment that the UK monetary authorities have paid much more attention to interest rates than US monetarists would have advocated, I would dispute his repeated claim that the UK authorities have operated (implicit) interest rate *targets*, a claim repeated several times. I cannot recall a period of open-loop fixed targets for interest rates in the UK in the last 18 years, during which I was personally involved, though there *have* been a very few occasions when Whitehall (not the Bank) enforced interest rate ceilings, largely on political grounds. It is certainly possible to claim that there were *closed-loop* targets for short-term interest rates, in which these were varied in response to contingent outcomes for exchange rates, the growth of the monetary aggregates, etc.; but I am not clear at what point complex and adjustable closed-loop policies merge indistinguishably into paying careful attention to some variable. As Fischer recognizes (p. 20), paying 'Attention to interest rates is far from sticking closely to interest rate targets'.

While it is certainly possible to argue that the British authorities may have given too much weight to smoothing, or stabilizing, interest rates and too little, say, to stabilizing exchange rates, that is not the same thing at all as making the unfounded claim that the authorities fixed interest rate *targets*.

As partial evidence of the authorities' excessive attachment to stable interest rates, Fischer cites the reluctance of the Bank to move to an auction system in the gilt market, and asks why the authorities did not trust that market. At least part of the answer is that the market structure then, with only two large, but still under-capitalized, jobbers and a dearth of well capitalized primary market-makers, was thought potentially too fragile to handle large auctions on adverse occasions. Moreover, actual experience with auctions of indexed gilts reinforced such caution. The change in structure after the 'big bang' has, however, allowed more of a shift towards auctions: and indeed has done (May 1987).

Fischer does not think that £M3 makes a good monetary target. There are several possible reasons for taking this view, but one that Fischer offers—that the choice of £M3 undesirably constrains fiscal policy—seems wrong to me and, I believe, also to my Treasury colleague, Terry Burns. It is indeed correct, as Fischer sets out earlier (p. 13), that the counterparts approach to the determination of the money stock (see Fischer's note 14) virtually requires that monetary and fiscal policies be co-ordinated. But forcing the authorities to think carefully about the *ex ante* balance between policies such as fiscal, funding, and interest rates, strikes me as one of the chief advantages of the adoption of a broad monetary target. It may be that, with the benefit of hindsight, the chosen policies were wrong, but at least they *were* co-ordinated *ex ante*, unlike in the United States.

Instead, the dominant reason for the partial abandonment of the £M3 target has, of course, been the breakdown of the stability of its velocity in practice; there is nothing wrong with treating it as a target in principle. When arguing for more attention to be paid to narrower aggregates, Fischer does note that all such velocity functions are subject to disturbances, for example from innovations, such as the innovation of interest-bearing sight deposits which is now subjecting M1 to even greater disturbances than those affecting £M3. But then, Fischer would place even greater weight than now on the monetary base. Which, alas, brings me to monetary base control. Let me start by noting that, for any set of given initial conditions, a particular level and path for the monetary base implies a given level and path for interest rates, and vice versa. If the short-term interest elasticity of the demand for money is, for example, very low, you cannot alter the money supply, say, by monetary base control methods, without causing a violent change in interest rates. I was a bit mystified by a passage on p. 19, and in note 34, where Fischer states that a monetarist would be happy with a totally interest-insensitive money target, but then wonders 'how monetary policy effects would be transmitted to the economy if the interest rate did not play that role'.

But they *would* still play that role. When the interest elasticity is very low, say zero, it is not the case that the transmission mechanism ceases to operate through interest rates, but that the mechanism becomes so violent, with interest rates forced instantaneously towards infinity, or zero, that nominal incomes have to adjust extremely rapidly towards the equilibrium level determined by the money supply.

Throw a few lags into such a system, and it is all too easy to see how a shift towards monetary base control, in a world of short-term interest inelasticity, would lead, as in the United States between 1979 and 1982, not only to far more volatile interest rates, but also to considerably more volatile monetary growth.

In a world with an inelastic interest demand function for money, the authorities' efforts to raise interest rates in the face of an overshoot above the monetary target would impinge directly on exchange rates, prices, and incomes, *before* they would affect the money stock. The chain of causation then runs from interest rates to nominal incomes to money demand, and would continue to do so, I should add, under monetary base control. In such a case, the evidence of whether the change in interest rates is about right for policy purposes would seem to be monitored more efficiently by looking directly at the course of nominal incomes than by observing the monetary aggregates.

The underlying argument in all the discussion about the technicalities of monetary operations is, I think, whether it would be desirable and acceptable to adopt a system that brought about greater volatility in interest rates in return for some *potential* dampening in another variable, such as a monetary aggregate or the exchange rate. As Fischer's note 32 reports, our chosen trade-off implied more volatility in interest rates than the United States had prior to 1979, and less than they had in the years 1979–82. Given their apparent dissatisfaction with the course of monetary policy in both these conditions, perhaps it goes to show that we had succeeded in reaching the happy mean.

Comment on 'Fiscal Policy'

Robert Gordon

Northwestern University, Illinois

In Chapter 2 above Begg does an excellent job, within a tight space constraint, of combining a critical overview of major UK fiscal policy actions since 1970 with a selective interpretation of the relevant theoretical literature. Rather than summarize the chapter or criticize it in detail, I shall focus on several major issues which either (1) receive short shrift or (2) can be illuminated by contrasting UK experience with that of the USA.

Demand Management

From an American perspective, most UK commentaries on fiscal demand management accept too uncritically that discretionary fiscal changes influence aggregate demand and fail to distinguish sufficiently between (1) tax changes and expenditure changes, (2) temporary v. permanent tax changes, and (3) fiscal changes with and without the reinforcement of monetary accommodation. An unsatisfactory element of the Begg chapter is its failure to address these issues or to cite evidence that indeed changes in his measure of 'fiscal stance' (which does not make distinction (1), (2), or (3)) have a significant impact on real demand.

In the USA, activist fiscal demand management was undermined by two simultaneous events. First was the failure of the 1968 temporary income tax surcharge to dampen demand. Second was the implication of the standard permanent income life-cycle (PI/LC) analysis, which distinguishes temporary and permanent income tax changes, with the former having no effect on consumer spending. My colleague Robert Eisner was the first, in 1968, to point to the PI/LC theory as the Achilles heel of activist fiscal demand management. And very recently, in 1985, Alan Blinder and Angus Deaton, in a monumental empirical study of US consumption behaviour, validate Eisner's initial insight by showing that there was no response at all of US consumption to any of the temporary tax change episodes in the past two decades. Begg provides a cursory claim that 'demand management is not an empty box or pointless exercise', but, in contrast to his discussion based on unrealistic market perfection, the US experience and evidence demonstrates that one does not need to base the argument against fiscal policy efficacy on perfect capital markets, perfectly flexible prices, or the extreme Barro–Ricardian equivalence proposition. Begg's case is further undermined by the complete absence of any citations that in fact discretionary shifts in UK fiscal policy are not either totally offset by movements in private saving or mainly attributable to accommodating swings in monetary policy.

The Monetary–Fiscal Mix

The US experience in the 1960s provided a sobering lession that the monetary environment of fiscal shifts dominates the outcome. The famous US income tax cut of 1964–5 boosted output because it was accompanied by an acceleration of monetary growth, but the income tax surcharge of 1968 failed to dampen output because it was accompanied by offsetting monetary ease rather than supportive monetary tightness, and the economy slowed only in 1969, when monetary contraction began in earnest. This background raises important questions about Begg's narrative of the post-1970 period; for instance, was the 1973 boom in the UK really due to a fiscal U-turn, or instead to a monetary explosion?

Begg's failure to address explicitly the feasibility of independent fiscal and monetary policies in the 1970s seems inconsistent with his commentary on the 1980s, which, by stating that PSBR control can be carried out without reference to an explicit target for money supply growth, implicitly assumes that independent monetary and fiscal policies are feasible in the UK context. Here one needs to be explicit about the twist in the monetary–fiscal mix that raised real interest rates after 1981, but one finds nothing about real interest rates in Begg's chapter. The real interest rate series presented by Fischer in Chapter 1 above makes one wonder why the full brunt of the UK recession was felt in 1980/1 instead of 1982/3. In light of the rapid growth rates of £M3 and nominal GNP evident to the end of 1980, I conclude that the British recession of 1980/1 was caused by the enormous real exchange rate appreciation of 1978–80, which in turn was due to North Sea oil, the supply shock effects of the indirect tax increases of 1979, and monetary tightness in the USA, rather than any direct effect of monetary or fiscal tightness in the UK, both of which came later.

Further on fiscal–monetary coordination, Begg seems to question the assumption of the MTFS that a reduction of inflation required tight fiscal policy. In the USA disinflation was achieved with a mix of loose fiscal and tight monetary policy. Again, one needs to learn why the Bank of England feels (according to Fischer) that it must peg long gilt rates, and one wonders whether the bond market is not broad enough to allow the independent conduct of monetary and fiscal policy in the UK.

Supply-side Issues

The paper's discussion of supply-side issues is cursory and lopsided, stressing effects on labour supply and investment, but with no word at all on labour productivity. I find the labour productivity numbers so striking that I reproduce them here (Table C1) for the UK, USA, and the weighted average of 10 European nations since 1961. This table is to be viewed in conjunction with the fact (shown in the conference version of the Begg chapter) that there have been no changes in average tax rates on UK income in the last 15 years, and that marginal tax rates have actually increased. Thus there have been no supply-side incentives in the UK, in contrast to the USA, in which marginal

Table C1
Average annual growth rates of output per hour, by sector
and internally, 1961–1984

	1961–72	1972–9	1979–84
Manufacturing			
UK	4.21	2.13	3.99
USA	3.10	2.00	2.67
Europe[a]	5.27	4.27	3.71
Non-manufacturing			
UK	3.17	2.14	2.17
USA	1.91	0.51	0.13
Europe[a]	4.51	3.05	1.48

[a]'Europe' includes Austria, Belgium, Denmark, France, West Germany, Italy, Netherlands, Norway, Sweden, and Switzerland.

Source: Data compiled from OECD and IMF sources. Details available from author on request.

tax rates have been decisively reduced in the Reagan era. Yet look at the productivity numbers. In both manufacturing and non-manufacturing, the UK has experienced a sharp acceleration of productivity growth since 1979 and has actually exceeded the European average, while the USA has remained a laggard, and in fact exhibits no productivity growth at all in non-manufacturing (about three-quarters of the economy) for almost 20 years.

The fact that the UK has outperformed the USA in both sectors and all three intervals in the table, after 90 years between 1870 and 1960 when the USA raced far ahead of the UK in its standard of living and output per hour, not only raises questions about the dubious claims of US supply-side proponents of tax rate reductions, but should restrain those who bemoan Britain's performance and point to the miracles that are achieved daily in North America. Rather, it appears that the second prize for macroeconomic puzzles, after the persistence of European unemployment, goes to the 17-year near-cessation of US productivity growth outside of manufacturing, probably the first time since the Industrial Revolution that a major nation has failed to advance its standard of living for so long in so large a part of its economy. If the USA had achieved the UK rate of productivity growth in non-manufacturing since 1972, at present we'd have 13 million fewer employees, and an unemployment rate equal to 17 per cent. In short, the USA now needs a reverse Marshall plan.

Comment on 'The Labour Market'

Patrick Minford

University of Liverpool

Chapter 5 above represents an impressive (as might be expected from this team) marshalling of voluminous data within a neoclassical theory of economic behaviour. The theory is neoclassical, rather than New Classical, in that unions' and firms' bargaining sets wages while firms set prices; quantities are set by demand, and then feed back into the wage/price-setting process in the long run. The NAIRU occurs where the bargaining real wage equates *ex ante* with firms' offered real wage.

The long-run equilibrium is conceptually not differentiable from Friedman's 'natiural rate'; and the disequilibrium dynamics are not dissimilar in kind to Friedman's or indeed to many 'Austrian' economists or older classical economists such as Irving Fisher. Whether one labels the labour and goods market quadrant curves 'supply' and 'demand' or 'wage-' and 'price-setting' equations seems to be a matter of indifference. Of course, the long-run equilibrium in Layard and Nickell's chapter is heavily distorted by a variety of 'pressures', including union behaviour and the operation of the tax and benefit system; but so was it in the mainstream classical account of long-run unemployment.

In the early part of the chapter much is made of the dynamic behaviour of the model; unanticipated inflation and quantity movements drive this. There is also an interaction between the average duration of unemployment and the wage bargain; the longer people have been unemployed, the less is the downward effect of unemployment on real wages. Nevertheless, this discussion suffers from vagueness because of the absence of a fully specified macro-model in which the relevant interactions are filled in; we are not even told how expectations are formed. And the 'puzzle' the authors refer to of inflation failing to fall rapidly with unemployment above the NAIRU is not a puzzle if expectations are rational.

The chapter's interest lies in its estimate of the NAIRU, which can be arrived at by specifying merely the *partial* dynamics of the wage and price equations. The easiest way for me to comment on this is to 'compare and contrast' it with my own 1983 estimate, which was arrived at within a New Classical model—different, as I shall arque, not in the nature of its long-run equilibrium, but only in its dynamic specification.

Table C2 gives the basic comparison. In reaching the breakdown of my own natural rate, I have deducted the effects of world trade and time trends ('rising productivity') from the effects of taxes and benefits (which are trended); the former variable can be thought of as determining a sort of 'warranted' rise in

Table C2
Comparison of Layard/Nickell (L/N) and Minford NAIRU estimates: % point rise, 1955–1983

	L/N (males)		Minford (males & females)
	Model 1	Model 2	
Taxes/benefits (model 1)	3.7	—	4.5
u/v shift (model 2)	—	4.8	—
Union mark-up	3.8	2.7	3.3
Other (esp. mismatch)	1.5	1.7	—
	9.0	9.2	7.9

Sources: Layard and Nickell (1985); Minford (1983).

benefits matching productivity. Layard and Nickell solve this problem of trended variables by conditioning on the capital stock, a practice I would criticize on the grounds that capital is strictly endogenous, especially in an open economy (whose potential profitability determines both the level of activity and investment, including inward capital flows).

Nevertheless, it turns out, as the table shows, to make little difference in practice. Considering that Layard and Nickell use male unemployment while I use total, the figures are remarkably similar, and the breakdown likewise. Their model 2 is distinguished by the substitution of the shift in the unemployment/vacancies ratio for taxes and benefits in the wage equation. They identify this shift with a reduced willingness of the unemployed to take jobs or to search at given levels of demand. Notice the very large importance in both accounts of union power, and the small importance of 'mismatch'. Finally, note the *total* absence of demand; this is inherent in a long-run equilibrium solution, for of course in the long run demand has to move to equality with whatever 'supply potential' the economy generates, and, since this is determined by the exogenous 'supply' (my words) or 'pressure' (Layard and Nickell's words), it follows that demand is wholly exogenous.

Two last comments. There is much talk in this chapter of 'insiders' keeping 'outsiders' out of jobs, implying that unemployment is 'involuntary'. Yet there is a large non-union sector in the UK, and such a view requires that jobless outsiders are excluded by unions or government regulation from offering themselves for jobs, which by definition they can do if there is a non-union sector free of such control. Besides, Layard and Nickell's own account of the u/v ratio emphasizes the greater work-shyness of the long-term unemployed; Layard himself has frequently stressed the separation of job centres from DHSS offices and the decay of the 'work test' (whereby failure to take a job forfeits benefit). In Layard and Nickell's model, implicitly, were these people not work-shy they would drive down wages in the non-union sector, and these in turn would reduce union real wages assuming a roughly constant mark-up at given union power.

Second, Layard and Nickell claim that their theory embodies 'hysteresis' because longer-duation unemployment reduces wage pressure and duration depends on unemployment history. The term is sufficiently imprecise for their claim to carry. Nevertheless, in the context of the NAIRU, we require that past unemployment affect the equilibrium; *this* sort of hysteresis plainly does not obtain in the Layard/Nickell model, for the NAIRU depends only on pressure variables.

In general, much of the hysteresis discussion in 'popular economics' has suffered from damaging vagueness about the mechanisms involved. Layard and Nickell, to their credit, have a theory of the NAIRU, and clearly, since there is no feedback of unemployment on to the pressure variables, their mechanism is purely dynamic. It is nevertheless vague even in that respect. *Why* do the long-term unemployed generate less wage pressure? As already noted, if there is an answer, it lies in the tax/benefit system in their chapter. Perhaps one could also discover some effects of actual unemployment on the public's knowledge of the benefit system (and the shadow economy?) and its attitudes (stigma, etc.) to unemployment. These could contribute to a proper micro-theory of hysteresis. But of course, the policy implications of such a mechanism are not encouraging to those who hope not to have to change the benefit system, since neither knowledge nor attitudes will be reversed by expansionary policies.

I conclude that Layard and Nickell have a traditionally classical view of the causes of non-cyclical unemployment. I find this congenial and convincing; when two of the best Keynesian labour economists have reached this view, is it not time for the others to join them?

References

Layard, R. and Nickell, S. (1985), 'The Causes of British Unemployment', *National Institute Economic Review*, no. 1, 62–85.

Minford, P. (1983), 'Labour Market Equilibrium in an Open Economy', *Oxford Economic Papers*, 35, 531–67.

Index